CHILE throug[h]

by CLAUDE G. BOWE[RS]

mbassy windows: 1939-1953

MON AND SCHUSTER   NEW YORK   1958

FIRST PRINTING

LIBRARY OF CONGRESS CATALOG CARD NUMBER: 58-6273
MANUFACTURED IN THE UNITED STATES OF AMERICA
BY H. WOLFF BOOK MFG. CO., INC., NEW YORK

Foreword

I served for more than fourteen consecutive years as Ambassador to Chile under three United States Presidents, Roosevelt, Truman, and Eisenhower, and four Chilean Presidents, Aguirre Cerda, Juan Antonio Ríos, González Videla and Carlos Ibáñez. These years, 1939 to 1953, cover the most critical time the free world had known in a century.

I have dealt in some detail with the controversy over Chile's diplomatic rupture with the Axis, less in criticism of Chile than in explanation and justification of its adherence to the democratic process. We were almost rapturous in praise of the South American dictatorships that acted more promptly because they did not have to consult public opinion, await congressional approval and act in conformity with a constitution.

Meanwhile, Chile collaborated with us in every practical way, precisely as we collaborated with England for two years prior to Pearl Harbor before we broke diplomatic relations with the Axis. The delay in both countries was imposed by the democratic process—requiring the crystallization of public opinion and congressional action. While the delay of action was annoying, it was a source of gratification to me that Chile did

v

not deviate one hair breadth from the democratic process we were fighting to preserve.

After the rupture the Communists took up where the Axis left off, with exactly the same slogans and propaganda, and this phase is covered in later chapters.

I have tried to give my impression of the Chilean people, their institutions, their literature and culture, their free press, their important cities too seldom seen by casual tourists, the majestic beauty of the mountains and the primeval forests, the charm of the famous lake region, the lovely coast line and its resorts, the appeal of the countryside, the industrial growth of the country, the part the women, noted for their beauty and intelligence, have played in the onward march.

Necessarily this narrative is partly personal. It is based on intimate contacts and observations, on personal correspondence and on seven or eight volumes of my Chilean diary.

A foreign minister, distressed by our ignorance of Chilean institutions, once asked me: "Is it impossible to persuade your people that Chile is not a dictatorship or totalitarian state but one of the only two bastions of democracy in South America?" If I have not succeeded in making this crystal clear, I have failed in my purpose.

—CLAUDE G. BOWERS

NEW YORK, 1957

Contents

vii

Contents

Contents

I

Between the Mountains and the Sea

Leaving New York in mid-August on the *Santa Maria,* we
reached Valparaiso the first of September 1939. Having declined another post because of the strain of my Spanish mission during the war in Spain, I looked forward to a peaceful
life in an entrancing country, among a charming, democratic
people in Chile when, at the President's personal request, I accepted the mission to that country. Unhappily, the day after
our arrival Hitler broke the armistice after the Spanish phase
of World War II, and the totalitarian crusade against democracy was resumed.

Never having been in South America, I shared the appalling
ignorance of my fellow countrymen about this great, rich continent. I had accepted the North American fallacy that all

Latin-American nations are exactly alike in psychology, ideology, traditions and aspirations—though Bolívar knew better much more than a century ago.

Arriving by sea or air, the visitor's first impression of Chile, far famed for beauty and fertility, is disappointing since all one sees is a desert of lonesome sand and rocks. No greenery. Grim desolation. And yet in this rich region billions in wealth have been extracted, since here is found copper and nitrate. We spent a day in Arica, a small city where General Pershing made his headquarters while acting on the commission to settle a boundary dispute between Chile and Peru. This little city by the sea is dominated by the high hill of Morro, from the summit of which the defeated Peruvian officer in the War of the Pacific spurred his horse into the ocean, never to be seen again. Behind the town is the desert, which seems to swoon in the sun. To the tourist the prospect must seem bleak. Sea gulls floating in the air above the Morro hill do nothing to relieve the feeling of loneliness with their weird, sad cries. Driving into the country to a small oasis, we found no trace of a road in the shifting sand. Some girls and women rode by on mules or donkeys, as in Spain, but here no one bade us "Go with God." In a small building near the house of the owner of the oasis we found women, most of them middle-aged and worn with work, busily packing olives. Beside one of the patient workers was a cradle in which a baby smiled and gurgled.

It was on returning that our attention was called to some rusty iron in the sand, and we were told the story of the American warship *Waterlee* that had been swept inland on a tidal wave sixty years before and deposited far back in the desert. Since it was impossible to get the ship back to the sea it was finally abandoned, and it found its grave in the Arica sand.

The next stop in Chile was at Antofagasta, also on the edge of the desert but throbbing with activity since it is a port at which millions of tons of copper and nitrate have been loaded for the United States and Europe. To the transient

4

tourist the city may seem drab, but I was to find that executives of the copper and nitrate companies, once stationed in Antofagasta, looked back with nostalgia to the pleasant days of their residence there. Today they have a club looking out on the beach, where they entertain their friends and swim. An agreeable society is composed of officers of the mining companies, the consuls of various nations, the officers of the army stationed there and prosperous Chilean businessmen.

Rain seldom falls in Antofagasta, and the temperature varies little through the year. When the winter rains and cold make Santiago dreary, many seek relief in the brilliant sunshine on the sands of this city by the sea, with the desert stretching out behind.

2

Then on to Valparaiso, the most important port of the South Pacific and famous for centuries in history. Without lingering, however, we were soon rolling toward Santiago across three minor mountain ranges, over a paved road with many curves—a solid wall of stone heights on one side and a precipitate fall of hundreds of feet into a pleasant valley on the other.

This drive is scenically beautiful, with trees, shrubbery and flowers on the mountain side and cultivated fields and pastures on the other. Here sheep and cattle grazed in the shade and lifted their heads to greet us as we passed.

Just before reaching Casablanca, a thriving market town, we were surprised to find by the roadside a sweet little church set in a garden shaded by trees and fragrant with flowers. Motorists usually pull up a moment at this church to drop an offering in a box provided at the entrance, since prayers are said here for the safety of travelers. We were never to fail to make our contribution. Somehow that little church, so simple and yet attractive, suggested a smiling hostess greeting friends.

We were wondering why so many family groups were having alfresco luncheons on the roadside, or just beyond in the field, and then quickly came the explanation. A picturesque religious procession was approaching down the road. The usually serene countryside was quivering with animation, and the bells of the little church were pealing joyously. The *carabineros* rode ahead directing traffic. Then came men bearing banners, and behind them women and children marching out of step; and then, on a platform borne on the backs of stalwarts of the faith, came the figure of the Virgin, her blond tresses disheveled by the breeze. This was my introduction to the religious side of Chile.

The procession over, we drove on again into the mountains, and when we reached the top of the last range before descending into the valley a picture spread before us so startlingly beautiful that we stopped the car for an unhurried view. Below us, reaching far, was a rich valley, the fields under perfect cultivation and divided, not by fences, but by rows of poplars and Lombardy pines. It was so perfect that it seemed like an idealized painting in a frame. Never in fourteen years did we fail to stop to enjoy this charming picture.

3

It was evening when we drove through the gate of the grounds of the American Embassy, which had housed our ambassadors since 1922. Across the Merced, in front, was the green-shaded Parque Forestal, a miniature Bois in the heart of the city. On an intersecting street to the side of the house were many Japanese cherry trees, which were lovely when in blossom. The garden was not large, but an old dedicated gardener who loved his work coaxed flowers of many varieties and hues both summer and winter.

The house may be described as a palace or a large mansion. We liked especially the spacious dining room, with its deeply carved wooden ceiling and a sweet little room adjoining which had been designed by the builder as a chapel. Although we converted it into a library, it was too dark to read there without artificial light. The front salon, where guests were received at receptions, dinners and luncheons, was furnished then in the French style and was connected with the dining room by a long corridor which caused no end of trouble when hundreds crowded the embassy at receptions and created an embarrassing congestion. I recall that on one occasion I had to send strong-armed members of my staff to force a way out when President Juan Antonio Ríos was leaving.

The Ambassador's Room was never used by me since I preferred a study on the second floor, and it was used by the social secretary. It had been flamboyantly decorated by the widow of an ambassador or minister of the 1860s in memory of him and she had made the eagle scream.

Although the embassy had been ideally situated at the time of its purchase, business had encroached upon it and high apartment houses close by deprived the garden of privacy. During my tenure I signed the papers for the purchase of an ideal site on a hill adjoining the Los Leones Golf Club for a new ambassador's residence. I could not look forward without regret to the demolishing of the old residence, with all its associations of the years, and the erection of an apartment house. Lass, our dog who had been with us through Spain, died in Santiago and we buried her in a bed of roses against the house. We shall be sorry to have her rest disturbed.

4

The presentation of the credentials of ambassadors in Chile is colorful. We found ornate and stately coaches drawn by four horses, accompanied by mounted officers with pennants, waiting for us at the gate, and the procession moved toward the Moneda, the presidential palace. Beside me sat Leon Subercaseaux, chief of protocol, who later had a brilliant diplomatic career in London during the war. A crowd of the curious in front of the Moneda cheered when we arrived, smart soldiers presented arms in the court, and we were conducted to the Red Room, where President Aguirre Cerda and his ministers were waiting. The President exuded cordiality, which was to prove sincere. After the usual brief speeches, followed by an informal chat, the ceremony was over.

A few days later, on Chile's anniversary, I was introduced to one of the most animated of celebrations when I was to see the Chileans en masse. These ceremonies began with a *Te Deum* in the cathedral. The diplomats were ordered to wear uniforms, and since ours is full evening dress and the ceremony was in the morning, I hurried to a tailor to have a light overcoat made to hide my shame. I could not rid myself of the notion that street urchins, seeing a man in full evening dress at eleven in the morning, would conclude that he had been out on the town all night and had not had time to change.

Facing the cathedral, soldiers were lined up, immovable as stone images. The red and white plumes and caps of the boys of the army academy enlivened the scene.

Then the rolling of drums, the sound of a trumpet and the stirring national anthem announced the arrival of the President, who took his place on a platform with the President of the Senate and the Chief Justice of the Supreme Court. Since the President's legs were short, I noticed that he was provided with a footstool for his comfort.

That evening we attended the President's reception at the palace. The diplomats found him and his ministers lined up in the Red Room to receive them. A word of congratulations, and we mingled with the guests until we were conducted into the dining room, where tables laden with food and champagne offered refreshment. The chatter in the crowded room was deafening, for the diplomats were not at all at a loss for a conversational topic since Hitler had marched into Poland, and there was much speculation as to what Mussolini would do. Commander Webb, my Naval Attaché, asked the Italian Attaché what Italy would do. In an arrogant Fascist manner he replied that he did not know, but that "whatever happens Italy is ready." Irritated by his manner, Webb snapped, "So are we"—and the Italian blinked.

Back now to full evening dress for the traditional opera at the Municipal Theater. This year it was *Rigoletto*. The President was a little late in arriving and the gallery was impatient. When he appeared the entire audience rose and cheered, the orchestra played the national anthem and the curtain rose.

5

The next day the celebration continued at Cousiño Park with the grand review of the armed forces. I was convinced from what I saw that day that Chile can defend its independence and territorial integrity. At first, far across the field, the men of the infantry, artillery and cavalry were lined up awaiting the President. A stir in the crowd, and a murmur, announced his arrival in an open carriage drawn by four horses, and he rode slowly down the line, across the field and then took his place in the reviewing stand.

Immediately the infantry regiments were sweeping by, the officers saluting with their swords, the uniforms of the soldiers immaculate, all moving in unison, the bright sun glistening on their bayonets—a scene that touched the emotions. It was then I had my first view of the goose step, for as the officers saluted with their swords, the soldiers fell into the goose step, and the multitude responded with thunderous applause.

The infantry passed, and then, to the stirring music of another military band, the artillery approached; it rushed by with a mighty roar. Then the music of another military band, this time mounted, for it was the band of the cavalry. The grace and beauty of the Chilean horses and the superb horsemanship of the riders were spectacular. Meanwhile the air force zoomed above. We observed these with special interest since we had an air mission in Chile officered by Colonel Niergarth, aided by Burns and Kelly, who, with their charming wives, had earned the confidence and affection of the Chilean fliers.

In three hours the review was over, the President entered his carriage, the enormous throng spread toward the exits and the streets were lined with cheering people. I had seen Chilean patriotism *en fête*.

6

The celebration over? Not at all. The next day, Sunday, came the races at the Hípico, attended by the President, the Diplomatic Corps and thousands from all segments of society. No race course could have been more beautiful. Not far away the mountains climb high in the sky. In a section of the big concrete grandstand reserved for the President and his guests we awaited his arrival, which was announced with shouts that called attention to an unusual scene. The President had dismissed his car and was walking toward the stand, surrounded and followed by the *rotos,* the most picturesque segment of the masses. But that day other interests took precedence over the races, since politics was rampant and the war was on.

7

For four weeks I had been entranced by the beauty spread about me by the mountains—the Andes—outlined against the sky, but now I was to see them more intimately in crossing the highest hump in the world, on my way to Argentina as chairman of our delegation to the first All-American Housing Conference. I went part of the way by train; halfway over the grim heights the tracks had been swept away in a landslide, and it was necessary to make the last half of the journey over the mountains in a car. It was not a pleasing prospect. We left Los Andes, at the foot of the mountains, at dawn. I had in mind the journey over the mountains of Joel

Poinsett, the first American diplomat in South America, many years before, when there were neither trains nor planes. The grim heights had startled him, the loneliness had depressed him, as had the perils. The scenery could not have been much different after a century—still ruggedly beautiful, still menacing. Halfway over I was transferred to a little Ford car, and all afternoon we rode along a narrow, winding, unpaved road, the threatening mountains rising above us on one side, a frightening fall of thousands of feet on the other. My confidence in the driver was put to a supreme test as we approached the descent to Mendoza. There a heavy white cloud settled on the winding road and we could not see the curves or the ground. With the experienced driver going it blind, as it seemed, we passed the crisis and descended safely to the plains. The railroad tracks were restored a little later, but most tourists now prefer crossing by plane.

8

I added something to my knowledge of South American psychology at the Housing Conference in Buenos Aires. I was supported by a number of specialists on housing projects who took the conference seriously and had prepared an elaborate report, but the Latin-American delegates were not in the least interested. I was astonished to find them bitterly divided on whether the buildings should be individual houses or apartment houses. It seemed simple to me. If land were abundant, individual houses; if the area were crowded, apartment houses. This suggestion made no impression, and I finally pressed a bitter opponent of apartment housing for an explanation. He thought that apartment houses for the workers could be "dangerous" since it would be more difficult to keep an eye on the workers, who would be cooped up together and could "conspire." If they were provided with individual houses, the authorities could more easily keep them under surveillance. Then I knew that these delegates were thinking of the workers' apartment houses in Vienna and of the time these strong buildings were converted into bastions in a bitter social struggle.

9

I returned to Chile via Bariloche, the entrance to the region of the lakes. Crossing into Chile, we drove several miles along a beautiful lake and through primeval forests of enormous trees that seemed almost impenetrable. We lunched at Bahía, and then took a motorboat ride on the lake Nahuel Huapí. From Puerto Blest we began a long drive over the Continental Divide, a memorable journey along narrow roads shut in by dense woods, with the snow-capped Andes looming near.

It was evening when we reached the village of Peulla, where we were to spend the night. The inn was a frame building looking much like a large farmhouse, but it was impeccably clean, comfortable and homey. The manager, an artistic Swiss who loved nature and its moods, roamed the woods and mountains in search of rare flowers found nowhere else. Proudly he showed me his paintings of these flowers; but with even more pride he brought out the register to show me the signature of Cordell Hull, who had lodged there en route home from the famous conference in Uruguay.

The next morning in a brilliant sunshine we embarked on a large launch with its German owner, who had lived in the neighborhood for forty years. We were on the delectable Lake of All the Saints, which is fed by the springs and melting snows of the mountains. The water is an indigo blue and so crystal clear that it reflects the mountains on the surface. Suddenly we found we were approaching a very large island in the middle of the lake, the greenery of the trees and the foliage vivid in the sun. Our host was the owner of the island and he had just put up an attractive house for a home. During the war, when rumors were rife, it was said that this island would be an ideal nest for espionage, but there was positively nothing to explain the silly suspicion. We found our host more concerned with mice than with spies because of a recent scourge of mice that had emerged from the woods when the bamboo trees were in bloom to feed upon the blossoms. They had appeared "by the millions," and men had worked day and night on their extermination, since, with the passing of the blossoms, the desperately hungry mice attacked animals and were dangerous. I was not to hear of another scourge of mice during my fourteen years in Chile.

When I commented to my host on the cleanliness and comforts of the little taverns in the lake region, he told me a story of an innkeeper there who had advertised "All languages spoken here." An Englishman tried English on the keeper without results; then French, to no avail; then Italian, and there was no response. Thoroughly annoyed, the traveler referred to the advertisement and asked, in Spanish, who spoke "all languages" there. The tavern keeper replied, honestly enough, "Why, our guests, of course."

In one of these little taverns run by a German we had a delicious lunch at Petrohué, where we left the launch and took a car for a long drive over fields covered with lava from the old volcanoes not far away (they are still active at infrequent intervals) until we reached green pastures and cultivated fields and the city of Osorno.

Since I knew that this city was predominantly German I was curious to get the sentiment of the community on the war then in progress for six weeks. I was most favorably impressed by the town itself; it was so neat, clean and orderly.

In search of popular sentiment I went to the cinema. The house was filled before the picture was shown, and the conversation was all in German. When, in the newsreel, Hitler was shown leaving his plane in Poland there were scattered cheers, but I noticed they came entirely from a few groups of young men, and there was a little whistling in disapproval. When Churchill's picture appeared on the screen there was a hum of conversation but no demonstration. I had seen and heard enough to know that in Chile sentiment on the war would be divided. But in the midst of the loveliness of the scenery in the incomparable lake region this did not then seem too ugly.

Visiting this same region on his return from Africa, Theodore Roosevelt looked about him and exclaimed, "The most beautiful in the world—more beautiful than Switzerland." Here the mountains seem higher, the lakes deeper. In some places the peaks rise almost precipitately from the lake shore. The largest of the lakes, Llanquihue, is like a sea studded with islands rich in vegetation, and in the background loom the mountains and the volcanoes of Osorno and Calbuco that spout at infrequent intervals. Swans and ducks float gracefully on the water. In calm weather the lakes are smooth and serene, but when strong winds rise they can become tumultuous and dangerous.

10

We were now on the last lap of our journey back to Santiago. From Osorno I had my first experience with Chilean trains. The Pullmans were not the shoddy ones we had used in Argentina but were staunchly built, clean and comfortable, the rooms pleasant, but I was especially impressed by the quality and quantity of the food served in the dining car and by the service. Before lunch or dinner, the steward passed through the cars inquiring if, and when, the passenger wished service, and he was given a ticket reserving a table for him when he reached the dining car—no standing in the aisle of a swaying coach waiting for a seat at a table. The cost of an excellent meal was astonishingly low. Most of the fast trains, which are run by electricity, are kept clean.

The journey back to Santiago took us through a large part of the famously rich Central Valley of the great, intensively cultivated *fundos*, with enormous droves of cattle and sheep grazing in the pastures. In the small towns we passed we found high piles of sawed lumber, foretelling the ultimate development of a better-organized lumber industry. The scenes on the station platforms of the little towns, with the villagers meeting the train out of curiosity, evoked nostalgic memories of just such scenes during my boyhood in the small towns of Indiana.

Thus circumstances had made it possible for me to learn, within two months, something of the topography and scenery of Chile, its desolate and yet opulent desert of the north, the lovely lakes mirroring the mighty mountains, and the great forests and rich vegetation of the south, but I was still curious about the people, so different in so many ways from those of surrounding countries. At length I worked out my theory about the people.

II

The Chilean People

When Pizarro, conquerer of Peru, looked southward into Chile, with its grim desert, its towering, rugged mountains, and its fierce natives, the Araucanians, he shivered and drew back, and when that gallant warrior, Valdivia, proposed to brave the difficulties of conquest, Pizarro sought to dissuade him. The mass of Spaniards who fought in Peru found nothing to attract them to an incursion into Chile. They knew that only the hardiest and most determined could withstand the heat and torture of the desert, to be crossed to reach the Central Valley, of which they had heard, and the terrifying mountains, where no trails had been blazed, gave them pause. Then, too, the fame of the Araucanian Indians had reached them.

These Indians had easily held back the Incas north of the river Maule and were known to be an infinitely tougher breed than the red men of Peru. Broad-chested men, of medium height, with shaggy black hair, narrow foreheads, prominent cheekbones and piercing, rather oblique eyes, they seemed formidable. They were copper-colored, and there was nothing in their sad, somber countenance to inspire confidence. In battle, incomparably fearless and ferocious, they fought with arrows and javelins tipped with flint or stone, and they flung themselves into battle with bloodcurdling shouts. Despite the then modern weapons of the invaders, they challenged the whites to combat. Their physical endurance was phenomenal. When food was plentiful they gorged themselves, but when food was scarce they could live and struggle, march and fight, for many days with nothing more to sustain them than a little water and toasted grain. Though not noted generally for their intellect, they had among them born orators. Each tribe had its spokesman, a master of natural eloquence. Their orations were narratives or tales and legends. They were steeped in superstition and had complete faith in enchantments and sorcery.

For two centuries and more they withstood the whites. With an intrepidity that resembled madness, they contested every inch of ground. At first terrorized by the invaders' horses and intimidated by their firearms, their confidence returned when their arrows laid low the whites they had thought immortal.

After his earliest battles, Valdivia wrote Charles V that in all the fighting he had seen, of all the warriors he had known, these men were "stiff in battle" beyond comparison. The most famous of their warriors was Lautaro, after whom the Chileans named their biggest battleship, and in honor of whom they have raised a monument. These red men fought to kill. Prisoners were dispatched without mercy and were usually tortured. Valdivia himself, when captured, was clubbed to death, and his heart, cut into small pieces, was eaten by the Indian chiefs.

Among all the Spanish conquerors none approached Valdivia

in intelligence. His dispatches to the King were lucid, wise and remarkably well phrased. These, in his own handwriting, recently published in Madrid, would do credit to a seasoned, enlightened statesman of any age.

Since, in the nature of things, the two races remained aloof in hostile camps, there was less mingling of their blood than elsewhere, though women, red or white, when captured, were victims of the lust of the captors.

It was not until the nineteenth century that the struggle between the races ended with the acquiescence of the natives to defeat, though not defeat in battle. The old passion for fighting had died out. The periodic parleys through the centuries accomplished little, and yet something. Agreements were made and broken on both sides. The influence of the Jesuit missionaries, in whom the natives had confidence, made them tend toward conciliation. Diplomacy and tact took over the work of sword, gun and arrow, and O'Higgins issued an edict pronouncing the natives "Chilean citizens and free, like the other inhabitants of the country, with whom they shall have equal voice and equal representation." This was followed, a year later, with another edict granting them the secure and perpetual ownership of the land allotted them.

Today these red men dwell, for the most part, in a portion of the southern section, near Temuco. Some have been converted to Christianity; many retain their old beliefs and superstitions; some cultivate their land but others rent it to the whites and live in idleness, though the women are industrious. In fourteen years I never recognized as an Indian anyone I saw in the streets of Santiago or Valparaiso, but in Temuco, the nearest city to the Indian reservation, they were much in evidence, and I have seen their women in the stores bartering their beautiful handiwork for food and clothing.

The long struggle with the red men did something toward making the Chileans a race of fighters, and the courage, determination, passion for freedom and the nobility of the Araucanians have entered into the molding of the Chilean people.

The small band that followed the sword of Valdivia came from all parts of Spain, at first mostly from the southern section, but later, when the immigration began, the greater part came from the Basque country. Tough, independent, resourceful, industrious, liberty-loving, they helped set the pattern for the molding of the Chilean people. In the Basques, Spain gave of her best to Chile. These turned to trade, to industry, to farming, and in the early days they formed the society of the country.

Inevitably, among the first of the settlers came the English —always English but always loyal to the land of their adoption. In the halcyon days of the Empire, when the sun never set on all the British possessions, when Valparaiso was world-famous as a port of trade, this Chilean city by the sea had some annoying visits from Drake and other English buccaneers, but more significant, and of lasting influence, were the British who came to trade. More, I think, than any other race, these had a determining influence on business. Merchants, importers and exporters, manufacturers, they settled in the beginning mostly in Valparaiso, in whose harbor flew the flags of all nations, and to this day the city impresses me as distinctly British in tone and appearance.

These British, found now in all parts of the country, have, for the most part, come to stay and have intermarried with the Chileans. Some of the oldest and most distinguished families have English names. Some return to the homeland to retire, but most remain. They have brought with them respect for law and order, for democracy, a love of liberty and a dependable business integrity. English capital has made notable contributions to Chilean development, and the nation, with 2,800 miles of Pacific coast making it naturally maritime in spirit, has never forgotten that Lord Cochrane created the Chilean Navy, which compares favorably, in training and personnel, with any in the world.

Along with the English came the Scotch and the Irish, and

not a few old leading families have Scottish and Irish names. One of my most pleasant memories is of evenings spent with the Scotch on St. Andrews Day, when I spoke every year for eight years at their dinners and was finally rewarded with a tartan and identified as of the "McBowers clan."

3

The English and the Basques were the most important settlers until after the revolutionary troubles in Germany in 1848, when the Germans began to pour into the country. They went originally in search of freedom and escape from military domination, and they brought with them the best the German race has produced—industrious men, organizers, disciplinarians, redeemers of the wilderness, who, in the south, felled the forests, cultivated the fields, bridged the streams, drained the swamps and built the roads in a rich region previously a primeval forest. No one can visit the thriving cities of Osorno and Valdivia without the feeling that Germany is not remote. German order and cleanliness are conspicuous. German culture is here predominant. The German emigrants, encouraged to come in the 1850s, redeemed the waste land and became proprietors of large *fundos* and small farms; and then, grown prosperous, they branched out to become leaders in commerce, industry and banking. They intermarried with Chilean families and became a strong factor in the direction of Chilean thinking.

More than any other race, the Germans realized the potentialities of the country long before we North Americans discovered Chile's great possibilities, and the German influence was felt. It was a German officer who for two decades trained the Chilean Army. Chilean officers were invited to Germany for special training. Chilean physicians and surgeons went to work in German hospitals and laboratories. German machinery was imported and has long been preferred. The trade with Germany became of great importance to Chilean economy. And out of all this came a natural admiration and appreciation of the German character, and today, in seeking immigrants, the Germans are preferred.

4

Along with the Germans came many Dutch and Scandinavians, more important for their quality than quantity. Then, later, came another people to mingle their blood with the Latins: the Yugoslavs settled in the south, and the word went back to the homeland that Chile was a land of beauty and opportunity. Then the Yugoslavs began to pour in. These have not a few of the qualities of the Germans. Intensely industrious, they turned to farming and sheep raising, to commerce and industry, and soon they too prospered and waxed rich. The great *fundo* of Chacabuco, with almost a hundred thousand acres, is owned and operated by a Yugoslav family. During my time in Chile one of the richest men in the country was a Yugoslav who, on his death, left a fine bequest to the land of his adoption. In Magellan the Yugoslavs vie with the British in the sheep industry. These are all stout fellows of the stuff of pioneers.

The Italian immigrants, and there are many, are in business on a moderate scale, but they have given to public life such significant figures as Arturo Alessandri Palma, twice President, sponsor of the most advanced social legislation on the continent, who played a conspicuous part in the writing of Chile's excellent democratic Constitution. Many leaders in the professions of law and medicine are of Italian origin. In very recent years, during my tenure in Chile, Italian agricultural workers have been sought, and a large colony has been settled in the region of La Serena.

5

It will be noted that for years the greater part of the immigrants to Chile have come from northern European nations. Comparatively few Spaniards have migrated to Chile in recent years. The mingling of the blood of these northern non-Latin races with that of Chileans of Spanish origin has created a distinct race. Chile today is no more Spanish, except for language, than the United States is English. The political thinking of the Chileans today is no more Spanish than it was when they declared their independence from Spain. They are instinctively democratic, tolerant in politics, and they look to the future and not to the past. Proud of their heritage of Spanish culture and of the achievements of the race, they nevertheless have a more cosmopolitan psychology. It is this mingling of the northern European blood with the Spanish that is probably responsible for the fact that the Chileans are more mature politically than any other people on the continent; more democratic, more innately hostile to totalitarian or dictatorial rule. It has also made the Chileans less explosive and more serene; less imaginative and more realistic; less romantic and more utilitarian; and they fit into the mart and factory more easily.

Thus Chile is the beneficiary of numerous races and nationalities:

The Araucanians have set an example in courage and stubborn fighting.

The Basques have given her some of the same qualities, along with practical business sense, industry and ambition.

The British have contributed a model for commercial organizations and business integrity.

The Germans have been an example of orderliness, perseverance, discipline and culture.

So, too, the Scandinavians and the Dutch.

The Yugoslavs have reinforced the qualities furnished by the Germans.

And all these qualities, thrown into the melting pot, have

produced the Chilean people of today, who differ in character from the people of surrounding nations.

6

The manner of the Chilean is a mixture of Yankee breeziness and Spanish courtesy. They are a courtly people. When meeting male acquaintances on the street the old-school Chilean is apt to lift his hat. Like the Spaniards, they are given to much handshaking. The guest rises to leave and shakes hands; the host accompanies him to the door and again shakes hands; here a pause for some parting words, and, this over, another handshake. If the host lives in an apartment house or hotel, he sees his guest to the elevator for a final handshake. Whereas in the United States the host parts with his guest at the door, the courtly Chilean is apt to accompany him to the gate or even to the car to wave and smile as the car moves off. This is not an affectation but an ingrained sense of courtesy.

When North Americans and Chileans mingle at receptions and cocktail parties one would be hard pressed to tell which are the Yankees and which the Chileans, since their social manner, their dress, height, and color are almost identical.

In some countries the stranger is made to feel, by the aloofness and coldness of his reception, that he does not "belong" —although there are exceptions—but in Chile he is made to feel at home and among understanding friends at once. This is a common observation of tourists and businessmen. Then, too, the stranger is judged more by his intrinsic worth than by his possessions.

In nothing do the Chileans resemble the North Americans more than in their business dealings and psychology. Across the counter they speak the same language and understand each other. Both are noteworthy for their business acumen, their hard bargaining qualities, and if there are any resentments over negotiations it is due to the inability of either to "put a fast one" over on the other. They have a common respect for the sanctity of a contract. I think Chile incapable of repudiating an honest national debt. When the crash came in the late twenties and the bottom fell out of the nitrate market, when the catastrophic earthquake of 1938 brought enormous losses, when, during World War II, millions in trade with Germany were wiped out and Chile understandably was unable to make the stipulated payments on its debts, she paid what she could as a token of recognition of her debts as an obligation of honor.

Nothing pleases the North American more than the discovery that the Chileans have a Yankee sense of humor. The Frenchman may turn a puzzled frown on a Yankee joke, the English may take it home to sleep on and the laugh comes in the morning, but the Chilean anticipates the point of the story before it reaches its climax. I am sure this sense of humor goes far to explain the political stability of the country. While some countries of the continent become hysterical over political differences, the Chilean laughs. This is one reason why the Chileans are not given to comic-opera coups and conspiracies. Political enemies can mingle socially and joke and laugh over their political disagreements.

Like all peoples, the Chileans have their faults and weaknesses. If asked to put a finger on the most outstanding fault I would point to their extreme optimism, a fault they have discovered in themselves in recent years. "Sufficient unto the day is the evil thereof." Relying for years on the income from copper and nitrate, they long overlooked the need for a diversification of industry to take up the slack should these sources fail. Even so, this optimism, this cheery outlook, contributes greatly to the Chilean's charm in social contacts. He is always gay. He would not think of weeping over his woes and wiping his eyes on his companion's coat.

There are gradations in the social scale in Chile as in all other countries. Not very long ago the peak was the great landowning aristocracy, dating back to feudalistic days. These live part of the year on their *fundos* and part in their town houses in Santiago. For the most part they are cosmopolitans, to be found, in season, on the Riviera, at Biarritz or in Switzerland. Most of these are cultivated persons with a great deal of charm. The passing of their political pre-eminence is accepted philosophically by them since they are very intelligent and adjustable. The autocrat of fifty years ago is seldom seen. The attitude of the very few who remain is illustrated in the story of a land baron, a very picturesque old man who spent most of his time in the city and could be found almost any day at the Union Club having his lunch or toddy. One day a telegram was handed him from the supervisor of his estate which read: "The peasants have locked me in the barn and say unless they are assured of increased pay within six hours they will kill me." The old man grew red in the face, the cords stood out on his neck as he called for a telegraph blank. Then, shaking his head and muttering to himself, he wrote his reply: "Tell those communist SOBs *they can't intimidate me.*" But this old man is interesting only as a relic.

Meanwhile, a large and prosperous middle class possesses more political power today than the old aristocracy. It is composed of what we North Americans call "self-made men." The legal, medical, architectural and engineering professions and writers are recruited largely from families of ordinary means. These furnish, too, a large majority of the successful businessmen and industrialists. Among recent Presidents, Aguirre Cerda and Juan Antonio Ríos spent their boyhoods on small farms, where they followed the plow and milked the cows.

The condition and status of the industrial workers in mines and factories are much superior to that of the peasants. These workers are keenly and intelligently conscious of their economic rights and interests. They have been strongly organized into unions that embrace every branch of industry. On my arrival in Chile the labor syndicates were intelligently led and were concerned solely with the protection of the legitimate rights of labor. Before I left, the communists had infiltrated systematically into the unions, with the single purpose of using them for the revolutionary, antidemocratic purposes handed down from Moscow. This has weakened public confidence. After their infiltration, the political overshadowed the economic motives, in revolutionary, illegal strikes, in defiance of the vital interest of the country. Every strike in the copper mines means a tremendous loss in revenue to the government.

The peasantry is gradually securing a greater recognition of its needs, and under the pressure of intelligent public opinion, better housing is being furnished on the *fundos*. Many, if not most, of the peasants are uneducated, some superstitious, and while they are, in general, Catholic, not a few have a religious psychology difficult to define. This may be due in a measure to some Indian blood dating back many generations. Until recently they were political ciphers, responding unquestioningly at the polls to the instruction of their employers, but this, too, is passing, and today politicians cannot afford to take the vote of the peasants for granted.

There is still another class, more picturesque than any other, known as the *rotos*. These are the first cousins of the *inquilinos,* the descendants of the mixed races of centuries ago who were long slaves of the soil on the great feudalistic estates. They long accepted their status, giving loyalty and respect to their masters in return for none-too-good food and rather wretched shelter. Whether their instinctive spirit of independence when the more spirited rebelled was due to their Spanish or Araucanian blood is conjectural. Resenting a life that offered no entertainment or liberty of action, these stout individualists left the land and flocked to the cities, where, at the time, they did not fit in with the social and economic system. Some few found their way to the mines, but the majority clung to the more pleasant life of the cities. No other element is more distinctly Chilean. Uncompromising individualists, proud and independent, and fiercely jealous of their freedoms, they won the respect and admiration of the nation. Forced for years to live by their wits, they are naturally clever and resourceful. In some ways they bear a resemblance to the Cockneys of London, for they are good-natured and always ready with a joke or a searing bit of repartee. Because they are so Chilean, *Topaze,* the brilliant magazine of satire, symbolizes "the people" with cartoons of the *roto* with a taunting, cynical grin, and with devastating comments on political leaders and scenes. In the celebration of national holidays the *roto* plays a conspicuous part, dancing in the plaza and parks as an outer expression of his deep-rooted patriotism. On my first attendance at the traditional military review in Cousino Park, it was a *roto* who received special attention. I was startled to see one of these approaching the presidential stand shouting and waving his arms. There was no indication of alarm. Everyone in the reviewing stand was smiling, and army officers made way for the *roto* as he approached. When he reached the presidential stand, Aguirre Cerda, the President, reached over the railing with outstretched hand and the two shook hands and exchanged sharp repartee, as the presidential party roared with laughter. I then got the impression—later verified—that the Chileans as a people have a real affection for the *roto,* who, elementally, reflects the national spirit. They are a cheerful people, and to see them at their gayest one should look in on their celebrations of the national holiday in the Plaza Bulnes, when the streets are swirling with the cueca, the Chilean dance of the masses. No element loves Chile more than the *roto.*

8

No visitor to Chile should fail to see the cueca. The dance has been variously described in attempts to interpret its meaning. Joaquín Edwards finds it "music intoxication that no

Creole can see without feeling drunk with the indefinable, a dance of history and conquest and submission," in which "the sexes remain barbarously defined." Eugenio Pereira Salas, historian of Chilean folklore, sees in it "the expression not only of lyricism, eroticism and satyrism, but Chile's whole history." Louis Durand sees in it "the soul of the people" surging up "from the depths of its ancestral boredom and apathy to prove that there is still in every breast a strong tincture of sane and robust optimism, a spiritual energy." Erna Fergusson finds it fascinating but beyond the interpretation of an unimaginative Yankee.

Many attempts have been made to fix its origin. One finds something like it in the Africa of long ago, and a few believe it was brought to Chile by the very few Negro slaves who were in the country in colonial days. Some trace its introduction to Chile to a Negro battalion which visited Chile and presented it originally in the "lowest cantinas and dives," as Erna Fergusson heard. More than a century ago the dance was frowned upon by the middle class, but even then it was seen when friends gathered in fashionable drawing rooms. If I were called upon to describe it—and no Chileans were about—I would call it a flirtation aimed at seduction. It certainly is an exciting and passionate dance. While it is danced by all classes, to see it at its wildest, in its primitive abandon, one must see it in the Plaza Bulnes, for there the impact on the emotions of the masses is manifest.

The cueca is not easy to describe. It begins with a mild flirtation, turns into a wooing and ends with the conquering of the lady and her surrender. I have seen it danced in different costumes, by charming women beautifully gowned and by women of the masses in torn and dowdy skirts. In exhibition dances the men are usually dressed as *huasos*—cowboys—with cowboy hats and flashing spurs. The handkerchief plays a major part in the flirtation, the man and woman waving it provocatively and gracefully. The man is supposedly indifferent, and the woman uses all her wiles and appeal to arouse his interest. Demurely but with a seductive smile, she lifts her skirts to display her ankles, and the man retreats before her attack. Gradually she melts his heart of stone, and as he now advances, she coyly retreats, but not for long. The cool calculations of the consummate flirt concerned solely with the domination of the male slowly give way to the awakened fervor of her partner. Now she is no longer the artist in coquetry but a true daughter of Eve. The dance quickens, intensifies, art gives way to passion, and now, the conquest achieved, they encircle each other with their arms in a warm embrace. Such, at any rate, is the drama as it appeared to me. Some have described it as a barnyard courtship between a rooster and a hen.

The effect on the bystander is similar to that of the gypsy dances in the Granada caves, when the spectators shout encouragement, clapping their hands in unison, and the caves resound with the shrill shout *"Olé."* So it is in the dancing of the cueca in the fiestas of the masses. The bystanders clap their hands to the movement of the dance, taunt the male for his timidity and compliment the woman—sometimes a bit too frankly. The scene is sensual. With the blood warmed with wine and the senses excited by the movements of the dance, these popular fiestas can lead to trouble, born of jealousy, resentment or unrealized desire. Occasionally, but happily not often, a knife does flash and a flying fist makes contact, but such incidents must be charged less to the dance than to the popular drink, which is potent.

The cueca is rarely seen in formal dances in the homes. Sometimes, however, it is announced that if the dancers will momentarily retire, the Señorita Lucila and the Caballero Luis, who have kindly agreed to dance the cueca, will perform, and there is always rapturous applause.

These, then, are the people. And now for their political institutions, aspirations, ideals and philosophy, since these will determine the policy of Chile in the war and explain many things of which we North Americans are ignorant.

III

Government and Politics

The day before an election, after a fiercely fought campaign, a group of North American correspondents stationed in Buenos Aires who had not manifested any special interest in Chile trooped into the embassy. Suspecting that they expected rioting at the polls, and a possible *coup d'état* attempt by the defeated, I told them that such events were incompatible with Chilean democracy. The next day the polls closed at four, the result was known by eight, and at nine the defeated candidate sent his congratulations to the victor. This, so unusual in South America, impressed me as "news," but the correspondents took their departure without sending a line to their papers. Good news is not "news" from South America.

I cite this as an illustration of the appalling ignorance we

North Americans display about our neighbors of the south. We have acted too long on the stupid assumption that all the Latin-American Republics have the same racial mixture, the same psychology, the same traditions and aspirations. More than a century ago, Bolívar was more intelligent. In speculating on the probable future trends of the newly emancipated Spanish colonies, he thought Peru would be ruled by an oligarcy of the aristocracy, that Argentina would be partial to dictatorial regimes, Mexico to military rule and that Chile would follow the line of law and constitutional government. For the most part, Chile has vindicated the foresight of Bolivar, and, along with Uruguay, it has been a "bastion of democracy" in South America.

In the first days of the Republic, some liberal views of the liberator encountered bitter opposition. The nation was too close to the old Spanish concept of society, the great landed interests, with a feudalistic outlook, were powerful because of their wealth and influence, and the great emancipator retired before the attack to prevent bloodshed and went into voluntary exile in Peru, where he died.

This left a powerful segment of the population in possession of the field to establish a system primarily intended to perpetuate the domination of the landed interests. For a time this seemed ideal to the beneficiaries, but all was not serene. The democratic element was constantly in revolt. The government was honeycombed with corruption, the administration crippled by the incompetence of the bureaucracy, and for years the only safe investment was in land. Because of the constant turmoil and lawlessness, even in the law-enforcing agencies, business, in general, suffered.

It was at this juncture that a really great constructive statesman of vision and democratic ideals, though essentially a conservative, appeared upon the scene. This was Diego Portales. His business as a merchant had been demoralized by the anarchy of the times and he went into politics in the hope of bringing order out of chaos and making investments in commerce and industry reasonably safe.

He was made Minister of the Interior, and with grim determination he set himself the dangerous task of forcing corruption from the public service, of establishing stability in government and of imposing efficiency on public servants. He was not an enemy of the landed interests but he knew that the welfare of the state would ultimately rest on commerce and industry as well. His purpose was to persuade men of means to invest their money in constructive enterprises by giving them a sense of security. Finding that the continuing feud between the followers and the enemies of O'Higgins diverted attention from the pending political, administrative and social problems, he applied his power of persuasion with success. When, by tireless effort, he had restored confidence in administration and given a sense of security to business enterprise, he retired to private life. Thinking primarily of the country and not of his own selfish interests, he had no personal political aspirations. He refused to consider the Presidency when it was within his grasp. Retiring to his farm, he lived quietly until, in his absence, anarchy reared its ugly head, and he returned to the ministry to put down the mischief-makers with an iron hand. Though the acknowledged leader of the conservative element and absolute master of the government, he generously credited President Joaquín Prieto, a good man but untrained in statecraft, with all his own policies.

He had never been more popular than on the day he started on a journey through the country. He was to be overtaken by some army officers and assassinated on the highway, as Cicero had been murdered.

Mark that name—Portales. It is one of the greatest in South American history, and, more than any other man of his time, he symbolized modern Chile. I was never to visit the Ministry of the Interior without pausing a moment to look at the bronze bust of this truly great man.

For ninety years the Constitution imposed by the conservative landed interests remained in force. It established a strong

Presidential government in control of the aristocratic olig-
archy, and the power of parliament was almost nil. The struggle for power between the Executive and Legislative branches
reached a climax in the bloody collision between Congress and
President Balmaceda in 1891, ending in the triumph of the
Congressional party and the suicide of the President.

The struggle was renewed during the first administration of
Arturo Alessandri Palma in the second decade of the century.
Alessandri had a greater personal following than Balmaceda,
and he was a cleverer manipulator of men, with a better understanding of mass psychology. By sponsoring radical social
reforms, he arrayed against him the favored interests dominant in the Senate. With their power over the purse, his opponents had the whip hand, and their refusals to grant appropriations made it impossible for Alessandri to govern. Some
of his own followers began to desert under fire. Unable to
govern, he resigned. The army was on the point of knocking
on the door of the Moneda when he appeared at the United
States Embassy and was received, not as a refugee, but as
a "guest." One day many years later when he was my luncheon
guest, he placed his hand on the table in the library and said,
"It was on this table that I signed my abdication." Ambassador Collier personally drove him to the Argentine border,
and he sailed for Italy. But chaos followed; he was recalled
and received with popular acclaim. After this came the new
Constitution of 1925, which was written to include the views of
Alessandri.

2

During the early stages of World War II, Chile was criticized in the United States by the cheerleaders of the South
American dictators because it moved with the deliberation of a
real democracy toward rupture with the Axis. These cheerleaders of the dictators were either ignorant of the Chilean demo-

cratic Constitution of a sovereign state or they could see no reason why a Constitution should stand in the way of our immediate desire.

The Constitution of 1925 is thoroughly democratic. It describes the State of Chile as unitary, its government republican and representatively democratic, with sovereignty vested in the people. It denounces as treason any attempt by any person or assembly of persons to usurp authority.

The constitutional guarantees for the protection of the people against the abuse of executive or legislative power are all-embracing and might have been written by Jefferson. Note the words "Equality under the law"—no privileged class, no slaves. And these words: "He who sets foot on Chilean soil is free." Then ". . . freedom of conscience, religious freedom and toleration, with all church property exempt from taxation." Freedom of speech and of the press? "Freedom to express without prior censorship opinions, orally or in writing, through the medium of the press or in any other form." Freedom of assembly? "The right to assemble without prior license and without arms" in plazas and streets, governed only by police regulations for the preservation of order. The right of petition? "The right of presenting petitions to the constituted authorities upon any matter of public or private concern, without any other limitation than that of using respectful and suitable language." The right of teaching? "Primary education is obligatory." As to civil and military authority? "No armed body can make requisitions or exact any kind of aid except through the civil authorities and by order of the latter." Inviolability of property? "No one can be deprived of property under his control . . . except by virtue of a judicial decree or writ of expropriation on account of public interest, conformable to a law," and in cases of expropriation the owner shall be "indemnified in advance." The privacy of homes? "The house of any person can be entered forcibly only for a special purpose, determined by law, and by virtue of an order from a competent authority."

One will look far among the constitutions of nations to find one more considerate of the rights of the citizen. I was to find the Chileans holding their fundamental laws in reverence.

3

The governmental structure is very similar to our own. The three co-ordinate branches of government—Executive, Legislative and Judicial—each independent of the other, could have been patterned after our own system, with some minor modifications, perhaps after the French. The President is elected for six years instead of four and is ineligible for re-election, though after an intervening term he may serve again. The Senate is elected for eight years, instead of six, and the Deputies for four years instead of two—a distinct improvement on our own system. As in England, parliamentarians need not reside in the districts they represent, thus making easier the employment of the men best qualified for public service. Half the senators are elected every four years, and so the Senate is never without experienced lawmakers.

No elected President uses his position to continue himself in office after the conclusion of his six-year term. I was shocked one day when, on the terrace of the summer palace in Viña, an American congressman, assuming that all South American nations were alike, said to González Videla, "I suppose you are planning to stay in another term." The startled President turned on his interrogator an indignant stare. "You surely do not know that our Constitution, which we observe, forbids two consecutive terms, or you would not ask that question," he said, and turned his back and walked away from the gaping congressman.

While the Constitution of 1925 gave the President more power than he had before, he is still without autocratic authority. Legislation which he urges can be defeated in Congress; legislation enacted, he can veto; and Congress can negate an international agreement by refusing its ratification. In all this, the Chilean system runs parallel with our own.

Refreshingly free from politics and popular pressure are the courts, which are absolutely independent. This, perhaps, is to be expected in a country with a bar of the greatest ability and dignity. Only men of stature and character are appointed to the bench from the bar, which ranks high. The Supreme Court is composed of thirteen justices. Whenever the President is called upon to appoint a justice, the members of the court make a recommendation, and thus party politics does not dominate. The justices hold office through life, on good behavior. I had the privilege of knowing some of these jurists, all men of legal erudition, high professional ideals and impeccable character. I was to see legislation favored by the President, passed by the Congress, and signed by the President set aside on constitutional grounds by these courageous judges. As long as men of their caliber sit upon the bench and retain the respect and confidence of the people, the democracy of Chile is secure.

4

The people are politically minded, perhaps a wee bit too much so. It is conceded, I think, that they are more mature politically than any other people on the continent. Politics is a favorite conversational topic throughout the year. The women talk politics, national and international, with keen intelligence at dinners, luncheons and cocktails. I found the taxi drivers veritable encyclopedias, more dependable than most politicians in forecasting the result of elections. But this preoccupation of the mass of the people with politics has its disadvantage, as the ancient Greeks found centuries ago. In Chile, politics takes no vacation after an election. Scarcely has a new President entered on his functions when candidates for the succession, six years later, are in the field, if a bit under cover. Unhappily, as a result, legislation is often affected by the rivalries of contending aspirants.

Like most nations in Europe, Chile suffers from a multiplicity of political parties, which are often divided on methods rather than on principles or policies. The result is that it is practically impossible for any one party to receive a clear mandate from the people at the polls. Thus the party with a plurality, on taking office, is forced to form coalitions with other parties to form a government, and differences, often on minor issues, sometimes on patronage, force a reorganization of the ministry, creating the impression abroad of instability. These changes, due to what is described as a "crisis," create the false impression of weakness. Even so, the numerous changes in the personnel of the ministry have not thus far weakened the democracy of Chile.

5

For many years the Conservative party, composed in large part of the landowning aristocracy, was dominant. The ideology of this party is denoted in its name. Among its leaders from the time of Portales have been many of the ablest statesmen and rulers in modern Chilean history. Miguel Cruchaga, a leader in my time and a cherished friend of mine, was a wise statesman, distinguished diplomat and Foreign Minister. The Conservative position was shaken during my time when it split on issues of a social nature. The new school, led by Senators Cruz Coke and Horacio Walker, favored more advanced social reforms, mustered a majority, and the old-line Conservatives withdrew and formed another party, called the Traditionalists. It was being led, when I left, by Senator Prieto in the Senate and Juan Antonio Coloma in the House. The reunion of the two segments was soon inevitable.

The Liberal party, also conservative, is more liberal as to religion, and during the regime of Arturo Alessandri Palma it followed him, a bit reluctantly, on social legislation for the masses. During the period of its power it developed a group of leaders of the stature of statesmen.

Thus in 1938 Chile was governed by the Conservatives and Liberals; then came the electoral revolution, with the triumph of the Radical party under the leadership of Aguirre Cerda, and for fourteen years that party was to be in possession of the Presidency. It had split off from the Liberal party in the 1850s, when it recruited its members largely from the middle class favoring the *laissez-faire* economy, but in the 1920s it turned to state intervention and made its bid for proletarian support. Even so, it may be described as the party of the middle class. It became powerful by maintaining a closely knit organization reaching down to every hamlet. It was intensively active, putting emphasis on party discipline. When legislation of a controversial character was pending, and the party was not of one mind, representatives of the organization throughout the nation were summoned to a conference in the large clubhouse in Santiago, where the issue was debated, sometimes for days, behind closed doors, ending with a vote. This, the will of the majority, reached the party's members in Congress as an instruction on how to vote. These debates in the clubhouse seemed quite similar to those in the Jacobin Club in Paris during the Revolution, when the Jacobins in the National Assembly or Convention responded to the orders of the club. Being for some years the most powerful party and therefore offering the most promising returns for the ambitious, it had drawn to itself aspiring young men of both the right and left, and discipline alone could make for solidarity. It was in power throughout my fourteen years. Uniting the parties of the left, including the socialists and communists, it created the Popular Front coalition and won its first sensational victory with Aguirre Cerda in 1938, repeated its triumph under Juan Antonio Ríos in 1942, and again under González Videla in 1946. But often it was a thorn in the side of its presidents. Trained in opposition so many years, the habit was persistent.

The Socialist party was a strong organization when I arrived in Chile. Some of its former leaders were in retirement. The brilliant Carlos Dávila, whose tenure of a hundred days in the Moneda had been terminated by the army, had gone to New York, after having been Ambassador in Washington, to make a new career. He died years later when he was head of the Organization of American States. Marmaduke Grove had also served a few days as President before his expulsion by the army. I had heard such disturbing things about the "old man" that my first meeting with him at the Mexican Embassy was a revelation. I found an old, grandfatherly, soft-spoken, and kindly-looking man who seemed as dangerous as a dove picking crumbs in front of a cathedral, and not at all like the alleged conspirator who had once been exiled to a lonely island in the Pacific. He was then in the Senate and generally respected.

The Socialists, when I arrived, were united under the clever leadership of Oscar Schnake, who had a keen intelligence, sound judgment and a capacity for leadership. His appointment, first as Ambassador to Mexico, and then to France, had serious repercussions on the party, which had begun to split into segments. The ably edited Socialist paper, the *Crítica,* began to lose in circulation to its more sensational communist competitor. Marmaduke Grove called on me for help in securing a private loan in the United States to keep its flag afloat. This was impossible and, of course, improper, and soon thereafter the *Crítica* ceased to be. The party was completely split; the larger and more authentic section was under the leadership of Senator Allende, a physician, an able man of character and intelligence, but he had not been able to reunite the party when I left the country.

The Falangist party, composed of keen, intelligent, ambitious young men with a mission, was an offshoot of the old Conservative party. It interested me because of its resemblance to the "Fourth party" in the England of the 1880s, when Lord Randolph Churchill (brilliant father of a still more brilliant son), Arthur Balfour, Sir John Gorst and Sir Henry

Wolff, unable to persuade the Tories to take the lead in social legislation away from the Liberals, sat aside as a separate entity as the "Fourth party." The Falangists in Chile left their party for much the same reason. They were unhappy with the choice of a name, which suggested Fascism, but it had no remote resemblance to the party of the same name in Spain. Senator Frei, one of its leaders, was very able, and another, Senator Tomic, was eloquent; they all impressed me as young intellectuals with high ideals.

The Agrarian-Labor party was one of the new ones; it was ultraconservative and represented an important segment of the large landowning element. Since its special strength was in the south, where the Germans were numerous, it at first drew some Nazi elements to its support. Its first leader, Jaime Larraín, was a clever young aristocrat, possessor of broad acres that had come down to him as gifts of the Spanish monarchs to his forebears. It was in the cards for him to be the party's nominee for President in 1952, but General Carlos Ibáñez intervened and took over control.

6

Since I was the pet aversion of the communists, I will give them a separate section; then, too, the other groups would prefer it so. Because of the world struggle against Soviet imperialism, the Communist party is of special interest to the foreigner. A certain romantic interest invests the story of its founder, a self-taught printer, Luis Emilio Recabarren, who threw himself passionately into advancing the labor movement, then in its infancy, and in supporting popular education. He remains an unsolved mystery. Free from the soap-box technique, he impressed by his seeming sincerity, and he was elected to Congress. During the twenties, when the conditions of the poor were sad and not a few among the young began to look hopefully toward the experiment in Russia, the Gran Federación Obrera, with which he was connected, declared for communism.

It was after this that Recabarren went to Russia to study the new phenomena. Just what he really thought is also a mystery, but he seemed bitterly disappointed by what he saw, and, while suffering a nervous breakdown, he blew out his brains.

The sweeping social and economic reforms of Alessandri had cut the ground from beneath the communists, who began to lose face. The founder was succeeded by Senator Elias Lafferte, who remained the titular leader of the party during my time in Chile. I was introduced to him in the reception room of one of the ministers on whom I was calling. He seemed a tired old man and he gave me the impression that he did not feel flattered by the introduction. He was reputed to be a kindly soul, but I would not know. The story is told that when in party conclaves the disputation became threatening he diverted attention from the quarrel by dancing the cueca on the table.

In the Communist Congress of 1928 the party broke away from a democratic ideology and aligned itself wholly with Moscow, taking its orders from there. It was now a Russian, not a Chilean, party. During the war, the Secretary General of the party, who was most active on the surface, was Contreras Labarca, a lawyer with the appearance of intelligence and gentility. He called upon me once on a strange mission. One of the regimes in Argentina during the war was hostile to the United States, and he proposed that if we would furnish arms and ammunition, the opposition in Argentina could overthrow the government there. He seemed amazed when I told him that we could not thus interfere in the internal affairs of another country and least of all send arms and ammunition. He went as one of Chile's delegates to the San Francisco Conference for the creation of the United Nations, where, I understand, he conducted himself well. He signed the charter, but unhappily for him, this, the most historic act of his career, was to deprive him of his position in the party.

We shall hear much more about the communists as we go along.

7

Such were the major parties. I was to witness three presidential elections and the campaigns that preceded them. The candidates were nominated at conventions, as in the United States. Each candidate had his national organization, similar to our national committees. Party leaders and candidates traversed the country on speaking tours, and the speeches were reported reasonably well in the press. There was no rowdyism or violence. The speeches were mostly serious discussions of the actual issues, and, until the campaign of 1952, they were singularly free from vituperation. That year extremists of splinter parties did go beyond bounds in personal abuse.

I should have liked to have attended some of the rallies, to get the feel of the fight, but my presence at any one of them would have been open to misinterpretation. I saw, and heard, one meeting addressed in the Plaza Bulnes by Alessandri in support of Ríos, but I was standing at an open window in the Foreign Office, a full block from the platform, from which loud-speakers carried the words. That meeting, I could see, was enthusiastic but orderly.

In none of these elections was there rioting or trouble of any kind. The polls were guarded by soldiers under command of officers in whom all parties had confidence. They were instructed to maintain order and see that no one was denied his opportunity to vote. The polls closed at four, and by nine the result was usually known.

Since, with more than two candidates in the field, a clear majority for any one is almost impossible, the law provides that in the absence of a majority the election falls to Congress, which must choose between the two highest on the poll. Since, in two or three elections, the majority in Congress were not members of the party with the plurality, it would have been legal had Congress elected the second man on the poll. In every instance, however, Congress elected the candidate at the head of the poll.

It is this political maturity and judgment, together with Chilean self-control and sense of humor, that restrain the defeated from going out into the streets in an attempt to take over by force. The brilliant Colombian statesman and journalist, Eduardo Santos, after a short sojourn in Santiago, ascribed the absence of post-election uprisings to the Chileans' "civilized sense of humor."

This is enough to give the reader an idea of the governmental structure in Chile and of its political parties, which is necessary for an understanding of Chile's position in World War II. But before entering on political matters, it would be well to take a stroll in Santiago, the center of these activities.

IV

Santiago: City That Snubs the Past

The North American tourist, strolling through the streets of
Santiago with the thought of finding something picturesque
or exotic is doomed to disappointment. He will find the pedestrians bearing a striking resemblance to the people with whom
he is familiar at home. No beggars in rags displaying their
sores for money, no Indians or cowboys with forty-gallon
hats, no "color." If in his meandering he hopes to find colonial houses and palaces mellowed by the centuries, he may be
shocked to learn that there are scarcely any at all. And yet
Santiago is a very old city.

I was to witness the celebration of the four hundredth anniversary of the founding of the city by Valdivia, and to live
within a few blocks of the hill of Santa Lucia where he

fortified himself and his followers against the onslaught of the savages. Today, a town with nearly a million and a half population, it seems a strangely modern city, and, unlike Lima, which preserves and exploits its colonial treasures, Santiago, with a truly Yankee disregard for yesterday and living intensely for today, has wiped out most of the monuments of the past, and where a colorful colonial residence once stood, an apartment or office building has been raised.

The Spaniards in colonial days favored Lima as the capital of its South American empire and put most of its treasures there. It is often said that but for the trickery of the architect, Santiago would not have standing today the one official colonial palace it can boast. When the architect, who was famous, was ordered to build a mint, it was presumed that he knew it should be built in Lima, but it was halfway finished in Santiago before Madrid knew that he had used his own judgment. The truth is that Madrid had ordered the mint at Santiago. The palace resulting, the Moneda, is the residence and office of the President, and it houses the Foreign Office and the Ministry of the Interior. It is a two-story building of stone, covering a full city block and patterned after Somerset House in London.

During my stay in Chile I saw, with regret, the demolishing of not a few old colonial residences that had charm and color, and but few remain to conjure up the past. Frequently we went to lunch or dinner at one of the few that remain on the ancient narrow street of Santo Domingo, and this, being the property of an American corporation, reserved for its Chilean director, is immune from the ax of the wrecker. It is a delightful old house, with a fountain and flowers in the patio and a dining room with an overhanging balcony where musicians once played during the interminable meals of many courses.

The impressive cathedral, built on the site of the first church in Santiago, is modern, but there are some old churches steeped in history, though these are disappointing architecturally. Walking with a priest in the pleasant, serene cloister of the centuries-old Church of San Francisco, I was shocked to hear that it would probably be necessary to demolish the monastery, which, with the church, encloses the cloister, and sell the ground. The building, as church property, was exempt from taxation, but the unoccupied ground was subject to a tax too burdensome for the monks to pay. Unofficially, of course, I expressed my astonishment in a personal conversation with Ernesto Barros Jarpa, then Minister of Foreign Affairs, since it seemed to me a form of vandalism to destroy any part of the structure, so rich in memories of many generations. He looked his amazement and thanked me for my interest, though I was not sure this did not carry a rebuke. However, he asked me to put in a letter what I had said and he would see what could be done, if anything. A few days later I found in *El Mercurio* my letter to the minister and his reply, which I had not yet received, expressing his pleasure in assuring me that the monastery would not be molested and the sweet old cloister not disturbed. The Franciscans sent me a note of appreciation, and I have on my wall a painting of the Church of San Francisco, presented to me by the American colony in appreciation of this modest service. I have some pride in the fact that I was able to save one of the old landmarks from mutilation.

Even so, the old church which has withstood the storms and earthquakes of some centuries extends a little into the busy Alameda, and one still hears that it should be demolished for the convenience of motorists—a shocking thought!

During my first years in Chile a great flower market faced the church in the center of the wide thoroughfare, a fresh and fragrant spot in prosaic surroundings, where, for a song, one could carry away enough gorgeous flowers to fill a house. This gave a touch of color and beauty, with loads of roses, lilies, violets, jonquils, narcissuses, calla lilies, tulips, sweet peas —all flowers in season, summer and winter, with smiling women vendors busy with pretty housewives eagerly making selections for the adornment of their rooms. But, alas, this market, which attracted tourists, went the way of "progress" and has been relegated to an ugly section of the city near the railroad station.

The clever Benjamin Subercaseaux, in his unique book, *Chile: A Geographic Extravaganza,* attempts to explain this impatience with the past by describing Santiago as "more of an alert spirit, a whiter race, stronger and bolder than any other city on the coast." Thus charm and tradition give way to "progress," and something of romance passes from the scene. Not without reason are the Chileans called the "Yankees of South America."

But nature, and the works of God, cannot so easily be tampered with, and few cities are so beautifully placed as this capital, set in a fecund valley and sentineled through the centuries by the towering Andes in the background. Always one is conscious of these rugged and majestic mountains that are never out of sight. One gets a thrill, on warm days when the sun shines hotly in the streets, in looking up to the mountains, often glistening in a mantle of snow; and nothing can be more thrilling than the going down of the sun in the evening, with its veritable explosion of colors, red, silver and gold, on the peaks.

For nine months in the year, little rain falls in Santiago, and in fourteen years I saw snow in the streets but once. This was so sensational that the shops had to close since the clerks, with childish glee, rushed into the streets to indulge in snowball battles until the police had to end the frolic lest windows be broken.

2

Near the Embassy Residence rises the historic hill of Santa Lucía. It had only an historical interest for years until the eminent historian Benjamín Vicuña-Mackenna converted it into a place of beauty, with delightful gardens, a museum beloved by the children and an imposing entrance through ornamental iron gates at the foot of the hill.

On a rock at the entrance may be read Valdivia's letter to the Spanish King lauding the country of which he was then the master:

> Let the merchants and other folk who wish to come and settle here be told to come. For this land is such that there is none better in all the world for living and residing in; this I say because it is flat, very healthy and pleasant; it has no more than four months of winter, and even then it is only when the moon is at a quarter that it rains a day or two, and on all other days it is so temperate, with such delightful breezes, that a man can be out in the sun all day without suffering ill effects. It abounds in pastures and fields, and in yielding every kind of livestock and plant imaginable; such fine wood for building houses and an infinity of fire wood for use in them; and since very rich in gold, the whole land being full of it. And wherever men may wish to take land, there they will find a place to sow, and withall to build, and water, wood and grass for their beasts, and it seems God made it on purpose to be able to hold within the palm of His hand.

The old conquistador was clearly thinking of the country immediately around Santiago, for even his fertile imagination could not level the hills and mountains in other parts; and, alas, in my time Chile was not "very rich in gold."

Santa Lucía is easy of access to the cityfolk, but the loftier San Cristóbal, towering higher near the edge of the city, is difficult for visitors on foot, and these ascend by a funicular railway or in cars by a winding narrow road. From the heights one looks down on the city, which seems like a picture in a frame. Dominating the top looms a high statue of Our Lady. The figure was sculptured in France and sent in pieces to Chile. At the time of its erection great numbers of oxen could be seen straining as they hauled the heavy pieces to the top. The arms of the figure are extended, and its eyes are turned toward the skies. A chapel was made in a grotto at the base. Visitors ascending by car see numerous crosses with burning candles where men have been killed by accidents.

Through the city flows the Mapocho River—that is, when it flows at all, since in the dry season it is a tiny stream, sometimes entirely dry, but in the season of the rains, it can become tumultuous and even dangerous when it overflows its banks. Though not an impressive stream, the poets attune their harps to sing its praises, and Neruda's "Ode to the River Mapocho" is one of the best of his earlier days, before he turned from poetry to politics. The drive along the river to Los Leones, Providencia and the golf club is not without a certain charm which somehow evokes memories of Paris.

Not least among the many pleasant features of the city are its numerous parks. Across the Merced from the Embassy Residence, and stretching along for many blocks, is, as I have said, the Parque Forestal. There one finds nursemaids with small children in the morning, lovers when the sun goes down, and in the afternoons students from the universities, men and women parading up and down, books in hand, mumbling their lessons to themselves.

Under the trees of the Quinta Normal the poor seek shade. The once favored Cousino Park now seems to be dreaming of more gaudy days when women of the aristocracy in elegant equipages regularly rode under their parasols of lace, greeting their friends with nods and smiles and, no doubt, flirting a bit, and when men and women in riding attire cantered along the bridle paths. But the impersonal motorcars came to blot out this picture, and still more color was lost, as in New York's Central Park, where the opulent yielded this playground to the common folk, who may now be seen lolling on the grass or taking their siestas in the shade.

The most famous and historic thoroughfare, and one of great width, is the Avenue Bernardo O'Higgins, with a wide grass strip in the center with flowers and statues of the great and the not-so-great. Facing this avenue are the impressive buildings of the two universities and the Union Club. The mansions of the rich old families, farther out, are now being slowly abandoned to encroaching business. The streets, in general, are laid out in patterns, with long streets intersected by others at right angles. There are some cozy and intimate corners, and one of these, with a cobblestone plaza, a murmuring fountain and a few towering trees of pine and palm, was a favorite of mine. It suggested days long dead. In La Plaza del Corregidor, if the moon is shining and the mood is right, one may easily lose oneself in the eighteenth century. And so, after all, Santiago does tolerate some patches of the past.

3

Much of the political, cultural and business activity of the town centers in four buildings. That which houses the Congress has dignity and some beauty. It is set in large, enclosed grounds, a little lower than the street. If the stranger is curious about a depressing memorial on the grounds, he is told that years ago on this site a theater was burned to the ground, with an appalling loss of human life. The chambers of the senators and deputies are dignified and attractive. The Diplomatic Gallery of the Senate is small, the seats uncomfortable and so conspicuous from the floor that I seldom attended. However, I often visited the chamber of the President when Alessandri presided, and on numerous occasions I have conducted our visiting congressmen to the Senate restaurant to meet their Chilean colleagues. The members of the different political groups usually find separate tables, but good-natured repartee passes back and forth between them. I was surprised on one occasion when Senator Miguel Cruchaga, a leader of the Conservative party, rose to introduce my group to senators of the extreme left.

The presidential palace, the Moneda, is in the very center of the business section and has a paved patio with fountains but no grounds. More than half of this large palace is used by the President for his residence and office. At the great iron gates, sentinels are always on guard, as at Buckingham Palace in London. Beyond the gate one finds oneself in a coldly austere court, from which one ascends a wide stairway and is shown into a reception room. Finally one is admitted across the hall to a large, tastefully furnished salon where the President receives visitors. Most of the many rooms are ornately furnished, and I was told that some of the furniture came from the Tuileries in Paris after the fall of Napoleon III. When, on special occasions, the President received the Diplomatic Corps it was always in the Red Salon. Many times I have dined in the state dining room, a large room with a gallery for musicians, and with some old Spanish paintings on the wall. One of these aroused my curiosity. It showed Philip II in a drab apartment in the grim Escorial seated in a chair in a state of manifest depression or fear, while looming above him was a large, powerful monk laying down the law to the most powerful monarch in the world.

The residential rooms of the palace are attractively furnished and vary according to the taste of the occupants, but even these living rooms are not cheerful, since they are often dark and look out on paved streets and office buildings. To me, the most interesting room was a very small dark one in which the President and his council of Ministers had conferences; in a corner was a simple desk used by Bernardo O'Higgins in the dawning days of the Republic.

President Ríos could not abide the formal atmosphere of the place and he lived in his attractive country house and drove back and forth to his office. Soon after González Videla moved in I asked his wife how she liked her new home. She shook her head. "I miss the beautiful light apartment where we lived before," she said. In truth, the palace lacks the warmth or privacy of a home. The atmosphere is too tense and electric. On the many occasions I have been in the Moneda at night and even on Sundays, I have found the rooms and corridors swarming with senators, deputies and politicians feverishly busy in conferences. This was notably true during the administration of González Videla.

The entrance to the Foreign Office in the palace faces the Plaza Bulnes, and here sentinels are on guard. This entrance is as grim and cold as the corridors of the Escorial, but the offices above are furnished with taste. The Red Room of the ministry, where diplomats are received, conferences held and international agreements signed, is richly ornamented and more impressive than the drab office of Cordell Hull in the old State Department building in Washington. On the walls hang portraits of former ministers, and in the center is one of O'Higgins in a flaming-red uniform. During the short winter season one's blood congeals in the frigid cold of this room, and diplomats are received by the minister in his private room, where an electric heater takes off the chill.

Not far from the Moneda is the Municipal Theater, built years ago and patterned after the Opéra in Paris. Though very large, with boxes all around just above the pit, and with two galleries, I never saw it when it was not packed. Chileans of all social grades are discriminating lovers of music. Orchestras, piano, violin and harp concerts, the ballet and plays, crowd the theater to the top gallery. To me the top gallery was the most interesting. Since seats in this gallery are not reserved, one can always find a great number of students, and the poor, waiting patiently in a procession for the opening of the doors. It seemed to me that much of the appreciation came from high up. When artists like Marian Anderson sang and Claudio Arrau played, the enthusiasm was tumultuous. There was always perfect order in the top gallery, and with the opening notes there was absolute silence, but at the conclusion, if the work of the artist was outstanding, the most sincere ovations came from above; if the performance was disappointing, there was restrained applause; and if bad, there was no unmannerly whistling or hooting. These Santiago audiences were not typically Latin.

When Emma Grammatica, the great Italian actress, gave

her plays in Italian, and the French companies in French, this upper gallery, filled with many who understood neither language but were familiar with the drama, seemed to sense the meaning and reacted to its emotional appeal as much as when Margarita Xirgu, the distinguished Spanish actress, played in Spanish. It was quite clear that the Chilean love and understanding of music and drama is not confined to the opulent but is national. Much of the cultural activity centers in the Municipal.

Quite close to the Moneda and the Municipal is the Union Club, one of the finest in the hemisphere, built regardless of cost in the flush days when everyone was thriving on nitrate and money was not hard to find. It is a stone building with four floors and a roof garden, and it figured elaborately in gala social events, when one dined on the best and danced till dawn. Some diplomats, with dining rooms restricted in size, found it convenient to entertain their colleagues in one of the large dining rooms. Here too the government often gave dinners to visiting dignitaries. The cuisine was always superior, the service perfect, the cost moderate. Numerous small dining rooms, where privacy was possible, were favored by politicians who found it convenient to weave their web of intrigue behind closed doors, and by businessmen who liked to consummate their deals over wine and walnuts. The club is a crossroad where one is sure to meet one's friends and acquaintances. The bar is famous as one of the longest in the world, but even so, it is always crowded at the cocktail hours before lunch and dinner. All the amenities are strictly enforced, and if a stranger forgets to remove his hat in the barroom, he is discreetly reminded.

Because most of the aristocracy and the wealthy are members of the club, the extremists of the left try to create the impression that it is a "bastion of plutocracy," but I could not have qualified had that been true.

4

Of sports and popular entertainment there is an abundance. In many moving-picture houses all the best pictures may be seen with the North American predominating, although now there is competition from Italy, England, France and Mexico. Daily, at noon, and especially at teatime, the Crillon Hotel is packed, and at the Robinson Crusoe Bar of the Carrera, there is a gay, laughing crowd of the younger set late in the afternoon and at night.

The one unique restaurant of Santiago is the historic Posada, which only the more adventurous in search of color are apt to visit today. Outside, it has a formidable look, with its thick walls and barred windows, but, passing it in the night, the music of guitars within offers some enticement. The old house, once the residence of the Corregidor Zañartu, still bears the carving of his coat of arms above the door. One is apt to get the impression, on entering, of impenetrable darkness, but when the eyes become adjusted the visitor can see by the candlelight the musicians bending to their task and the wine bottles on the tables. The speciality of the house is hot wine. At the Posada one can get the feel of the past, with much the same entertainment as was presented a century ago, when the stoutest conservatives, like Portales, found it pleasant.

The business section of the city, with its high office buildings of concrete reinforced with steel against the always possible trembling of the earth, with its miles of shops and stores, resembles that of any large city in the United States. Here the streets are filled with shoppers in pursuit of bargains, women stopping to gossip, men to talk politics or business.

But the charm of the town to me is the residential sections of Los Leones and Providencia, the streets lined with trees, often overarching, with pleasant houses set back in their grounds and often concealed from the prying eyes of pedestrians on the street by walls or shrubbery. Behind the shrubbery or the walls are lovely lawns and flowers, and often swimming pools, with guests disporting themselves in the water or sitting in steamer chairs enjoying their sandwiches and drinks. The gates to the grounds of these houses are usually kept locked; the caller rings the bell at the gate, instead of at the door, and a servant runs to admit him.

When I went to Chile, the Las Condes road took us occasionally to the beautiful house of Helen Wessel. At that time there were only fields along this road, but later many attractive houses featuring beautiful gardens were built along it.

The Los Leones Golf Club is ideally situated. The course is excellent and the view superb from the wide, paved terrace where the fashionable have their tea or cocktails, or splash in the pool to one side. From the terrace one looks out over the vivid greenery of the course to the mountains. Because of the play of lights and shadows these never seem the same; they are always entrancing and stunningly beautiful when, toward evening, the sun dies on the mountain peaks.

More remote from the city is the Prince of Wales Club, which takes its name from the fact that Edward VIII, when Prince of Wales, laid the cornerstone. Here is real country, unspoiled nature, such as the English love. The old building, which I knew well, burned down in my time and a far more impressive clubhouse was finished just before I left. I attended its formal opening in celebration of the coronation of Elizabeth II.

Not far from the Los Leones Club is the charmingly located Polo Club, where one can lunch well and watch the sport. On Sundays the lovers of the races find their way to the Hípico Club, where one may go early and lunch facing the mountains in the background.

In the winter many go up into the mountains for the skiing, since the field of Farellones is so near the city that one may enjoy a day's sport and return to home or hotel in the evening. Others, with more time, prefer the less accessible skiing ground of Portillo, nine thousand feet up the Cordillera, where a thoroughly modern hotel offers accommodation for all who have the time to linger. Sometimes a heavy snowstorm surprises the skier in the mountains and he may be marooned for a time. My secretary was once caught in Portillo for three days and she reached the office on the fourth day by skiing part of the way and wading in snow up to her knees the rest.

Thus Santiago does not lack for entertainment. The moving-picture houses are crowded, the theaters packed, the shops well stocked, betting is brisk at the Hípico, and the streets teem with busy people with friendly faces. They seem so much like North Americans that I am sure a thousand people from Santiago could be set down in the streets of Cleveland or Indianapolis without attracting attention.

The Yankees and the British maintain the most cordial relations, and in my time the young among them formed a Little Theater group that put on popular plays with eminent success in a tiny theater. We of the embassy were pleased with their success since two or three members of the staff were among the players, and June Thomas, wife of Colonel Thomas, the Air Attaché, was almost professional in the artistry of her work.

5

Happily, in recent years we have begun, through personal contact, to learn something of the great pulsating continent to the south, with its impressive power, its great population and potentialities, for there has been a constant stream of bankers, industrialists, businessmen, professors and publishers pouring into Santiago. These, I am sure, have carried away pleasant memories of the warmhearted hospitality and the courtly courtesy of the Chilean people. With this expanding knowledge it will not be so easy for the fly-by-night reporter to write a book based on a wealth of misinformation. There have been exceptions among these—notably, Erna Fergusson, whose *Chile* is based on actual knowledge. She lingered long enough to meet the people in cities, towns and villages, to talk with intellectuals, artists and peasants, and, more than most, she caught the tone and temper of the country. There is no silly condescension in her book and there is an appreciation of the people based on personal experiences.

We now have some idea, I hope, of the Chilean people, their institutions, government and capital. Although Santiago is normally a serene city, I had just landed in Chile when an undercurrent of contention could be felt, because World War II, having finished in Spain, had moved on to Poland.

V

Before Pearl Harbor

During the interval between the outbreak of the war and the treacherous attack on Pearl Harbor, I dealt with a dizzying succession of foreign ministers due to the reorganization of the government because of minor differences between the parties in the governing coalition. Abraham Ortega was minister when I arrived, and I found him strongly democratic and friendly to my country. Dr. Cristóbal Sáenz, who succeeded him, was a wealthy landowner, instinctively and militantly democratic and friendly to the United States. He was followed by Marcial Mora, a lawyer and clever politician, afterward popular in Washington when he served as Ambassador. Later came Manuel Bianchi, a distinguished professional diplomat who was to attain high rank as Ambassador to England, and I found him sympathetic toward the cause of the Allies. Just before Pearl Harbor, Juan Rossetti was minister. Son of an Italian immigrant, a self-made man, he had distinguished himself at the university and in the House of Deputies. He had a quick mind, and his sharp tongue was dangerous in debate. His disposition to make instant decisions sometimes forced him to reverse himself on meditation. Intensely active, he usually remained in the Foreign Office until midnight and then went to his paper, *La Opinión*.

My relations with all these ministers were cordial.

2

Meanwhile, Hitler was on his triumphant march in Europe, and never had the German army seemed so irresistible. In June 1940 the friends of democracy in Chile were stunned by the shameful news from France when Pétain locked arms with Hitler, renounced democracy, and pledged his country to the degradation of furnishing the Nazis with the resources of France in material and men, while welcoming the German army to French soil. A Spanish writer, naturally in exile at the time, summed up the treason by saying that Pétain had "traded civilization for Paris," and that while Paris might be worth a Mass, it was not worth the loss of liberty. The Nazi troops had invaded Holland and Belgium and were bombing French towns. Neville Chamberlain, who had brought "peace in our time" from Munich, was being forced to resign, and Winston Churchill had stepped in at a desperate hour to pick up the pieces and put them together again. The pro-Nazi element in Chile was confident to the point of arrogance, and the new Chilean Ambassador to Germany was sent out with a resounding cheer.

The marked partiality for Germany, flamboyantly proclaimed by some, was not so remarkable in a nation with so many Germans who had been so advantageous to Chilean economy, but more disturbing was the manifest hostility to the

United States in numerous quarters. When the Executive Committee of the Popular Front passed a resolution aimed at the United States, with which it was then negotiating for money, even the Chilean Government was taken by surprise. I protested orally to Dr. Sáenz, the minister, who denounced the resolution and said it had so shocked President Aguirre Cerda that he had been unable to eat. He reiterated that the government would determine foreign policy and not the executive committee of a political group, and that its policy would be that of co-operation with the United States. The next day, *La Nación,* the government organ, denounced the resolution in a stinging editorial. Even so, the outlook was not encouraging.

With the British almost alone in holding back the Nazi flood, and with our help desperately needed, we had not drawn the sword. The heavens were dark with clouds when Sir Charles Bentinck came to my house to request me to transmit directly to Roosevelt a personal telegram:

> You are the only person in the world who can save humanity. The faith of all men who are threatened with enslavement rests in you. Will you not convince the American people that the Allies need their full and immediate help? The spirit of survival and the justice of our cause are not enough against overwhelming forces. The future of the civilized world depends on the United States. Without you, we shall all perish.

We were, of course, moving toward all-out military support of the Allies as rapidly as the processes of democracy would permit, and we were seriously concerned about South America. This concern was clear in a letter Roosevelt wrote me on May 20, 1940:

> I have read your letter of the fourteenth with a great deal of interest. I think there is no doubt that in the event of a continued German victory in Europe, German agents in many Latin-American countries will immedi-

ately undertake activities with the view to overthrowing existing governments. I know you will remain in close touch with the Chilean authorities and let me know by telegram, if necessary, all information of a disquieting nature. You will have received by now a telegram requesting you to suggest the desirability of confidential conversations with military and naval officers of the United States and officers of the Chilean army and navy, with regard to the co-ordination of measures for continental defense. I think it desirable that a step of this kind be undertaken as soon as possible in the light of existing conditions.

At this time the Nazis were busy all over the continent with espionage and with plans of sabotage. These agents were concentrating their hate on the American republics that had pledged themselves, with the active collaboration of the United States, to a unified defense. My colleague could not have known at the time he sent the telegram that plans had already been made for our active assistance in defense of the continent. It was understood that Hitler planned to strike at South America from Dakar. Should Chile be attacked, it would be our obligation of honor to join in her defense by land and sea and air. Such a defense could not be improvised in a moment. A military plan had to be agreed upon by the general staffs of the two countries.

For manifest reasons it was necessary that the utmost secrecy be observed about the joint meeting of the two staffs. I presented Roosevelt's plan for such a meeting to Dr. Sáenz, who conveyed it at once to President Aguirre Cerda, and an agreement was reached. Officers from the general staff, dressed in business suits, arrived quietly in commercial planes, and when they left after a few days of intensive planning for a common defense if Chile were attacked, the blueprints were ready. The Chilean officers agreed to the purely military plans but said that political and policy features could be accepted only by the President.

With the North American officers waiting at my house, I sent Cecil Lyon, of my staff, to Aguirre Cerda with the plan. I expected a delay, possibly of some days, but in less than an hour Lyon returned, reporting that the President had accepted. Certain assurances were asked and given. If Chile were attacked, she would defend herself to the utmost; if the United States were attacked and Chile could be of help, she would respond to the utmost. It was a temporary military alliance *to become operative only if the Nazis attempted to overthrow by force the Chilean Government and impose Nazi rule on the Chilean people.* The President had made the pledge while leaning against a table and emphasizing what he said by pounding his right fist into the palm of his left hand. The officers waiting at the Embassy Residence were delighted. They left as quietly as they had come.

3

My first official contact with Rossetti was in connection with the German Consul in Valparaiso, who had been caught red-handed in a violation of Chilean law and ordered from the country not long before. He had given fraudulent passports to the fugitive members of the crew of the German warship *Graf Spee,* which had fallen foul of the British Navy in South American waters. Just before Rossetti took office the consul had returned to Chile and nonchalantly resumed his functions in Valparaiso, in disregard of the order of expulsion. This seemed a bad omen in Washington. I had seen the minister before he formally received the Diplomatic Corps and he had promised an immediate investigation. At the reception the next day he said the case of the consul would be speedily settled. A few days later he summoned the German Ambassador, who said the consul had returned to resume his functions with the permission of Rossetti's predecessor. A search of the archives failed to uncover any such permission, and the former minister, when asked, made a sweeping denial.

After this I am sure Rossetti insisted on the man's expulsion, but powerful pressure was being applied to protect him, and there was a long delay. During this period I had two letters from Roosevelt touching on the case. Though the second expulsion finally came, it was clear that the Axis influence was powerful and persistent.

4

It was after Rossetti became minister that we resorted to the "Black List" to deal with individuals and businesses that were contributing through trade, or otherwise, to the war efforts of the Axis and interfering with our own. In informing him of our purpose, I assured him of our interest in the economic welfare of Chile and our willingness to give special consideration to cases that would be embarrassing politically or likely to aggravate economic troubles. Businessmen and politicians flooded the Foreign Office with their protests, but from the hour we announced our purpose until Chile broke relations with the Axis, the Chilean Government admitted our right to trade, or not to trade, with our enemies. This was not so true in other American nations. The Brazilian Government in Rio approached the Chilean Embassy there with the proposal that the Republican governments of Latin America join in a denunciation of the Black List. At a reception at the Brazilian Embassy in Santiago, Señor Aranha, the Foreign Minister of Brazil and, in general, a friend of ours, took me aside to speak angrily against the Black List.

5

Even after this, many Chileans vehemently denied the existence of a Fifth Column. This was especially true of Aguirre Cerda, who, though a democrat and an ardent admirer of Roosevelt, could not bring himself to believe that Chileans he knew and respected could possibly engage in a conspiracy against a democratic regime. One day I gave him the names and addresses of four agents from Germany, and he seemed seriously concerned. Much later, however, while walking with him on the grounds of the summer palace in a drizzle of rain, I found him vehemently scouting the idea that there was a Fifth Column in Chile. Then his state of mind became clear to me. "Hitler" he said, "is a madman, and, in his insanity, he could be provoked into actions he might not otherwise undertake." Thus the fear of "provoking Hitler" which had driven the world toward an inevitable war between 1935 and 1939 persisted. He admitted that Hitler might have designs on South America but he still could not bring himself to believe that there were people in Chile willing to support these designs.

6

Meanwhile the activities of the Nazis, supported by the communists until Hitler attacked Russia, were quite open. In crowds collected before the bulletin boards of newspapers I learned that at frequent intervals someone in the crowd would shout, with simulated indignation, "There you have the damn Yankee imperialism!" Or, "How is that for British colonialism?" An investigation disclosed that these irate patriots were communists who had been systematically assigned for the purpose.

At this time, the German Embassy seemed to be functioning smoothly and efficiently, but Berlin was taking a dim view of German diplomacy in South America. This resulted in what was intended to be a secret meeting of German diplomats in Chile. We learned of the meeting when word reached us that the German Ambassador in Buenos Aires had just taken a plane for Chile. Here was one of the rare opportunities we had to serve our friends of the press, and on the Ambassador's arrival at the airport he was startled to find a reception committee of reporters waiting to receive him. Without pausing for protocol requirements, without even leaving a card at the Foreign Office, he hurried away to the south, where the Nazi element was strongest. The Minister of the Interior severely rebuked the German Embassy for its failure to inform the Chilean Government of the visit. And, on the heels of this diplomat came German diplomats from Peru and Bolivia. When *La Defensa,* a pro-Ally paper, commented sharply on the strange migration of German diplomats, Von Pochhammer, the most militant of the Nazis in the German Embassy, protested bitterly. The Ambassador to Argentina, he explained, had arrived for a "vacation," and his colleagues from Peru and Bolivia had crossed the mountains merely to extend fraternal greetings. No one believed it. Von Pochhammer, a clever man, should have done better.

Nazi spies and agents from Germany were now pouring in, and throughout the war Chile was to be infested with them. The Fifth Column was organized under the direction of Walter Boettger, who arrived in Santiago disguised as a "Commercial Attaché" of the embassy. He was tireless and effective, and at times a bit arrogant with Chilean officials. After the war I was more astonished than amused to find our military people in Germany had given Boettger a clean bill of health, finding him untouched by the Nazi brush, though the reports on file in the State Department were hardly in accord.

The spies, and rumors of spies, gave an Oppenheim touch that offered some comic relief to the work of the embassy. We had become accustomed to espionage and counterespionage, but I had one encounter with a spy who was at once so daring and so stupid that the story may brighten a page. I had met a young Englishman who was posing as a reporter, with some slight justification, and whose manner seemed a bit peculiar. One day the Mexican Ambassador told me that this man had shown him documents that were "very important if authentic." A little later this man came to see me with the same amazing stories, for the verification of which he claimed to have documentary proof. I asked if I could see the documents. Yes, indeed, but in his house only, since they were too important to carry about. My colleague advised me against going, since when he went he had noticed a photographer taking his picture, and my picture would doubtless be taken and shown to increase the spy's prestige and remuneration. The mystery man finally agreed to show me photostatic copies, and he did.

These were right out of a thriller. They were startling enough. Most were letters *on the stationery of the British Embassy,* and some had the forged signature of the Ambassador. "I have received instructions for you from Lord Halifax" ran one from Buenos Aires. "In the event of your requiring assistance, H. M.'s Embassy in B.A. will be at your disposal." Another: "We have made all necessary preparations and we hope to start the political work soon." More startling: "It is advisable that you communicate with General ———— today and notify our Military Attaché immediately."

Another, also on embassy stationery, purported to be a set of resolutions adopted in Santiago. One directed that "His Majesty's ambassadors in South America should use the Spanish Government's diplomatic pouch for all political matters and orders." At this time Franco had his Blue Division fighting beside the Axis forces, and the evident purpose was to create suspicions between the British Embassy and my own, since we were working cheek by jowl.

It was clear at a glance that these papers were fakes, but I was puzzled about the stationery of the British Embassy. A little later, when we were verging on the rupture with the Axis, this agent—if such he was—came to see me in a state of pretended excitement and indignation. Posing as my "friend," he showed me, *on the stationery of the Presidencia,* some insulting references to Roosevelt and the United States. This, he said, he had found on the desk of the President (Ríos) and slipped into his pocket. I knew this too was a fake. About this time, when I called on the Foreign Minister, I found him throwing up his arms and roaring with laughter. To explain his mirth, he showed me, *on the stationery of my embassy,* a coarse and insulting attack on Ríos and Chile which the same man had said he had found on my desk "and slipped into his pocket." It was clear enough that while posing as a journalist he had stolen the stationery from the two embassies and the Presidencia, to which he had been admitted in the role of a reporter. It was crude, but daring, in that the little man had been able to steal the stationery. He was not worth his salt if he was an agent, but it was quite different with the real agents trained in Germany.

Then, too, at this time there was much whispering about a *coup d'état,* and while that was most improbable, the rumors could not be safely ignored. The most bizarre story was one about a man, posing as a Spanish priest, who had been assured by one Alde Kapute, a Nazi spy, that one "Munstredt," an alleged American registered at the Carrera, had been sent to Chile by Roosevelt to organize a conspiracy to overthrow the government and establish "a good one." The alleged priest was eager to assist in the noble enterprise, and all he asked from the embassy was ten thousand pesos for expenses for a conspiratorial visit to the north.

Since a spy story, to be romantic, must have a lady, one appeared in Santiago. A very beautiful young woman, who undoubtedly was a traveling saleswoman for a North American business, attracted much attention because of her charm and beauty. Reports came in that she spent much of her time at cocktail bars with young men notoriously Nazi, and when the Americans began to snub her she came to me with tears in her eyes to protest against the unjust suspicions. Her father and mother would be shocked, she said. Evidently her absorbing interest was in men, not in ideologies, and she was dismissed with the reminder that there was a war on and that it would be wise to give some attention to her associations. A little later a United States Army officer traveling on some assignment and registered at a hotel was intrigued by a conversation in an adjoining room between the lady and some unknown man. Her companion warned her that unless she were more careful she could get into serious trouble. The lady laughed. "No danger," she said. "The Ambassador is my friend. He was very kind and I can count on him for protection." The officer ragged me about it until the next day, when, on taking a plane at the airport, to which I had driven him, he found that this lady was the only other passenger. I warned the colonel that his conduct and associations were unbecoming an officer and a gentleman, and we were even. The lady never returned.

7

Meanwhile, the democratic sentiment of the Chileans was beginning to urge a rupture with the Axis Powers. With the prospects gloomy overseas, the Chileans staged a patriotic demonstration at the O'Higgins monument. A great crowd assembled. A red carpet had been spread for the chairs of the members of the Diplomatic Corps facing the speaker's platform. President Aguirre Cerda made a ringing speech in support of the democratic ideology. Senator Miguel Cruchaga, then president of the Senate, followed along the same line. A general and an admiral spoke in a similar vein. The ceremony closed with a military parade.

The German Ambassador did not appear but was represented by the most militant Nazi on his staff, who seemed in some distress. I sat beside Ambassador Boscarelli, the Italian, who smoked incessantly and kept plying me with cigarettes. He was no more Fascist than the German Ambassador was Nazi. He loved France, where he had been stationed a long time, and his friends were almost entirely among the French, the British and the Americans. He was an unhappy man, but he seemed pleased that day.

The cordiality of the Chileans for my country was unexpectedly impressed upon me on the initial showing of the picture *Gone with the Wind*. The plaza in front of the theater was congested, and our car moved at a snail's pace. Press photographers snapped pictures. When the President arrived he received a standing ovation from an audience composed in large part of the foes of his domestic policies. When, following the Chilean anthem, that of the United States was played, and the crowd cheered, the spirit of the occasion was clear. We were guests in the presidential box, and when we reached our car on the way home we found a huge basket of flowers so arranged as to make an American flag. It was an American picture, on American history, and its showing was made the occasion for a popular demonstration of solidarity.

My faith in Chilean democracy had never faltered. Chile had supported our position at the conferences in Lima and Havana, and we had assurances of similar support at the conference in Rio, though in that conference Rossetti shifted to the position of Argentina, to the embarrassment of most Chileans.

8

At this time I ventured into the allegedly pro-Nazi section of the country—to Concepción—accompanied by Cecil Lyon. The occasion was the opening of an exhibit of paintings of American nations collected by an American millionaire. Prepared to be snubbed, we were surprised by the warm welcome we received; there was no unpleasantness. We were guests at the attractive colonial house of British Consul Cooper, who had looked after British interests there for almost two generations. We visited the university, whose brilliant president was an understanding friend, and on the first night the mayor, who, years before, had worked in a lead mine in Missouri, gave a banquet for me.

But, on second thought, there was an "incident." The evening we left we accompanied our host to the British Club for farewell libations, and we were there when the American in charge of the exhibit rushed into the room with a flushed face and in a state of great excitement. He had taken a taxi and directed that he be driven to the British Club. The car stopped in front of a building that clearly was a club, and he rang the bell. The door opened. "Is the American Ambassador here?" he asked. "Hell, no. He can't come here" came in a chorus from the men inside. Then only did the startled Yankee notice a large picture of Hitler on the wall, and he knew that he had been driven to the German Club by mistake or design. We all laughed heartily and agreed that this "incident" was the most entertaining of our visit.

Though we were not yet at war, the United States had become the pet aversion of the Nazis. For some time they were able to prevent the showing of *Parson Hall* and other pro-Ally pictures that had been unanimously passed by the official board of censors. The situation was all the more intolerable because pro-Nazi pictures were being shown in numerous theaters, and there had actually been one showing in the barracks of the army. This discrimination was ended after a fight.

Meanwhile, I was the victim of a whispering campaign of absurd proportions. The *Zig Zag* magazine had published a picture of a girl of German blood who had won a jumping contest at a horse show, and the rumor spread that I had threatened to deprive the magazine of paper, and not a few whisperers had "seen the letter with the threat above [my] signature." I sent for the editor, who protested that he had "never heard of the letter or the threat."

Then, from the cave of the winds, the rumor spread that I had daily conferences with the leader of the Communist party, and that I wrote his speeches and directed his strategy. At the same time a rabidly Nazi paper, *La Patria,* was running personal attacks on Roosevelt and promising the extermination of the "moribund democracies."

However, every annoyance has its comic relief, and this was furnished when Franco thought to make a contribution to the Axis cause by breaking diplomatic relations with Chile in a note charging it with "anarchy" and, far worse, apparently, with "liberalism." The Chilean press denounced the note, and the Foreign Minister sent a sizzling reply. He suggested that the Franco regime, born of a bloody army uprising against the constituted authority, was scarcely in position to indict a regime in Chile which had a mandate from the people. The man in the street was merely amused by the impertinence of the note. Soon it was thought more advantageous to the Axis to have the Ambassador in Chile rather than outside, and diplomatic relations were restored. But the irreverent people in the street still laughed.

The sentiment favorable to the allied democracies increased steadily. A huge demonstration, with thousands marching with flags and banners, demanded rupture with the Axis. This brought to the government, awaiting public opinion, tangible proof of Chile's adherence to the democratic cause. Many reactions to totalitarian arrogance could be cited, but my favorite involves an attractive woman of social standing who, in conversation with a woman companion at the cocktail lounge of the Crillon, was speaking about Hitler in terms less than complimentary. An attaché of a totalitarian country seated at a near-by table thereupon rose, slapped the lady and flamboyantly placed his card on the table with the observation that if she had a father, husband or lover, there was his card. "I can look after myself," replied the lady as she brought a bottle down on his head with a resounding whack. He was out of social circulation until the scar healed.

About this time I found Rossetti in a state of nerves and much concerned about law and order. It was common knowledge that the communists and the Nazis had joined forces, the function of the communists being to incite illegal strikes in order to reduce, or stop, the production of war material that was pouring from Chile into the United States. These totalitarian allies staged a hostile demonstration in front of the Embassy Residence, and as my daughter was entering the gate one gallant youth warned her that there would be another demonstration on the morrow, this time "with guns." No one was alarmed.

More significant and important was the fact that Japan

was now showing its colors. It was offering impossible prices for war material, with the reassuring knowledge that its delivery would be impossible. One day the Foreign Minister asked me if we were going to war with Japan. I replied that it was for Japan to decide. He added that the Japanese Ambassador had told him that Japan had no thought of going to war with the United States. I was then reporting fully on the activities of the Japanese Embassy, and this interested Roosevelt. "Your comment on the Japanese situation in Chile is particularly pertinent at this moment," he wrote. "I appreciate your courtesy in having sent me the detailed information which you included in your letter to Sumner Welles. This whole problem is now receiving special consideration, and your comments are very helpful in deciding on the proper line of action." This was written on June 2, 1941, just six months before the treacherous attack on Pearl Harbor. The embassy was to receive other warnings of Japanese plans and transmitted them to Washington at once.

9

This was a short time before the death of Aguirre Cerda. When it was common knowledge that he was on his deathbed, an American magazine published a scurrilous article misrepresenting the cause of his illness. The magazine reached Santiago on the day of his death, and there was general indignation. I cabled Roosevelt that while we could look after our enemies in front, American snipers in the rear were more dangerous, and he denounced the article at a press conference. Even so, this incredible attack was water on the wheels of our foes. Only a few days before, there had been a midnight conference at the Moneda, for the President had asked for a leave of absence because of the gravity of his illness. Since in the event of the President's death or illness the Minister of the Interior assumes his functions, and Dr. Guzmán, the minister, was a militant supporter of the United States and the democracies, he stepped aside for Dr. Mendez, who could be counted on to sit impartially on the lid, pending an election.

The President's condition became rapidly worse, and the end was expected. Our chancellery faced the Moneda, and a member of my staff was assigned to watch for the lowering of the flag on the palace. I was at lunch at my house when I was informed that the flag had that minute been lowered to half mast; at that instant the flag of the embassy was similarly lowered. But the whispering campaign was on full blast, and the next day a woman telephoned the embassy denouncing the United States, the first to lower the flag, because its flag had been "the last to be lowered." This tirade no doubt was delivered in the presence of curious bystanders, who were expected to put her story into circulation.

10

I have never seen a demonstration so moving and impressive as the funeral of Aguirre Cerda. The ceremonies began when the Diplomatic Corps assembled in the plaza of the Moneda to accompany the casket to the Salon of Honor in the capitol for the lying in state. Soldiers lined the streets holding back the pressing throng, composed mostly of the masses, who looked upon the dead President as their friend.

A bugle sounded, the band struck up a funeral march, and then, from the entrance of the palace, emerged the ministers, followed by midshipmen, who acted as the guard of honor. Following these, the bearers of the casket, which was covered with the Chilean flag. During the whole of the following day a procession, mostly of the poor, filed by the casket in the capitol.

The next day the funeral service was held in the cathedral. The great columns of the church were draped in black cloth. The Mass, with all the color and tradition of centuries, was moving. In his tribute, the cardinal dwelled on the dead leader's humanity and humility, and especially on his services to the children of the poor. The Diplomatic Corps was to march all the way to the cemetery, a long, slow trail through streets densely packed. The sun beat down unmercifully on bare heads, and, to save themselves from sunstroke, the members of the corps held their silk hats between the sun's rays and their heads. "Look at the American Ambassador," I heard from the crowd. "He is holding his hat so he will not have to look at the German Ambassador." In truth, I marched beside Baron von Schoen, and we talked in undertones all the way. At close intervals along the line of march military bands played funeral dirges, but it was a crude little band from an orphan asylum the dead statesman had befriended that moved me most. Far back, on a distant hill, the crowd looked like swarming ants. Flower blossoms dropped on the casket from roofs and balconies.

Thus Aguirre Cerda reached the end of his journey. With his death the voice of partisanship was momentarily stilled. At a critical moment we of the embassy knew that an understanding friend had passed and that little could be done on war issues pending an election and the reorganization of the government.

II

The activities of the Japanese were now becoming more interesting. One of the Axis ambassadors, in talking with the Yugoslav Minister, expressed bitterness against Roosevelt "for prolonging the war." When the Yugoslav suggested it would be a mistake to draw Japan into the war, the Ambassador disagreed. "Oh, no," he said. "Japan is the only power before which the United States trembles. She can do infinite harm in the Pacific." With the Japanese Ambassador in Washington treacherously posing before Cordell Hull as an emissary of peace, the attack on Pearl Harbor came.

This was on December 7, 1941. I had been authoritatively informed on December 3 that the Japanese Ambassador had called at the Foreign Office to say that "war with the United States is inevitable" and to ask refuge in Chile for the Japanese in Panama. He was instantly refused, and instructions were sent to Panama to refuse visas to the Japanese.

Two days later I was informed that Baron von Schoen had called at the Foreign Office to reinforce the request of his Japanese colleague. He, too, was refused. These requests, made five and three days before the attack on Pearl Harbor, were cabled to Washington immediately. Thus it was clearly shown that the Japanese diplomats had been forewarned.

Immediately after the attack, President Roosevelt cabled instructions to prepare for war. At midnight I went to the Moneda to inform Foreign Minister Rossetti that we were at war with Japan. He had already sent instructions that extraordinary precautions be taken in guarding the copper and nitrate mines. In conformity with prearrangements, Germany and Italy declared war on the United States.

Aside from the frankly Nazi propaganda sheets, the Santiago press denounced the treachery of Japan and unreservedly aligned themselves with the United States. A stream of colleagues poured into the embassy to express their indignation and pledge solidarity with us. Two days later Congress approved a public declaration that Chile associated itself absolutely with the United States. Japanese funds in Chilean banks were blocked, and the government declared the United States a victim of aggression.

Meanwhile the embassy was put upon a war footing and the staff had grown to include about three hundred persons. With the declaration of war, the activities of the Axis spy ring intensified and the most extraordinary precautions were taken. Immediately after Hitler marched into Poland, I noticed, when calling on the British Ambassador, that he disconnected the telephone before saying a word. Our experts on espionage insisted that some member of the staff be assigned to keep a vigilant eye on each office to make sure that all drawers were locked, that all papers not locked away and all pads on which anything had been written were destroyed through five or six pages. I was impressed when instructions were given that in reading or writing documents the blinds should be drawn, since from a building across the street it would be possible to read what was written. The presence of spies was impressed upon us when the manager of All-American cables warned us that one of his employees, on leaving work the previous evening, had been approached by a well-dressed stranger and offered 500 pesos a day if he would furnish copies of my telegrams. When the employee pretended to consider, the bribe was raised to 1,000 a day. "It means 30,000 pesos a month," said the agent, "and it will set you up for life." The employee reported the incident to the manager, and thereafter messengers taking telegrams to the cable offices were always accompanied by guards.

While circumstances incidental to the death of Aguirre Cerda held back negotiations for rupture with the Axis, Chile had acted as a friend. We had arranged for the purchase of all Chile's strategic material—nitrate, copper, mercury and cobalt—but it was evident that Chile did not want to become militarily involved. Rossetti made it clear that Chile did not want to declare war—something we had not asked—though he had no doubt that the war would ultimately reach Chilean waters and force Chile into the conflict. In the meanwhile, without declaring war or breaking diplomatic relations, Chile would be in a better position to send an uninterrupted stream of ships to the United States with war material. This, I found, was the feeling of a large part of the Chilean people, including warm partisans of the United States.

It was not at all absurd that Chileans feared Japan would attack if an excuse could be found. The government was not without cause for concern. The Chilean Ambassador in Tokyo had been summoned to the Foreign Office there and asked to explain the arrest and imprisonment of "a hundred Japanese in Antofagasta." Since no such arrests had been made or contemplated, it appeared that Japan was seeking a quarrel. Sending for the Japanese Ambassador in Santiago, the Foreign

Minister, to get his reaction, bluntly asked him if Japan intended to attack the mines near the coast with submarines. Melodramatically, almost hysterically, the Ambassador denied such intentions. If such an attack were made, he said, he would kill himself!

The importance of Chile to the democracies at this time has never been quite understood in the United States. Too many South American countries were under dictatorial domini-nation, and efforts were being made by the enemy to force American nations into the totalitarian crusade. Chile, one of the two staunch democracies, was of vital importance, since its alienation from the cause of the democratic allies would be a great incentive to enemy activity on the continent. Roosevelt was keenly conscious of this danger, as was the State Department.

Meanwhile, an agreement had been made in the conference at Havana that an attack on one American nation would be considered an attack on all. An attempt to impair or destroy the mines near the coast was so possible that without awaiting Chile's ratification of the agreement, we sent some new coastal batteries. More than any other nation in South America, except Brazil, Chile was in danger. She had 2,800 miles of Pacific Coast, and at one time it seemed probable that the Pacific in the south would become a seat of war. Along with the batteries went experts on coastal defense, and a hundred soldiers to set up the installations. The public was to learn about the batteries from our enemies. Their press opened vicious attacks on the United States for "forcing on a reluctant sovereign nation inferior war material," and the public was urged to register indignation because a hundred soldiers trained in coastal defense were nothing less than "an army of occupation." Chileans were asked to "hang their heads in shame as long as the foot of the invader is on their soil."

These were the gloomiest days in the fight for rupture with the Axis. The agreements at Lima and Havana had not been sent to Congress for ratification—as had been promised—since

Dr. Mendez had recessed the Congress to permit members to visit their constituencies for the electoral campaign. The real, and not unnatural, reason, I am sure, is that Dr. Mendez had been asked to do nothing that might embarrass the incoming government's foreign policy.

12

In the presidential election, the Conservatives and Liberals had nominated General Carlos Ibáñez, and the Radicals and their allies had nominated Juan Antonio Ríos. The issues of the war were not openly discussed in the campaign, but it was known that Ríos favored the democracies and suspected that Ibáñez was partial to the Axis. Despite the undercurrent of intense feeling on the war and the vigor of the verbal combats from the platform, the campaign was conducted on a high level and there was no violence. Ríos was elected, but two months were to intervene before his inauguration, and in the meantime we could only mark time.

Under these circumstances, the Axis element was pushing its advantage. The war had caught the Germans with one of their naval training ships in Chilean waters, with no possibility of getting it back to home base, and so they presented the ship to the Chilean Navy as a regal gesture of disinterested friendship. The German Ambassador and others spoke. The German flag shared the breeze with the Chilean banner. The Nazi salute was given repeatedly in the presence of embarrassed Chilean officers. The press carried the story to the United States, arousing some resentment, and even President Roosevelt wrote me personally for an interpretation.

The gloom was not lightened at the time by our inability to see eye to eye with the British on the issue of rupture with the Axis. Argentina, notoriously pro-Nazi, was trying to pressure Chile against such a break. The English, from necessity, were pouring gold into the Argentine coffers for meat and wheat they absolutely had to have for their gallant army, and, though they were forced to pay fantastic prices, they were not in position to quarrel with Argentina and felt they could not afford to affront Buenos Aires at this juncture. I could understand and sympathize with their embarrassment. Even so, we were, otherwise, working in very close collaboration with our English friends.

13

At the inauguration of Ríos, Argentina appeared with a large delegation headed by its Vice-President and Foreign Minister. The Vice-President was a rich farmer, large and inelegant, but not unlikable. An incessant smoker, he carried with him cigars made for his special use—long, fat and deadly ones. Every time he gave me one I would light it with an expression of delight, wander into the crowd, and drop it on the ground. This strategy failed at an alfresco luncheon where I was seated directly across the table from him. "Ah, you have no cigar," the old man said. "Try this one." Ecstatically lighting it, I awaited an opportunity to drop it under the table. At length he noticed that I was not smoking. "Ah, you have finished your cigar. Take this one." With his eyes upon me, I had to smoke it through if it killed me. I am sure the old gentleman would have preferred the life on his farm, seated on the veranda with a box of his cigars, and with whisky and a siphon on the table.

But the Argentine Foreign Minister, Guiñazú, was a horse of another color. He had arrived with a flourish of trumpets, and with many in his party. He was notoriously pro-Nazi. The announcement of his coming was not without embarrassment to the Chilean Government, since, in the absence of any other guest of similar rank, he would have to be featured under the rules of protocol, and this would be susceptible to misinterpretation.

He came and saw, was seen, but he did not conquer. He made a bad impression and was utterly ignored by the general public that had given popular acclaim to Dr. Aranha, the democratic Foreign Minister of Brazil, a little before. But Dr. Ruiz Guiñazú was fascinating as a study in pomposity. His manner was not endearing. The scene at the reception in his honor at the Argentine Embassy was illuminating. It might have been in the Berlin of Hitler. The totalitarian ambassadors of Germany, Italy, Japan and Spain, who, for some time, had made themselves inconspicuous on public occasions were here cocks of the walk, in their element, the center and soul of the party, all in fine fettle, as though conscious that they were in the house of an ally.

Before the attack on Pearl Harbor we had spent our summer vacation on the coast in the lovely summer resort of Zapallar, about forty miles north of Valparaiso. Because of the difficulties of communication, Pearl Harbor made it impossible for us to remain. But before we continue the story of the problems of the war, we shall now relax a moment in this village of great charm and beauty.

VI

Social Treadmill and Escape

Because of the hectic social activities, in addition to the work of the embassy, when the hot days came in January and February, the diplomats sought the breezes and beaches of the coast. Near the beginning of our first summer we set out by car in search of a quiet retreat, remote from dinners, luncheons and cocktails, and found perhaps the loveliest spot in Chile at Zapallar. Many years ago, a French architect, finding this region so suggestive of the Italian Riviera and a choice spot, built the first house in what was to become the favorite summering place of many old Chilean families. These followed rapidly, building attractive summer houses on the hillside looking down on the little bay and beach. In the winter, when these houses are boarded up, the village seems desolate and deserted. Sir George Graham, my friend of Madrid days, wrote me that he had seen the village when the only thing attractive about it was the woods and the sea. Now all this was changed. The Chileans there, putting aside all business cares in summer, wanted no easy means of communication, and there was but one telephone in the village at the hotel run by a French woman. The road from Viña del Mar was perfect as far as Concon, halfway, but from there, it was a dirt road with ruts and rocks, and the one long bridge that spanned more land than water was in such a state of dilapidation that motorists were warned to drive across it slowly. We always held our breath in crossing. But whenever the government proposed to pave the road, the property owners of Zapallar appeared en masse to protest vehemently, and the project was abandoned. Jealous of their privacy, they knew that with a paved road picnickers from Valparaiso would descend upon the beach on Sundays and holidays with their lunch baskets.

The house we found was the "Casa Benoit," the first one built by the architect for himself. The house was modest, though the living room had windows looking out over the garden and the sea, and with its sixty panes the slightest temblor gave the impression of a cavalry on the charge. The kitchen was in a small stone house near by. More amusing, the bathroom was in another small concrete house which we never thought to lock at night, and one night a burglar appeared and rifled the contents, taking a toothbrush, some facial cream and two bath towels. In this small house was also the machinery that generated our electricity.

Since in dry weather the water supply of the village was low, our water was piped down from the hills, and we had an abundance for sprinkling and domestic use, with water plugs over the grounds. One morning, Luis, the butler, came to me with a sour expression to announce a shortage of water. I looked my surprise. "Our neighbors are light-fingered," he said indignantly. I awaited an explanation of the grave charge. "At night," he said, "when we are all asleep, they send their servants over with buckets and fill them from our taps." Thereafter we had locks put on the water plugs as a protection against some of the nicest people in Chile.

If our house was simple, the large grounds were beautiful and picturesque, with little hills and valleys, with ravines spanned by rustic bridges. Pines and palms furnished shade. Flowers of many hues blossomed everywhere. Looking far down on the sea was a fine tennis court, and facing the highway, but protected from the prying eyes of the curious by trees and shrubbery, was a croquet ground. Noticing a narrow path that wound around a small stone peak, we explored and came upon a paved pavilion over the sea, with flowers blooming in great stone vases. Below, huge rocks against which the waters sang angry songs. Yellow seaweed, moving back and forth with the tide, looked like a mermaid's golden hair. From the grounds a path descended many feet to the beach, the rocky wall on one side colorful with clinging flowers, and, at the bottom, a small plot of ground with a spring-fed pool from which a naked lady in stone emerged.

There we were to spend three delightful summers. Once a week we drove to Viña to meet Lucy Lentz, my secretary, who brought us the mail and papers, but otherwise we seldom left the grounds. My daughter Patricia could not resist the beach, but, lazy in a comfortable steamer chair, I regaled myself with biographies and detective stories. Backgammon helped to pass the hours. Occasionally we climbed out on the huge rocks in the sea and had our lunch served there, with the water lapping the rocks for music.

Guests at the hotel were wont to go toward evening to a stone bench at the edge of the village to look out over the sea and watch the sun go down in a splash of vivid colors. We could get the same effect from our grounds. These sunsets were memorable. Seen through the branches of the trees, the sky, with its coloring of gold and purple reflected on the sea, was glorious. The scene on the beach was one of festive animation, with pretty women swimming or sunbathing on the sands. A friendly beach bar, where light lunches could be had, added to the attraction.

Our most immediate neighbor, Matías Errázuris, was a man of charm and distinction. He had built a castle bordering our grounds that might, from its appearance, have been moved intact from Italy or Spain. On its wide, paved terrace facing the sea were beautiful marble columns from an old castle in Italy. The first day we arrived this gallant old gentleman sent over a basket of flowers from his garden. He had been a diplomat with ambassadorial missions, but he was now an old man in retirement, though his erect, sturdy frame gave no indication of age. Daily he could be seen on his horse, as erect as one of the pillars on his terrace, riding about the village or to the beach, the wind playing with his beard. He looked like a baron of old surveying his domain, gallantly greeting the pretty women, pausing to chat with the children, stopping in front of the one general store to exchange news and gossip with the loungers.

Quite another character, not at all in keeping with the aristocratic tone of the village, who never ceased to amuse us, was the driver of the garbage wagon. Twice a day he passed our place, his approach always heralded by the barking of many dogs, the snapping of a whip, the shouts of the driver, and then, in a cloud of dust, he came and passed, the wheels of his dilapidated cart wobbling as if it had St. Vitus's dance and threatening a momentary collapse, four or five large dogs barking behind, the driver shouting to the horses, abusing the dogs, cracking his whip. In aristocratic Zapallar he was an exotic, and I should be sorry to hear that he has gone.

But in a search for characters we did not have to go outside our own household. On reaching Chile we had found a chef, a man who had long presided over the kitchen of a distinguished politician. He was of gargantuan proportions, and he had a high regard for the dignity of his calling. He demanded two assistants. That he knew how to spare himself physically was manifest when, on visiting the kitchen, I found him lolling comfortably in a huge chair with thick cushions and giving minute instructions to his assistant. He was so supercilious that we gave him a wide berth, but he was a master of his craft, and we respected his resourcefulness. Since the meat cart from Viña entered the village at the far end of the town and ours was the last house reached, we seemed doomed to get the cuts scorned by our neighbors. Noting this dire danger before we did, he had already had a "conference" with the butcher boy and had arranged for the choicest cuts to be concealed and saved for us. We concluded that during his long connection with the politician he had learned the tricks of the political trade. He had been with us for some years when, after a very small dinner, he presented the grocery bill and we were puzzled to find that four dozen eggs had been bought for the dinner. When I inquired if any eggs were left he asked if I had thought of the cakes and sauces. Not wishing to offend his majesty, I attempted an indirect approach to a rebuke by telling him the experience in China of a Belgian colleague of mine in Spain who, on opening his seaside villa, had sent his wife ahead one day with the very young second cook. On joining his wife the next day, he was interested to find on the grocery bill three dozen eggs. "You must have a lot left," he said to the cook. "No, no, all gone," said the young man, who had not learned the art of moderation in graft. "Gone? Where?" demanded the Ambassador. "Madame's breakfast," replied the boy, with a disarming Oriental smile.

But our chef was not amused and, fearing the worst, he resigned. We learned later that all the time he was with us he had been running a restaurant of his own and doing very well.

During the first days of the war the sentiment of most of the summer residents in Zapallar was frankly pro-German, and the reception of the American Ambassador was a little less than heartening. One night at 4 A.M. we were awakened by the sound of beating on tin cans and shouts from young men of the summer colony. We were a bit puzzled by the demonstration but were not annoyed, and in the morning we heard the explanation of the serenade before dawn. It was the night of the world championship battle between Joe Louis and Godoy, the Chilean heavyweight, and through some misunderstanding the impression reached Zapallar that Godoy had won. Assuming the bitter disappointment of the Yankee diplomat, the boys fared forth to humiliate him. In truth I had hoped for the triumph of Godoy since my patriotism does not go beyond the ropes that enclose the fighting arena, and had I known the reason for the demonstration I might have joined in the celebration.

Life in Zapallar is not always confined to cocktail parties, bridge and the pleasures of the beach. In the presidential election of 1942 between Ibáñez, the Conservative and Liberal nominee, and Ríos, the summer colony was almost unanimously for Ibáñez, but Ríos had one ardent supporter in a woman whose large house looked down upon the beach. Defying the popular sentiment for Ibáñez, she decorated her beach tent with a huge poster of Ríos, and the enemy, mostly among the young, made repeated efforts to capture the poster, resulting in rough scrimmages. The boys were motivated by a love for fun and mischief, but the lady, personally well liked, could not see the fun. She demanded protection from the *carabineros,* and one day she was accompanied by a guard. The triumph of her candidate offered sweet revenge on her tormentors, and the day following the election she jubilantly appeared on the beach with Ríos posters and was not molested, since this day the lady appeared with a gun.

As the summer waned we left Zapallar with sorrow, but we returned to Santiago refreshed and reinforced for the physical ordeal of the social obligations of the capital.

2

I soon found that these were far more enervating than the official duties. The scoffer's concept of a diplomat as a "cooky pusher"—pompous, snobbish and empty-headed—has no remote relation to the realities. My intimate observation of scores of foreign-service officers who served with me for twenty years proved to me that, with scarcely an exception, all were serious-minded, conscientious, efficient and industrious. Of course they attended cocktail parties, dinners, luncheons and receptions, since their absence would have been resented. It was part of their job. Daniel Vare, a clever Italian diplomat, says, in his amusing memoirs, that "the life of a diplomat is made up of just two things—protocol and purgatives." Thus he grinds his teeth over the protocol that prescribes an endless procession of rich, heavy dinners. I soon found that, in comparison, the social life of Madrid had been simple. The season there began in January and ended in June, but in Santiago there was no intermission for twelve months in the year. After two months I was forced to consult a doctor. "I will give you the advice I gave your predecessor—eat your dinner before going to the dinner, and there play with the food," he said. Even so, for some years, until I became hardened to the punishment, I was glad to confine my dinners at home to the delicious *cazuela,* a wholesome Chilean soup.

Unhappily there was no curtailment of entertaining during the war, but it resulted in embarrassing social situations. The German, Italian and Japanese ambassadors could not be brought into contact with the diplomats of nations at war with the Axis. A neutral embassy or legation could entertain the diplomats of both sides if they were invited separately, and before Pearl Harbor this was my method. But at one of my first receptions in war days I noticed that the German Ambassador appeared and left early to avoid the British, who came late, though before the war they were the best of friends.

It was when the government gave a dinner and the entire corps was invited that the Chief of Protocol had his headaches. He had but one course possible—to place the diplomats of the Axis at a single table alone, and so the German, Italian, Japanese and Spanish ambassadors were seated together, along with the Portuguese Minister. This was bitterly resented by the spirited wife of the Portuguese, who, on emerging from the dining room, seethed with indignation and exclaimed to me in the presence of the harassed Chief of Protocol that she was "tired of being shoved into the company of these Nazis and Fascists at every dinner." Perhaps it was the penalty the Portuguese had to pay for their support of Franco and the Axis in the Spanish war.

The embarrassment was not confined to protocol, since Baron von Schoen and Raffaele Boscarelli, the Italian Ambassador, were personally popular with the entire corps, and neither was believed to be in sympathy with the ideology of their governments. The German Ambassador was a charming man of culture, and his American wife was popular. Boscarelli was especially unhappy, for reasons we have given.

3

The Diplomatic Corps when I arrived in Chile impressed me as being of a high character. During my fourteen years, there were many changes. Great Britain was to have five ambassadors and France more. My personal connections after Pearl Harbor were entirely with colleagues aligned with the democracies, and the nuncio, who stood aloof.

Monsignor Aldo Laghi, the nuncio, who established the American convent school of Villa Maria, first became my friend in that connection. He was a heavily built man, but his expression reflected his dedication to the spiritual side of his mission. He never mixed in domestic politics. We became rather close confidential friends, and on his deathbed he instructed his secretary to give me a beautiful, heavy, silver cigar box, the lid of which was gaily embossed with the "Intérieur de Cabaret" by P. Gasson.

After his death and burial in the crypt of the cathedral, his successor was Monsignor Mario Zanin, who had spent many years in China. He was a tall, slender man with graying hair. He was highly cultivated, exceptionally able and brilliant, and much loved and admired as *doyen*. His wit and humor enlivened his conversation. We were the best of friends until his transfer to Argentina.

Sir Charles Bentinck, the British Ambassador when I arrived in Chile, was unique. He came from a distinguished family, well known in English history. He was tall, slender, in manner courteous and soft-spoken, and intensely religious. A kindly man, a real Christian, he frowned on the disposition of some of his staff to be "rough on Hitler" because it was "not Christian charity." Nature intended him for the religious life, and on his retirement he prepared himself for the ministry and was sent to Brussels as chaplain of the embassy.

Any thought of Bentinck evokes memories of his dog. One day a mongrel in the street followed Bentinck home, adopted him and became his passionate guardian. When I called, I was usually asked to wait before entering the room, since an unannounced visitor who entered before the master could explain that the visitor was a friend was certain to be attacked. The Ambassador, who adored the dog, liked to dress it in fancy raiment—coat, vest, high hat and cane—and after dinners he would sometimes entertain his guests by sitting on the floor while dressing the dog and putting it through its paces. On retiring and returning to England, he was distressed because the dog would have a prolonged stay in quarantine and would be lonesome, and he settled down in the immediate neighborhood through this period and made daily calls upon his pet. Sir Charles had a really sweet personality.

Lady Bentinck was a pretty and artistic woman, much loved by all who knew her. She was a talented artist and her paintings of scenes near Sofia, where her husband had been stationed, were much sought after, but she refused to sell them.

The Bentincks left Chile at the beginning of the war, to be succeeded by Sir Charles Orde, who was to be the wartime Ambassador in Santiago. It was with him that I collaborated closely throughout the war, and though we did not see eye to eye on rupture with the Axis, or on the 300-mile safety zone in the Pacific, we worked generally in close co-operation. He was not physically strong, but he had a valiant and efficient collaborator in Lady Orde, a remarkable woman who threw herself into the war activities and thereby shortened her life.

So conspicuous was she in these activities that when children in a school were asked to name the British Ambassador, one little mite chirped, "Lady Orde." The Ordes served throughout the war and well into the postwar period.

Sir John Hurleston Leche, who succeeded Orde, I had known in Madrid, where he had been the First Secretary in the British Embassy. Transferred soon after my arrival there, he returned to Spain during the Spanish war as Chargé in Barcelona. He was refreshingly free from the flamboyancy of some diplomats and was very human. He had a keen sense of humor, which protocol frowns upon, and a caustic wit, and I long thought he was Irish until, in giving me William Hickey's rollicking memoirs as a going-away present when he left, he inscribed it to me thus:

> *The book's begetter was an Irish Mickey.*
> *Who at his birth was christened William Hickey.*
> *But as I have no Paddy blood, gorblimey,*
> *You'll have to take this offering from a Limey.*

I thought of him as a man from the gay days of the Regency.

His immediate successor, Sir Charles Stirling, could also break through the crust of hard-core conventionalism too often associated with diplomacy. Very tall and slender, he loomed impressively above all others in a crowded reception. In the years when we had giants in the Senate in Washington and many, if not most, used snuff, they had snuffboxes on the wall by the doors, and while the snuff habit has passed, these boxes are regularly filled to this day as an act of sentiment. I had never seen anyone use snuff, however, until Sir Charles made his initial call on me and I was momentarily puzzled when, at frequent intervals, he took out a little horn-shaped box, extracted a pinch of the contents and applied it to his nostrils. He was amused by the surprise of some, and we were close enough to permit me to twit him occasionally on the good old-fashioned habit, and I sent him a press clipping of an article by Harriet Wilson describing the ornate snuffboxes given diplomats by monarchs in the eighteenth century. His acknowledgment came in the form of a rhyme:

> *The Foreign envoys in the courts of old,*
> *Were given jeweled snuffboxes of pure gold.*
> *Today we're lucky when we take our leave*
> *A silver cigarette box to receive.*
> *But since, as history is by Harriet seen,*
> *These gewgaws lead men to the guillotine,*
> *It seems to me we are safer far,*
> *I with my fog horn, you with your cigar.*

The popular notion that the English have no sense of humor is not borne out in my experience with English diplomats, with whom I had more fun than with any others.

The French Ambassador when I arrived was Count Louis Sartiges, a man of broad culture and much charm, who was unhappy over the trend in France during the first days of the war, and when Pétain became Hitler's cup-bearer he resigned. His grandfather, a French Minister in Washington before our Civil War, had married a Boston girl, and Sartiges seemed proud of his North American blood. He knew Washington intimately, having served on the staff of the brilliant Jusserand. He was succeeded by an appointee of Pétain's, and I had few contacts with him.

During the war my closest contacts with South American diplomats were with Eduardo Labougle of Argentina; Samuel de Souza Leao Gracie, the Brazilian; Dr. Hugo Pena, the Uruguayan; and Reyes Spindola, the Mexican.

Labougle was perhaps the ranking man in the foreign service of his country. He had been Ambassador in Berlin for six years immediately preceding the war and had written his memoirs of these years. He was an able diplomat, clever and far-sighted, a man of real distinction. When his country was tending toward Perónism he resigned.

Ambassador Gracie, also a clever diplomat, is now (1957) Ambassador in London. He was most *simpático*, courtly and co-operative. Since Washington and Rio were in complete agreement, we exchanged news and views constantly and worked together to align Chile officially with the democracies.

Ambassador Pena, who was educated in the United States when his father was the Uruguayan Minister there, understood the United States and its psychology better than most, and he was militantly with us on the war issue.

One of the staunchest friends of the democracies in the war was the Bolivian Ambassador, Alberto Ostria Gutiérrez, who, when he was Foreign Minister in his country, was the first to send a conspiring Nazi diplomat on his travels. He was a staunch democrat of courage and character.

These were the colleagues with whom we maintained the closest relations throughout the war, when the support of the South American nations was of vital importance—an importance not suspected by the North American people or press.

4

During the war days, events of significance crowded each other. As late as September 1941 the Legation of Czechoslovakia kept the seal of the Republic on the gate and its flag afloat. The Czech Minister, Jan Havlasa, a popular novelist of his country and a lover of flowers, spent much of his time meandering in the mountains in search of rare specimens, and occasionally he came to the house after these excursions with flowers for my wife. He came in one day in December 1941 because a police officer had made the demand that he remove the seal and cease flying the flag. The officer had apologetically explained that the demand came from the German Embassy. I suggested that he positively refuse to act on the orders of the German Embassy and comply only when he received orders in writing from the Chilean Government.

More disturbing to diplomats aligned with the democratic forces were accumulating indications of a plan to overthrow the democratic regime in Chile and to set up one subservient to the Axis. The *coup d'état* in Bolivia in 1943 had the bad odor of Nazi inspiration, with the full knowledge of the Argentine Government, which was in complete sympathy with the Hitler crusade. When the democratic government in Bolivia was overthrown, it was significant that none of its supporters sought refuge in the Argentine Embassy. Meanwhile the pro-Nazi government in Buenos Aires was urging a speedy recognition of the new Bolivian regime, and pressure was being brought by the Argentine army, at that time strongly pro-Nazi. When the Brazilian Ambassador inquired what course Chile would take, he was told that it would do nothing until the part played by the Nazis was determined; and when the Chilean Ambassador in Buenos Aires reported that inquiries were being made as to what Chile and Brazil would do, he was informed from Santiago that Chile would go along with the United States.

So threatening seemed the outlook that on December 23, 1943, an experimental air raid was made over Santiago, with numerous Chilean planes flying over, to ascertain the dependability of the searchlights in picking them out. We witnessed this spectacular experiment from the roof garden of the embassy.

With little of this known in the United States outside the State Department, the secretary of President Ríos had publicly warned that Chile, in supporting the democracies, was "surrounded by erupting volcanoes." While Chile maintained a discreet silence, it would be sheer nonsense to deny that at this time there was concern over Argentina. She had greatly increased her armed forces on the Chilean border, and when Perón, then Minister of Defense, was asked his intentions, he replied that there were no differences between the two nations that could not be amicably settled. All Chile would have to do would be to concede some islands in the far south to Argentina and give her a port on the Pacific! Perón modestly explained that no nation can be truly great without ports on both the Atlantic and Pacific—but he was not offering a port for Chile on the Atlantic.

These threats to the security of Chile at this time figured largely in the exchange of views among the diplomats in Santiago.

5

Meanwhile, along with the troublesome diplomatic problems there was a superabundance of "cakes and ale," since the social treadmill of diplomatic society was constantly in motion. Interminable exchanges of dinners and luncheons sapped the vitality of the strongest. The luncheons announced for one o'clock were usually late in starting, since some thought it impressive to arrive late. One of Perón's ambassadors was notably obnoxious: it seemed his fixed policy to keep all the guests waiting until he could make his grand entree, with nothing lacking but the blast of a trumpet and the rolling of drums. On one occasion the indignant host consulted with his colleagues among the guests on the propriety of sitting down without him. This time the tardy guest arrived fifty minutes late, entering with the utmost complacency and without apology.

These luncheons were not an ideal preparation for work in the afternoon, since it was impossible to leave before three o'clock. Cocktails—too many if some guests were late—rich food, with three wines, liqueurs and coffee left the victim soggy and sleepy, and he found concentration on his problems difficult.

The dinners were more elaborate, though not so trying, since a night's repose intervened between the dinner table and the desk. Invitations for nine or nine-thirty usually meant getting to the table by ten or ten-thirty, and by twelve the guests filed into the drawing room for coffee, liqueurs and cigars. If one could start home by one o'clock one was lucky.

The formal receptions at the embassies and legations in observance of national holidays were usually an abomination. The rooms were packed to suffocation, the chatter deafening, and yet, in the confusion, nothing worth while was said. Buffet dinners were often served, and servants forcing their way through the mass with drinks not infrequently splashed the dresses of the women.

During our first years we invited diplomats, government officials, officers of the armed forces, Chilean society and the American colony to the reception on the Fourth of July, but with almost a thousand persons crowding the rooms the congestion was impossible, and we were forced to give two receptions, one at noon and the other at night.

As enervating as the dinners and luncheons were, they were mild compared with the unbroken stream of cocktail parties; there were often two or three a night in the embassies. This meant standing in a jam, with aching feet, exchanging small talk with people one had left an hour before. Beginning at seven-thirty, these parties seemed to have no ending, and, with the younger set, they sometimes went on far into the night. Only in the summer when such parties could be held in the gardens, lighted by Chinese lanterns scented with the perfume of flowers, with chairs and sofas for rest and comfort, and attractive women for companions, could a cocktail party have real charm.

6

I often wondered why these charming gardens were not used more often for entertainment. They lent themselves ideally to the presentation of plays. However, I recall but two that were given. In the lovely garden of the British Embassy, *A Midsummer Night's Dream* was performed in a perfect setting. The full moon threw a mystic light on the scene, and the women in their gay dresses were seated in comfortable armchairs. The amateur players were astonishingly good, especially Geoffrey McDermott, First Secretary of the Embassy, in the role of Bottom, and Mrs. McDermott, who gave a lively interpretation of Titania.

In the beautiful garden of the Agustín Edwardses another play was given by the light of the moon when the Little Theater Company was invited to present *Caligula*. The air was sweet with fragrance, and the setting, with the big house in the background, was picturesque. After the play there was a reception and a buffet supper, at which an amusing incident took place. The French Ambassador appeared in a white dress coat, and one of the guests, mistaking him for a servant, nonchalantly passed him a soiled plate. Without batting an eye, the diplomat bowed profoundly, took the plate with true Gallic courtliness and carried it to a table.

We shall now return to the political scene and the rupture with the Axis.

VII

Moving toward Rupture with the Axis

After the attack on Pearl Harbor our problems in Chile changed. The United States had been treacherously attacked by Japan, probably by prearrangement with the Axis, and Germany and Italy declared war on us. As I have said, under the agreement made by the American nations an attack on any one American republic was to be taken as an attack on all, but this agreement had not yet been ratified by the Chilean Congress, nor had it been sent to the Senate for action. Now more than ever Axis espionage and sabotage became matters of serious concern to us.

However, it was not remarkable or, in my opinion, unreasonable that Chile did not act at once, for reasons which I have already pointed out. President Ríos would not take office for two months. Ernesto Barros Jarpa had been announced as the new Foreign Minister by the President-elect. He was so well known as a friend of the United States that on the day of the announcement many of my colleagues telephoned me their congratulations, but I was to find immediately that he could see no reason for or advantage in breaking diplomatic relations with the Axis Powers under the existing conditions.

Some time before I went to Chile, when, in the organization of the Chile-American Cultural Institute, our people were looking for a President distinguished in Chilean life and friendly to the United States, they found in Ernesto Barros Jarpa the man who met all the requirements. I had known him in this role for some time and had found him clever, charming and friendly. He had an attractive personality and was a man of medium height, with a good physique, dark hair, graceful in bearing, fluent in speech. He had some claim to elegance in attire, since long before he had introduced a style of coat that came to be known as "the Barros Jarpa."

He was a member of the Liberal party, and this made his presence in the ministry of a Radical President a bit incongruous. At a very early age he had been Minister of Foreign Affairs in the administration of Arturo Alessandri Palma. He was one of the leaders of the bar and a professor of international law in the university. He was plausible, forceful and sometimes eloquent. Professionally he had, at one time or another, represented most of the North American interests in Chile. My personal relations with him were most cordial, and they have remained so ever since. In the midst of the prolonged controversy over rupture with the Axis, *Topaze,* the incomparable magazine of political satire, cartooned us in violent combat at a time when nothing had diminished the cordiality of our personal relations.

He had called upon me before taking office and had left me in no doubt. He was against the rupture. I ascribed it, at first, to the possible conviction, not at all rare in Chile at the time, that the war would end in a German victory or in a draw, and in either event Chile would be in a better position to profit in postwar trade if it maintained the appearance of official neutrality.

In our conversation, he compared Chile's position regarding the United States with our attitude toward England before Pearl Harbor. Our sympathies, he said, were with England, just as Chile's sympathy was with us; we thought that by not breaking relations with the Axis we would have less difficulty in getting war material across the water, and Chile felt the same way about getting war material to the United States; we did not break with the Axis for more than two years, and then only when we were attacked, and if Chile were attacked she would follow our example. This ignored the fact that the American nations had agreed at Havana that an attack on one would be an attack on all, but the Chilean Congress had not ratified the agreement, and until it was ratified it was not binding. And why not? *Because public opinion, which determines the actions of a democracy, was not yet prepared for such a step.*

When, after Pearl Harbor, some American republics, under dictators, broke relations because neither Congress nor public opinion had to be consulted, a portion of the North American press, ignorant of the institutional system of Chile, pointed an accusing finger at her, while praising the dictatorships. These accusations ignored the very essential fact that Chile is a democracy, a government of law, not men, with a Constitution that is respected, and that no one man, by a scratch of the pen, could commit the nation on an international issue. It was clear to me that there would have to be a definite crystallization of public opinion. After all, we were fighting a war for the maintenance of just such democratic institutions as Chile had, and against dictatorships, such as had been imposed on some nations that we lauded to the heavens.

Now public opinion was not keen on breaking relations with Germany, with which Chile had long had close commercial and cultural relations, and it could not ignore the fact that German immigrants had redeemed by cultivation much of the rich region of the south. Then, too, Chile had had no unpleasant incidents with Germany, and, unhappily, that could not be said about us.

Immediately after Barros Jarpa's designation, the President-elect told me he was sending him to Washington at once to discuss the relations of the two countries under war conditions, but I was convinced that Barros Jarpa would not go, and so it developed. At a luncheon given by our air mission for Yankee fliers who had flown planes to Chile for its air force, he told me frankly why he was opposed to going to Washington at the time. He thought, in view of Chile's opposition to immediate rupture with the Axis, he would be unable to satisfy the North American press in interviews and that the visit would do more harm than good. I am sure he was right.

Meanwhile I was fearful of the cooling of the relations between the two countries because of incidents not easy to explain to Washington, and I asked permission to discuss these frankly with the President-elect in the presence of Barros Jarpa. In Buenos Aires the Chilean Ambassador had given a farewell dinner to the departing German Ambassador, who was Hitler's most offensive diplomat in South America. Following a Nazi and Japanese demonstration in Buenos Aires, the mob had marched to the Chilean Embassy shouting insults at Roosevelt and the United States, and the Ambassador had appeared on the balcony to smile upon the crowd and to thank them for their attentions. These incidents, reported in North American papers, caused concern. Meanwhile, in Chile, the Nazi papers were constantly attacking the United States indecently, and the reputable papers had not seen fit to take up a defense. The country was infested with Nazi spies and agents who were transmitting information on the movement of ships carrying war material, and while there had been some arrests the offenders had found legal loopholes by which to escape.

I got the impression from my audience of two that they thought the enumeration impertinent or unimportant, though I knew the damage that was being done to Chile in the United States.

However, the new President in his opening speech to Congress laid special stress on the harmful effect of press denunciations of a friendly country, and when Congress named a committee to investigate Nazi activities, he told me that he had informed the committee in charge that all information in possession of the government would be turned over to it.

But it was just here that we had another shock when Minister of the Interior Morales reported that he had found no charges and no evidence of Nazi activities in the files of the ministry, though I knew that much such evidence had been submitted. The papers had evidently been withdrawn by someone some time before Morales, who was our friend, took office. The Nazis were then riding so high and mighty that the German Ambassador had the temerity to protest formally to Barros Jarpa against any investigation of Nazi activities on the ground that the Nazi party had been disbanded. The minister replied that the investigation was not aimed at a party but at Nazi activities, and that if there were none, the Ambassador should be pleased to have it proven.

About this time another issue appeared when the quisling in Denmark proposed to dismiss the King's Minister to Chile, Fin Lund, and replace him with a traitor. I had discussed this with the Foreign Minister, who had implied that Lund would not be disturbed. But there were complications. A ship was being built for Chile in Copenhagen, and there was a possibility that the construction or delivery would be stopped if the Chileans refused to receive the quisling appointee. Lund, stationed in Buenos Aires, came to see me on reaching Santiago, and I was able to reassure him with the assurances of the Foreign Minister. Lund thanked Washington for my interest.

2

Our most pressing need at this time was for action by the Chilean Government to stop the telecommunication of the Axis embassies and agents—which had been pledged at Rio. In early August 1942 I was shown the first draft of a decree, strong and satisfactory, but nothing more was heard of it, and, in the meanwhile, secret information via transradio was reaching Nazi agents in Cuba, and ships bearing war material were being sunk. In early September I sent a strong note to the Foreign Office urging that action be taken. In this fight we were receiving no support from the British Embassy, and Washington so informed London, since Sir Charles Orde called to say that he had just received instructions from his government to co-operate with us. Some days later, when I was asked if the co-operation had been forthcoming, I was compelled to report that it had not and that no appointment with the Foreign Minister had been asked for. Ten days later I found Sir Charles at his residence looking seedy from a cold and playing the piano. His explanation did not seem valid to me, and for a time we had to carry the burden alone.

With the transmission station "somewhere in or near Valparaiso" flashing reports via Cuba to Nazi submarines in waiting to sink ships carrying war material, with a prominent public man making a pro-Nazi speech at the War College, the propagandists were busily circulating falsehoods to confuse the public. Thus the Chileans were told that we were sending war material to Bolivia and Peru to be used against Chile, and I went to the Foreign Office to protest. I found that the Peruvian and Bolivian ambassadors had joined in a denunciation of this canard. More incredible was the story Barros Jarpa heard in the Senate that the embassy had ordered parachutes and bombs! *These had been ordered* and apparently had been addressed to the "Mission," meaning the air mission, but the word *mission* had been interpreted to mean embassy. The material ordered was for the Chilean Air Force.

But public opinion was mobilizing. The supporters of rupture in the Senate were more numerous and outspoken. The Socialist party had published a powerful manifesto, written by Oscar Schnake, demanding rupture. The Brazilian Ambassador had called at the Foreign Office to inform it that Brazil had declared war on Germany because of the sinking of Brazilian ships by Axis submarines. The government itself was divided on the issue of rupture. When the Executive Committee of the Radical party, thinking in terms of domestic politics, passed a resolution against rupture, Marcial Mora, the head of the party, resigned in protest.

At length something was being done to mobilize public opinion and make it articulate and effective. The minority, supporting the Axis, had been compact, thoroughly organized and financed. The formation of the Union for Victory changed the picture. Its membership was drawn from all political parties, from workers, farmers, country merchants, with its tentacles reaching into the most remote hamlets. Its headquarters was a beehive. Reports on people and events poured in. When a teacher was dismissed because of his opposition to the Axis, the Union for Victory aroused and mobilized the people of the community. The activities of the Axis were being exposed. Large mass meetings were organized where fighting speeches fired the blood of the democrats.

The effect of these meetings persuaded the Nazis that it was necessary to hold a counterdemonstration which would overshadow that of the democrats, but as the time approached for their meeting the managers feared that the attendance would fall short of their rosy prediction. Planning their excuse in advance, they announced that because of a nonexistent "epidemic" only half or two thirds of the theater could be filled. However, the theater was packed—but with the opposition, which heckled the speakers and made the demonstration a fiasco. Mounted *carabineros* were near to prevent any interference from without, for feeling was now running high. At this time, Luis, our butler, warned my daughter not to go into the park across the Merced since the German Embassy had just been stoned, and trouble was expected.

The Nazis scored one triumph, though it was neither intentional nor real. General George Marshall had sent a beautiful silk American flag to the Chilean War College and it was presented formally. The cadets were lined up against a wall facing the platform. I spoke at the presentation; General

Escudero replied, and then summoned the color-bearers. Three fine young soldiers marched to the platform and saluted. They were given the American flag. They marched to the end of the long line of cadets, parading along the line, the Stars and Stripes fluttering happily in the breeze. But there was a fly in the ointment. In accordance with the rules in reviews the color-bearers fell into the goose step. A photographer sent me a picture showing clearly the North American flag, borne by soldiers doing the goose step, and it looked as though the enemy had captured the flag. I treasure that picture.

3

President Roosevelt was deeply concerned over what could happen in South America that would have a disastrous effect on the inflow to the United States of strategical material. In his letter, previously quoted, he expressed his fear that the continued victories of the Axis armies would encourage attempts in some South American countries to overthrow the governments not subservient to Hitler. These activities were in full blast in Chile, but the inherent democracy of the people made their success improbable. My constant contact with the government convinced me that in essentials it was as sound as public opinion. I made no speeches, gave out no interviews criticizing the government, since this would, in my opinion, have been stupid and certain to defeat our purpose. I said what I had to say behind closed doors with the proper functionaries of a sovereign state that had the right to make its own decision without pressure or threats over its head. We had no reasonable basis for serious complaint. The members of our general staff had come, conferred, and agreed with the Chilean armed forces about methods of defense should an attack be made; our armed vessels were permitted to enter Chilean ports without advance notice; Chilean naval forces were keeping an eye on the coast near the mines; and three

American admirals had paid official visits and been most cordially received.

4

The first to come was Admiral Shafroth in his flagship, the *Concord*. He invited President Ríos to a luncheon on board at Valparaiso and I accompanied him. A short distance from the *Concord*, Chilean ships were lined up, with flags and pennants flying, the band playing as the launch bore the President to Shafroth's ship, while the presidential salute was being fired. The scene was colorful and dramatic.

The admiral was a real asset. Gargantuan in size, exuding good will, his thunderous laughter, which all but shook the Moneda, at first had startled Ríos and then captivated him. Often afterward Ríos spoke to me of Shafroth with admiration and affection.

But the luncheon had its comic relief. I was amused by the startled expression on the faces of the Chilean naval officers when, in the admiral's room, servants appeared proudly bearing tomato juice cocktails! During luncheon, the Minister of Finance, seated beside me, asked wonderingly, in an undertone, "Don't we get any wine?" They did not. They had to take water and like it.

When, during the visit of Admiral Whiting, later, I called on the President to invite him to luncheon on another warship, the conversation would have seemed peculiar to anyone listening in. "Mr. President," I said solemnly, "you have had luncheon on an American warship before, I think." He said he had. "Well, just inside Valparaiso there is a cocktail bar and you may wish to pause there on your way to the ship." He smiled. "You're telling *me?*" he replied.

I then told him the story of the dry White House during the Hayes Administration when Mrs. Hayes refused permission for wine to be served at dinners. When arrangements were being made for a dinner for the Diplomatic Corps, William Evarts, Secretary of State, called on Mrs. Hayes to explain that many, if not most, of the guests were accustomed to wine with their meals, and to ask her to make an exception in this case and to serve champagne. All in vain. The next day a friend of Evarts, who knew of his embarrassment, met him on the street and asked him how the dinner had gone. "Oh, fine, fine," said Evarts sourly. "Water flowed like champagne."

The exclusion by Daniels of wines and liquors from the naval vessels, and continued by the vote of the officers, may be wise, but when an American warship makes an official visit to a wine-drinking country, and a luncheon or dinner is served in honor of the Chief of State and his officers it would seem reasonable and courteous to treat such an occasion as an exception and to serve wine at the table.

5

At this time the battle for rupture with the Axis was being waged by a small but able group in the Senate in secret sessions, though I was informed in minute detail on what was being said and done. Alarmed by the drift away from them, the Nazis were now intensifying their activities. We were still having difficulty in getting telecommunications stopped, but we were most concerned about the mysterious transmitting station in or near Valparaiso. It was so well concealed that the experts required days of effort in detecting its whereabouts. We were now intercepting its messages, and the revelations were startling. It was at this time that Benjamin Subercaseaux wrote a powerful letter to *La Nación* charging that the Axis had a free hand and was informing Berlin on the movement of ships, which were being torpedoed by submarines in consequence. The Nazi papers, set up as propaganda sheets, were now going beyond all bounds of decency. An article appeared in one of these falsely attacking one of our consuls, charging that trucks followed our army with prostitutes, and picturing

Roosevelt on crutches and in a disrespectful manner. For the first time I made a formal protest.

But there was a brighter side to the picture. When a demonstration against rupture was organized, the demonstrators were prevented by the police from marching by the Embassy Residence, and when they then marched to the Moneda, President Ríos refused to appear on the balcony but agreed to receive a committee, which was bluntly told that he was in complete accord with the democracies and that he stood not only for continental but also for hemispheric solidarity.

In my conversations with the President at this time he left no doubt in my mind of his decision to break relations with the Axis soon. The impudence and smugness of the Japanese Ambassador in assuring Ríos that "should pressure be brought by the United States" Chile could count on the military support of Japan was not helpful to his cause. The President had not yet caught his breath after this astounding statement when the diplomat asked what Chile would do if the Japanese seized the Talara oil wells in Peru, which, he said, they easily could do.

"Is this a threat?" asked the President.

"Oh, no, just a friendly talk," replied the diplomat.

"But I can answer your question," said Ríos. "If Japan should molest any spot on the Pacific Coast, or on this continent, you will not only have to fight Chile but the whole of South America."

In the meantime, as I have said, we knew that the transmitting station in Valparaiso, the PSY, was informing German submarines in the Atlantic of the movement of ships to Chile and the United States, describing their cargo, destination and the probable time of their arrival in Atlantic waters, where they could be sunk. We knew the identity of some of these German agents, many of whom, if not most, had been trained in Germany. We knew that this espionage ring was under the direction of the German Embassy. But, unhappily, because the non-Nazi papers were silent about these activities, the mass of the people had been prone to discount the stories.

In June 1942 I placed in the hands of the Foreign Minister a long memorandum with detailed information as to the names of the Axis agents and spies, with evidence of their guilt. Information from the transmitting station sent to receiving stations in Hamburg and Cuba was also furnished, with as many as seventy intercepted messages showing conclusively that this Chilean station was reporting:

(1) The arrival and departure of boats from all ports on the western coast.

(2) The cargoes of the boats sailing from Chile, with the time of their arrival in Atlantic waters.

(3) Information as to imports from the United States and from South America.

(4) Facts as to defensive measures adopted by Latin-American nations.

(5) General information from the United States and political information from Chile.

(6) Administrative details as to the functioning of the station and the agents.

This memorandum showed conclusively that the station in Valparaiso was acting as the transmitter of information received from Axis agents in Peru, Argentina, Colombia, Ecuador, Guatemala and even Mexico.

We did not know until after the war, when we came into possession of the personal diary of the Japanese Ambassador, which had been strangely overlooked when all important papers were being destroyed after the rupture, that about this time one of my notes to the Foreign Office had mysteriously found its way to the German Embassy. The diary recorded that the Ambassador had been invited to the German Embassy to see the note.

The interceptions proved positively that the function of Ludwig von Bohlen, posing as the Commercial Attaché of the German Embassy, was to take charge of the espionage activities. One of the intercepts from Bohlen asked permission to turn over all information regarding ship movements to the Japanese Naval Attaché; and another granted permission.

Most significant was the disclosure of the close and constant communication between the ring in Chile and a similar ring in Cuba. No attack was to be made on ships from Chile in the Pacific, but when a ship left a Chilean port the agent in Cuba was informed as to the cargo and the probable day of its arrival in Atlantic waters, when the submarines, in waiting there, could sink it.

Barros Jarpa seemed impressed with this memorandum and promised to call it to the attention of the Minister of the Interior for appropriate action, but though he kept his promise, nothing was done about it. We were still feeding the government with intercepts on ship movements and information on the sinking of ships when a Nazi spy was arrested and executed in Cuba. He confessed that he had received his information and orders through the transmission station in Chile.

In July 1942 I showed President Ríos a personal letter from Roosevelt, who thought it "very dangerous for Chile" to continue diplomatic relations with the Axis, "as well as dangerous to the Allies in the war." Before I showed him the letter he had expressed views almost identical with those of the Roosevelt letter. "I am glad I said what I did before reading the letter," he said, "for these are my views." It was clear that he had determined on rupture with the Axis, though he thought it would take a little time to make arrangements and to prepare the public. He did not say, and I did not know at the time, that the Chilean Government was completing preparations for the arrest of spies and agents in the immediate future.

6

Washington was hopeful that President Ríos would visit the United States, where he could sit down across the table from Roosevelt and reach decisions important to both countries. An invitation was extended and accepted with evident satisfaction. Ríos had a deep admiration for Roosevelt and he was eager to visit the United States. Plans were made; the program for his entertainment was prepared and published; the visit was announced and the day set on which Ríos would take the plane to Washington; the Chilean Congress had granted the necessary permission for him to leave the country and had given him a going-away dinner; and I had invitations out for a dinner at the embassy on the Monday preceding his departure; my own preparations were made to accompany the President.

Then came the explosion.

At this juncture, Sumner Welles, thoroughly annoyed by the sinking of ships in the Atlantic and the seeming failure of Chile to act on my memorandum, made his speech in Boston referring to the presence of "spies in Argentina and Chile," though they were also in every other South American country. He charged that these spies were "stabbing the allied nations in the back." A part of this speech had been cabled to the embassy too late to make action possible, and after the speech had been given to the press. I find in my diary of that day my reaction: "It seems a shocking mistake, just as Ríos is about to leave for Washington as the guest of the nation, and I tremble at the inevitable reaction here."

This was water on the wheel of the element opposing rupture with the Axis. No phrase could have been more offensive to the Chileans than "stabbing in the back." While aimed at the German spies, it could be interpreted to mean that Chile was stabbing a friend in the back. The well-organized, completely equipped and financed Axis pounced on this statement with the eagerness of a cat jumping at a rat, and all its numerous avenues of publicity were put in service to persuade the Chileans that they had been flagrantly insulted.

The strange timing of the speech, as Ríos was about to take the plane, seemed incredible. The Chilean reaction was instantaneous, emphatic, furious and unanimous. All political parties united in resentment, and the press, without an exception, described it as an insult. The fact that Welles was greatly

admired in Chile as an understanding friend made the resentment all the more bitter.

The morning after the publication of the speech the Santiago papers screamed with headlines. *La Hora* was bitter editorially. *La Nación* insisted that Chile had done everything to
prove its adherence to the cause of the democracies, of which
she was one. *El Mercurio* carried a strong, dignified, though
conciliatory protest.

That day Barros Jarpa asked me to call. He said that without some satisfactory explanation he could not advise the President to act on his invitation since the atmosphere created
would be unfriendly; that Ambassador Michels in Washington had an appointment to see Roosevelt at ten o'clock, that
his report would be in Santiago by five, and that he would
inform me of the result.

That night there was a hostile demonstration of university
students in front of my house. We heard singing, but assumed boys were out on a lark and did not realize it was a
demonstration.

The next day was Sunday, and the press carried the bitter
protest of Arturo Alessandri Palma, twice President of the
Republic, attacking Sumner Welles without restraint. And that
night, at ten o'clock, the Foreign Office telephoned asking me
to receive Ambassador Ben Cohen, then home on leave, at
once. He brought a copy of President Ríos's telegram to
Roosevelt postponing his visit on the ground that the speech
had prepared an unsympathetic, if not a hostile, atmosphere,
and, of course he was right. I knew and admired Cohen, and
when he entered the room he seemed as unhappy as I felt.
He also brought a cancellation of Ríos's acceptance to my
dinner for him that was planned for the next night. It was
the end of a perfect day—for the Nazis.

During the next few days I saw no government officials.
The air was charged with bitterness. *La Crítica,* the Socialist
paper, was demanding the resignation of Barros Jarpa; the
Nazi papers were denouncing Ambassador Michels and de-

manding his recall; and a letter in praise of Barros Jarpa appeared in the press, signed by four former presidents: Alessandri, Carlos Davíla, Dr. Mendez and Barros Borgoño.

Nothing could have been more unfortunate at a time when we were nearing an understanding with the government and on the eve of the arrests of spies and agents *uncovered by Chile's Secret Service*. Even then, Washington asked my opinion about giving my memorandum to the press and I advised against it, with the request that if it were given out, it should be accompanied by an expression of appreciation to Chile for the arrests of the spies. However, the memorandum was published without the expression of appreciation, and in a telegram I insisted that such an expression be given out by either the President or Cordell Hull. Mr. Hull responded splendidly. *El Mercurio* published Hull's statement under large headlines on the first page, and that night, at dinner, President Ríos expressed his gratitude.

7

But there was even more to follow. President Roosevelt had immediately replied to Ríos's telegram in the most cordial terms, expressing the hope that the visit would be made soon, and I personally delivered it to the Foreign Office, with permission to give it to the press—but it did not appear. This gave the impression that Ríos's dignified telegram had been ignored and the Chilean President had been snubbed.

Resentment flamed again, especially among the students in the universities. Returning to the Embassy Residence from the chancellery, I found a great number of students in the Parque Forestal across the street and learned that there had been a demonstration, and that a letter had been sent in. The letter was couched in proper language but made clear the resentment that was felt because the Chilean President had been ignored. They would return on the morrow for an answer. When they returned the next day, I received a committee of ten or twelve. They were fine young men of intelligence and culture, and I saw at once that they had been moved by patriotic motives, with which I could sympathize. I assured them that Roosevelt had replied to Ríos in the most cordial manner and that they could verify this at the Foreign Office, where I had personally delivered the reply. I gave them the substance of it. This satisfied them that their President had not been snubbed, and, after an hour's conversation, we posed on the terrace for pictures and parted friends. The caliber and character of these students may be gathered from the fact that a very few years later I saw one of them a number of times when he was Minister of Finance. A little later, invited by the students to a celebration of the centennial of the university, I was surprised by the warmth of my reception and ascribed it to the treatment I had accorded the students who had called upon me with their protest.

8

Meanwhile, with a Nazi paper denouncing me for "directing the campaign for rupture with the Axis," thousands of men demonstrated against the Axis, marching to the Moneda bearing pictures of Roosevelt and Churchill, and President Ríos and Minister Morales appeared on the balcony to greet them with smiles.

With the ministry now divided on rupture, all the ministers resigned to permit the President to reorganize his government. I had found Barros Jarpa uniformly courteous and gracious, understanding my position as I understood his. Aside from a difference in the timing of the break with the Axis, he had been consistently helpful, and our friendship has continued to this day.

In the reorganization of the ministry, Joaquín Fernández y Fernández was summoned from his embassy in Uruguay to take over the Foreign Office.

VIII

Chile Breaks with the Axis

With the appointment of Joaquín Fernández as Foreign Minister there was little doubt that a rupture with the Axis would follow, since it was said that an agreement had been reached to break diplomatic relations within three months. Fernández was a slender man, his countenance distinctly Spanish, his hair black, his eyes shrewd, though he was inclined to squint a little when he was concentrating. He had a soft, modulated voice which I never was to hear raised in anger. I think I had his complete confidence, as I know he had mine. We were able to talk freely off the record, and it was possible to discuss the background of our problems without fear of misunderstanding. He never gave the impression of having "something up his sleeve" or of holding anything back. Best of all, he did not coddle himself with the delusion that Chile was isolated from international affairs and the war. For more than four years I was to see him frequently, sometimes twice a day, occasionally on Sundays and holidays. Soon, in public speeches, he had burned his bridges and taken his stand foursquare with us on the issues of the war. I have reason to believe that through these trying days of the war he rendered invaluable services to President Ríos, who, though a consummate national politician, had hitherto given little attention to international affairs. I know he had the President's confidence and affection.

2

With the realization that a rupture with the Axis was inevitable, the bitterness of the totalitarian sympathizers intensified. The last day of October 1942 a stone was thrown at the Embassy Residence from a neighboring apartment house. The police on guard rushed into the apartment house but did not find the culprits. Men dressed as mechanics had been seen in the halls and were assumed to be plumbers on a repair job, but these "mechanics" were missing, though they had not left the house. For some time, three Japanese living in the apartment house had been thought peculiar by their servants, who gossiped with my own. There was one room to which the servants were not admitted, even for cleaning, and the servants were convinced that their employers were spies.

In early November I had a long conversation with President Ríos. Though in a most cordial mood, he clearly felt humiliated by the Welles speech, since he had accepted invitations to visit most of the nations on the Pacific, en route to Washington, and the reason for the postponement of the visit would be circulated over the continent. Knowing that Welles's resentment was due in part to Chile's failure to act speedily on my espionage memorandum, he explained the reason. On taking office he had found the Secret Service disorganized and inefficient; it required time, patience and caution to effect a reorganization, and time was also needed for investigation, since, manifestly, we could not expect a sovereign state to make arrests on our representations without checking on our accusations. The men charged in my memorandum were being investigated, and the investigation had reached the point where arrests could be made; in fact, arrests were made within three days after the Welles speech. Obviously, the President's resentment had passed.

At this time forty thousand Chileans, in an impressive demonstration for rupture, passed the Moneda, with the President reviewing the marchers from the balcony of the palace. They then marched past the Embassy Residence shouting "Viva Roosevelt."

3

Then came the dramatic story of the landing of the American Army in French Morocco, and the enthusiasm in Chile could not have been surpassed anywhere. It was at this time that the always clever Joaquín Edwards Bello, in his column in *La Nación,* wrote that we had been hearing much about a "secret weapon," and the mystery had been solved. The "secret weapon" was the American Army! The Free French in Santiago came in a large group to the embassy to express their satisfaction. When I saw the President the next day, he congratulated me enthusiastically on the successful landing and on Roosevelt's message to the French people. He said the Chileans were partial to France because they associated it with liberty, and this move toward the liberation of France would be pleasing to them. He gave me a copy of the telegram he had sent to Roosevelt.

Especially impressive to me was the march of women workers of the syndicates to the Embassy Residence to extend congratulations, and I was asked to receive a committee. I gave instructions that *all* should be admitted. These women—

workers in factories, laundries and shops—were impressive, especially an old woman, whose years of toil had been carved deeply on her forehead, who stepped forward and spoke with a natural eloquence that astonished me.

That same evening, Fernández stopped at the Residence to say that orders had gone forth to close the Chilean Embassy in Vichy.

4

With the decision for action taken, the publishers of newspapers were informed and asked to help prepare the public for the announcement.

On December 18, 1942, the debate in the Senate began in secret session, but friends informed me minutely on the proceedings and the probable line-up. The small group of senators who had been valiantly pressing for action were now joined by others who, until this time, had steadfastly opposed the rupture. The opposition was bitter, and the extremists were threatening. A distinguished elder statesman, and a friend of mine, gave a long letter to the press urging a plebiscite— manifestly a delaying movement. Meanwhile, Raúl Morales, a young man of ability and promise, had gone to Washington, where he had been received by the highest functionaries of state, and the conversations had been eminently satisfactory.

With a pro-Nazi nation on the Chilean border, and with powerful Nazi elements within, there was some fear that a rupture with the Axis might be followed by an attempt to overthrow the democratic regime with the aid of a neighboring nation. To reassure Chile, Roosevelt sent me a letter, which I was to show to President Ríos on December 12, 1942.

Please take an early opportunity to inform President Ríos that if Chile is attacked by an Axis Power, or if trouble should be created in Chile by Axis nationals, or by elements instigated by Axis agents, after Chile has broken with the Axis, President Ríos may, of course, count on the support of the United States to the extent that the Chilean Government may request such support, and to the full extent of the ability of the United States.

There was really nothing confidential in this mere reiteration of the pledge we had made in Havana, but here was a positive assurance from Roosevelt personally that any attempt to overthrow the democratic regime in Chile and to set up another Axis satellite, would be met, if requested by the Chileans, with the armed might of the United States. President Ríos read the letter with satisfaction, but he had already determined on his course.

On January 12, 1943, he announced his purpose to the Council of Ministers, and at five o'clock that day, in presiding over the Council of Defense, Fernández made the announcement.

The former President, Carlos Ibáñez, who had opposed the rupture, then gave a statement to the press that since the President had decided on rupture it was the patriotic duty of every Chilean to support the government.

The government was then preparing for action, making lists of the more dangerous suspects. Ríos announced the establishment of emergency zones where attempts at sabotage might be expected. These included the mines producing war material for the Allies.

The debate in the Senate was drawing to a close, with the result certain, when I was honored with a full-page open letter addressed to me in a Nazi paper financed by the German Embassy. It paid me the exaggerated compliment of ascribing the approaching break in relations entirely to me. It was phrased in the best Goebbels style; the resemblance was amusing. It said that I had been responsible for "getting the communists to start the rebellion in Spain"—the rebellion notoriously launched by the pro-Fascist army against the constituted authority. I was threatened with a "heavy fist." I could "laugh now," but when Hitler triumphed, as he would, I "would be remembered."

On the day this choice bit appeared, the Senate approved the rupture by a vote of thirty to ten.

5

On January 20, Fernández summoned to the Moneda all chiefs of missions except those of the Axis. The reception room was crowded and merry. We were ushered in separately to the minister's private office, and I was summoned first. The minister read the decree breaking diplomatic relations, effective that day, and also his note to the German, Italian and Japanese ambassadors.

There was an immediate popular reaction. The next day the blare of bands drew me to the balcony of the Embassy Residence, and I found a long procession, with bands and banners, with detachments from every part of the city, marching to the Moneda and the Plaza Bulnes to pay tribute to Ríos. These were mostly workers from the syndicates. Some noticed me on the balcony and shouted "Viva Roosevelt" as they swept along.

But there was a big fly in the ointment as far as the embassy was concerned—no cable of appreciation to Ríos had arrived from Roosevelt! Shocked by what I thought an unpardonable neglect, my frantic cable brought a reply from Welles, with the very confidential information that Roosevelt was in Africa with Churchill, that the utmost secrecy was necessary for their protection, and that Roosevelt would cable Ríos immediately on his return. It was on his return from Africa that I heard from Roosevelt:

> You deserve all our congratulations for your part in
> the realignment of Chile's foreign policy. I know some-
> thing of the obstacles with which you have had to con-

tend. I know that the Axis, particularly the German partner, has spent years of effort in building up its position
in Chile. The victory which has been gained is as real as
though it had been won on the field of battle.

Thus giving me more credit than I deserved, he added his
thanks to the Chileans who had really borne the brunt of the
battle:

> You have had the aid of our many friends in Chile,
> both in and outside the government, who battered away
> incessantly for the break of relations. As you say in your
> letter, Chile is a country where democratic processes must
> be observed. Without public opinion behind rupture, the
> efforts of all of us would have been without avail. To
> those who bore the brunt, our friends in Chile, we owe
> a debt of profound gratitude. Again, with many thanks
> for your fruitful efforts. (February 10, 1943.)

After the rupture the members of the Axis diplomatic missions who had been a bit supercilious toward the Chilean government found it difficult, at first, to understand the altered
position. Ordered to remain in their houses, the German Ambassador was found making a call on the Japanese Embassy,
and the press published pictures of the Ambassador advancing
on press photographers with uplifted cane.

With public opinion behind it, the Chilean Government was
now going all the way in aligning itself with the democracies.
It broke relations with Rumania, Bulgaria and Hungary.

6

The time now seemed auspicious for President Ríos to
visit the United States, and all preparations had been made
when the pro-Fascist military *coup d'état* in Argentina occurred. There were still some Fascist enemies of democracy
in Chile, and the repercussions of the event in Argentina were

problematical. For the President to leave on a journey of almost two months under these circumstances would be of questionable wisdom. Embarrassed by the necessity of again postponing the trip, Fernández asked my opinion, and I advised against the President's leaving Chile at the moment. The visit could well await a more promising time. Since this was the feeling of both Ríos and Fernández, the official visit was postponed. Washington gave approval of my advice.

Meanwhile, with preparations for the invasion of Europe in progress, calling for every available means of transportation for troops, Washington was negotiating for the purchase from the Chilean Shipping Company of its three fine motor ships. Coming just when Chile, with its 2,800 miles of the Pacific Coast, was beginning to have a good merchant marine, it was not unnatural that many Chileans resented these negotiations. The government had to be reconciled to the sale and convinced of its ultimate advantage. For some time the negotiations tottered on the verge of failure, but at length an agreement was reached, and one Sunday morning in August 1943 I signed the papers with Fernández in his house. By this act, Chile made another contribution to the war effort of the Allies. Soon these Chilean ships were transporting our troops to the European battlefields.

This was in line with the heavy contributions Chile was making to the United States throughout the war. The North American press did not seem to realize the importance of these contributions. To be sure, there was some delay in the implementation of the rupture through economic and financial controls. If these did not come instantaneously it was because Chile, like the United States, is a democracy, ruled by law and courts, where minorities have their legal rights. While the government machinery was being set in motion for the controls, some North Americans who do not understand the processes of democracy, or have no respect for them, were impatient. In the beginning there were bureaucratic difficulties, since some of the control measures had to be sanctioned by several different departments of the government. One would agree, another hold back. Because of pride or jealousy, each dug in. At length the President created a new governmental functionary who would devote his entire time to ironing out these difficulties and expediting the work. Thus one day I was presented to Pablo Ramírez, who had undertaken the task. Years before he had shown unusual ability as Minister of Finance under President Carlos Ibáñez. With the fall of that regime, he had been excluded from the public service and had been in retirement since. He was a big man physically, and forceful, but with a gift of persuasion. He worked incessantly and successfully on his job. I liked and admired him.

The President of Chile could not put these controls into operation with an autocratic ukase. He had to go to Congress for legal authority, and, as I wrote Roosevelt at the time, the deliberations of that body were as annoying as similar deliberations in the Senate at Washington when it took a very long time to enact the Lend-Lease law that was so desperately needed.

Viewed from the outside, the misunderstanding about what Chile could or could not do, under its democratic Constitution, seemed appalling. This was impressed on me one day when I was waiting in the reception room at the White House with Averell Harriman, a man of great intelligence and international experience in Asia and Europe. I had given and defended the reasons for the delays. He made no comment at that time, but the next day when I passed him on the steps of the State Department, he turned back and said, "I was very much interested in what you said yesterday. You are right, of course. Our people should know." Most astonishing to me was the fact that with the lightning-fast transmission of news over the world, they did not know. It had become so irritating to note the applause that greeted dictators who did not have to regard public opinion, constitutions and laws that I wrote President Roosevelt that "in this war for the preservation of democratic institutions we might well restrain our enthusiasm for the methods of the dictators and pardon something to the orderly, legal processes of democracy."

I was impressed by Chile's attitude when constitutional governments were overthrown by military or Fascist methods in South America, since I found its desire for the recognition of these antidemocratic governments less precipitate than ours. The reason, of course, for our seeming precipitance was not clear to the Chileans. In our attempt to create and continue continental solidarity, we have sometimes thought it necessary to juggle a bit with elemental principles, lest the dictators charge us with interfering in the internal affairs of the Latin-American nations. After a *coup d'état* overthrowing governments, our policy is to consult all our South American neighbors and to follow the majority. Since much of the time the dictatorships have been much more numerous than the democracies, the effect at times is to line us up with dictatorial or pro-Fascist regimes against the few democracies who look to us for leadership.

It was about this time that the *coup d'état* in Bolivia, partly military, partly Nazi, came, and the American nations were confronted with a problem. No American nation co-operated more freely and honestly in the investigation to determine the wisdom of recognition than Chile. When Cordell Hull decided against recognition, Chile promptly aligned itself with us. When the Warren Report announced the absence of any Nazi influence, Fernández was plainly skeptical, but, reluctantly, Chile again joined us in according recognition—which was to prove disappointing.

In this field, I was to regret Chile's action but once. This was in connection with the military *coup d'état* in Argentina which overthrew the government of Ramírez and placed General Farrell in the Presidency. When the question of recognition rose, Chile was placed in a more delicate position than any of her sister American states. First, she was dependent on Argentina for her meat supply, which might be cut off; and, second, there was a threatening dispute as to boundaries along the Argentine border, especially in the far south. In that remote region, Argentina had recently built large barracks for the strong military force stationed there, and its military establishment in Mendoza, on the border, had been doubled. Much was being made of the Argentine "Alpine troops," trained by Italian experts in mountain fighting, and these, manifestly, could be used only in a war with Chile. Then, too, among the people there was a fraternal feeling dating from the days when the two nations, under O'Higgins and San Martín, had fought together for independence.

Again the exchange of views among the American nations began, with no decision reached, when Chile unexpectedly accorded recognition.

However, Fernández had imposed certain conditions that would have aligned Argentina with the other American republics on the war issue for the first time. With Chile then the only American nation in a position to talk with the Farrel government, I know that Fernández continued to urge on Argentina the acceptance of the Five Points of Stettinius, but the internal dissensions in Argentina, and the continuing power of the pro-Nazi element within the governing circle, defeated the major efforts of Chile.

During the interval, on several occasions arbitrary action was taken against North American interests in Argentina, and Chile strongly protested *without a request from us*. It was Chile's intervention that lifted the ban on the United Press; Chile's intervention that wrung from the Farrell regime the promise to discontinue the censorship of North American newsreels; Chile's remonstrance against a foul attack on Ambassador Armour by a frankly Nazi paper that brought upon it the fist of the government.

Though I regretted the recognition of the Farrel regime by Chile, the action of the Chilean Government throughout was that of a friend of the United States. The position of Chile was precisely like that of England on the issue of rupture—both were dependent on Argentine meat and wheat.

7

Meanwhile, the Chilean Secret Service was continuing the search for Axis spies and agents, and in February 1943 came the sensational discoveries of subversive activities involving the German Embassy. In the office of a physician in the Military Hospital were found $20,000 in United States currency which had been turned over to him by the head of the spy ring of the German Embassy before leaving the country. In the house of another, 300,000 pesos were found, and the possessor admitted that he had received the money from an alien enemy. In the village of Tobo, in a house owned by the confessed spy and agent, were found $45,000 in North American currency, and on the farm of this man's father were found 20,000 Argentine nacionales and 300,000 Chilean pesos. One man, to whom this agent admitted he had turned over $16,000 in North American currency, fled to Argentina along with others.

These revelations and arrests convinced thousands of Chileans for the first time of the gravity of the conspiracy against Chilean sovereignty and independence; public opinion stiffened, and the government was able to act more decisively. Cordial as the Chileans had been, I observed an increased cordiality on July 4, when the press teemed with friendly editorials and articles, and the embassy was so deluged with baskets of flowers that they overflowed all the rooms into the entrance hall, which was filled.

8

Conditions were auspicious when Fernández made his official visit to Washington and New York, accompanied by Ambassador Félix Nieto. He went by way of Argentina and Brazil, exchanging views with foreign ministers en route. I preceded him, in order to be of some possible service. He made an excellent impression on both political and business circles by his modest demeanor and his clear understanding of our point of view. President Roosevelt invited leading members of the House and Senate to meet him in the family sitting room of the White House for cocktails or tea. In offering tea, the President said that anyone preferring whisky and soda would find them on the table, and the guests moved en masse to the table. He seated Fernández beside him on a davenport, where they talked in French for an hour.

It is not with pleasure that I record the controversies of war days. When I left Chile in 1953 I had most cordial relations with the German, Italian and Japanese embassies, where the personnel and policies were vastly different from those of the war; and, as I hope I have shown, when the war began the German and the Italian ambassadors were not in sympathy with the policies of their governments and were merely the victims of their profession.

Throughout the war there was a heavy increase in the personnel of the embassy, with everyone alert. Even the Embassy Residence was converted into a workshop when the women of the American colony, with some English and Chileans, gathered for sewing and knitting for the soldiers. The entire third floor resembled a factory, crowded, busy, noisy, where sewing machines made a merry hum several days of the week. To expedite the sending of the finished material out, it was necessary for the American colony to found and finance a polyclinic under the Chilean Red Cross, and this soon became the best equipped in Chile. My wife, Sybil, and Mrs. Horace Graham were the founders, but the greatest credit for the operation must go to Mrs. Graham, the beautiful Crystal Abelli and above all Josefina Vial de Walker. These women worked like Trojans. Every afternoon a recess was called, and Sybil served tea and sandwiches. During the day the house had little privacy since it was overrun with women, many of them strangers to the family.

Aside from the war material they produced, these women rendered a service of the greatest value when our ships reached Chilean waters and the sailors had shore leave. This caused us no little concern, since the men would land in a hilarious mood, and we had not forgotten the incident of the *Balti-more*. Deprived of drink on board, the men would most likely sample the Chilean wines and beers, and there was the danger that their possible encounter with Nazi youths would result in a fight. The women faced this problem and solved it. In Valparaiso and Antofagasta canteens were opened where the sailors could find beer and entertainment, and dance with attractive girls invited by the women.

Another threat loomed when the men on shore leave were permitted to visit Santiago. Here the problem was to furnish them entertainment that would keep them off the streets, where they would almost certainly meet the enemy. Again the women had a plan. The visiting sailors would be divided among the North American families and taken in as guests in the women's houses, given food and beer, and nice girls would be invited in to dance. I heard of but one case where the sailor was not happy over the arrangement. He had been assigned as a guest at the home of a couple who were obsessed with religion and thought it their Christian duty to impose religion on him, with a grim reminder that, in war, death is always near. This youth, walking in the garden, took advantage of an opportunity to scale the wall and make his escape.

The experiment was not without its comic features. One day the attractive wife of a member of my staff, Mrs. Dick Buttrick, went to the railroad station to call for the boy assigned as her guest, who was arriving from Valparaiso. She was wearing a becoming poke bonnet, not unlike that of the Salvation Army and similar to the one worn by Mrs. Fiske in *Salvation Nell*. She found that the young men leaving the train had evidently had refreshments en route and she waited patiently while they joked and chatted among themselves, until at length her guest, remembering his manners, exclaimed, "Well, so long fellows. I have a date with Salvation Nell," and the lady remained Salvation Nell until her husband was transferred to another post.

If, with thousands of young men on shore leave in Chile,

there was not an unpleasant incident it must be ascribed to the women of the colony. That the men enjoyed their entertainment was manifested by the flood of letters of appreciation that poured in on the women who had been their hostesses.

At the beginning of the war, after we were involved, I appointed a co-ordination committee composed of leading North American industrialists and businessmen, under the chairmanship of Horace Graham, the head of the Chilean Nitrate Company. He was a warm friend of Chile and he understood the people. We looked to these men for advice and co-operation, and they, in their surveys of the situation and their response, rendered a real service in the war. This committee met frequently in the dining room of the embassy until after the victory was won.

No ambassador could have been more deeply indebted to his compatriots, both men and women.

9

Long before the war ended, Cordell Hull and Roosevelt had been busy planning the organization of the United Nations for the preservation of peace. As the time approached for the historic meeting in San Francisco, Roosevelt felt it of primary importance that all the nations of the hemisphere be members, and he was concerned lest those that had not declared war might be excluded on that account, on the objections of some European nations. Unhappily, through one of those unfortunate leaks too commonplace in Washington, a press association announced that Roosevelt had sent telegrams —not yet sent—to the American republics asking them to declare war lest they be excluded from the United Nations. Though this was intended as a friendly warning, it could be interpreted as a threat.

Fernández was shocked and felt that he, a friend, had been let down and his position made untenable. As far as Chile was concerned, the timing was unfortunate since a congressional election in March was just ahead, and President Ríos thought it unwise to inject a controversial international issue into the campaign. The foes of the Ríos administration, interpreting Roosevelt's warning as a threat, would make the most of "Yankee pressure." Ríos envisioned a prolonged congressional debate, with political parties playing politics, and demagogues running wild with protests against "Yankee insolence." Anyone on the ground, and with an elemental familiarity with politics, could understand the distress of the government, torn between a desire to retain the confidence of the United States and its fear of unpleasant political complications.

Fernández came to understand the motive behind Roosevelt's message, which was wholly in the interest of Chile. After it was made clear that Roosevelt was motivated solely by his eagerness to eliminate any possible objection from other countries in Europe, we met with President Ríos in the summer palace in Viña, in the room where I had had my interview with Aguirre Cerda during the first days of the war. He wanted Chile, a democratic country, in the United Nations. An agreement was reached by which Chile would declare a state of belligerency with Japan. When the purpose was made clear to Congress by Fernández, there was an immediate agreement in that quarter. I am sure that Roosevelt never gave Chile a better proof of his friendship.

The Chilean delegation to the San Francisco Conference, headed by Fernández, was composed of representatives of all political parties, and men of distinction. The embassy naturally had nothing to do with the selection of the delegation, though when Miguel Cruchaga, an able statesman and diplomat, hesitated because of his age about accepting a designation, I did all I could to persuade him to accept, and he did. The Chileans played their full part in the formation of the United Nations and signed the charter. In the intervening years, Chile has rendered distinguished service in this organization. As I write, Ben Cohen, an able diplomat in addition to being the administrative head of the United Nations, has been sent on delicate missions to Europe and Africa; and Senator José Maza has served as President of the Assembly.

During the war, Chile had, to my satisfaction, collaborated constantly with the democratic nations, and now, through the United Nations, it has made its contribution to the cause of peace.

Through all the controversies pertaining to the war, the Chileans were served by their sense of humor, and, for a change, we may now turn to their chuckles.

IX

The Chileans Chuckle

Except for a small segment of extremists the controversies over the war did not diminish the Chileans' sense of humor. I have often sat with them about a table enjoying refreshments and cigars, and have found them delightful when in a reminiscent mood. Many of their stories deserve recording, since they recall incidents, some of which happened long ago, that throw light on Chilean life. The first of those that I shall repeat does not reflect Chilean character, but it sheds some light on a phase of colonial life and the process of justice in those days.

I was a guest at a wedding on a *fundo* of La Ligua, not far from Santiago, where we gathered in a rambling colonial house which had been occupied for two centuries by the same family. The wedding ceremony was in the chapel, a small church that had served its religious purpose for many generations. As we were about to leave the chapel my attention was attracted to a bell with a rich mellow tone, and my companion asked me if I had heard it. On receiving an affirmative reply, he said, "Well, you have heard the bell presented to the chapel centuries ago by the Quintrala who owned this land for miles around." "And who was the Quintrala?" I asked, and then I heard the story of one of the most beautiful, wealthy and wicked women in Chilean history.

Her real name was Catalina de los Ríos, though her contemporaries preferred to call her the "Quintrala."

"And why the Quintrala?" I asked.

"Because of her resemblance to the scarlet-berried parasites whose embrace of death destroyed mighty trees and forests," my companion replied.

She was the daughter of a distinguished corregidor of Santiago, a member of a notable family which was prominent socially, politically and financially. The father was one of the richest feudalistic landowners of his time, married to the daughter of one of the wealthiest and most influential families of the realm. The mother of the Quintrala, Catalina Lisperguer, had died in giving birth to the child who was to become a problem for the eminently respectable father almost from her cradle. Tradition ascribes the wicked career of the child to her nurse, a favorite of her mother's, a slave reputed to be a sorceress, who gave the house of the conventional father a reputation for witchcraft.

This slave had real intelligence, but she began muttering spells over the babe in its cradle and soon so insinuated herself into its affections that it became passionately devoted to her. Observing the unwholesome influence of the slave, the father banished her to his large estate in La Ligua, which included the chapel in which I had heard the bell. Hysterically protesting the banishment of the slave, the nine-year-old child threw herself on the floor screaming, kicking and biting her father, who bent above her as she looked upon him with venomous hate. Even before she was eleven she had developed traits that were to make her infamous.

While of robust health, she was extremely temperamental, and in a frenzy of hate she attacked and injured the cook with a butcher knife. Later, when her hatred of her father intensified, she murdered him with a poisoned chicken when he was ill.

She had inherited some vicious blood. We have it on the authority of the then Bishop of Santiago, in a letter to the King, that she was a descendant of one of the concubines of Valdivia, the hero of colonial Chile, Maria de Encio. This none too lovely lady murdered her husband by pouring quicksilver into his ear when he was asleep. Another equally delectable lady of the family tried to kill the governor with water poisoned with herbs obtained from an Indian, and, when the venture failed, she killed the Indian she held responsible for the failure. That she whipped her stepdaughter to death was generally believed. Another ancestress had been tried as a witch before the Inquisition in Lima.

In addition to her great wealth, the Quintrala had extraordinary physical attraction and abnormal sex appeal, though contemporaries described her as "devilish." Her little chin was pointed, her eyebrows slanted, her hair a flaming red, her skin of a copper color, since, while she had predominantly German and Spanish blood, she had Indian blood as well. Her eyes were green and she knew how to use them, when to flash fire, and when to melt in the arms of a lover. Though her physical attraction was compelling, she increased it by the use of a seductive perfume.

There was one man only, and he a saintly soul, who had some influence over her. This was the Friar Pedro Figueroa, her confessor, who was noted as an orator. She admired him for his eloquence more than for his goodness. He was a good sculptor and miniaturist. When he was selected as her spiritual guide, she was in her fourteenth year, mature in mind and body, already a remarkable woman. She applied her seductive arts upon him without success. The priest found her a problem and he exerted all his persuasive power to keep her on the straight and narrow path, but one day when he rebuked her for her sacrilegious talk she flew into a fury and hurled a lighted candelabra at him, scratching his forehead and cutting one of his ears. Instantly, her frenzy spent, she was sorry and asked forgiveness.

She was more successful with other men, and she had her lovers. The remonstrances of the Church were without avail. They seemed to feed her passion for evil. When Don Juan de la Fuente Loarte, a teacher of the Holy Church and Vicar General of the Bishop, tried to restrain her licentiousness, she rushed upon him with a knife.

Though she spent much of her time on her great estate, she maintained a town house in Santiago that became the seat of her amours. Her love was that of an animal or a savage. One day, Enrique Enríquez, who was passionately in love with her, was delighted to receive a note summoning him to her house in the capital. On arriving, he was astonished when the servant told him his mistress awaited him in the cellar. He hurried to the basement, elated over the prospect of a passionate rendezvous. Never had he found her more fascinating, more deliberately provocative, as she walked about with a voluptuous swaying of her hips, smiling, laughing a bit wildly, but when he kissed her she slapped him. Then, smiling again, she put her face close to him and asked what he would give her for a kiss. He offered anything she wished. She chose the symbol of his knighthood, the Order of St. John. He pleaded to be spared, and a quarrel ensued, which she had obviously planned in advance. Simulating indignation, she thereupon called in some husky Negro slaves and ordered them to beat him to death. But before he expired, she drew a dagger from her dress and stabbed him to death with her own hand.

The murder of her father had cost her nothing, although her aunt had denounced her as a murderess to the authorities, but the family prestige was such that nothing was done about it. But the cold-blooded murder of her lover led to her arrest. Her trial was sensational in its revelations and it dragged on through a year. Though one of the judges would have given her over to the executioner, the others, unduly influenced by the prestige of the family, drew back from the death sentence and found ways to postpone the issue indefinitely. Much more effective than the family influence was the appeal of her confessor, whom she had attacked with the flaming candelabra. He insisted that she had repented. She had based her defense in court on the claim that she had been grossly insulted by her lover, and, becoming ill, she had no recollection of anything that had happened afterward. This was not consistent with her deliberate summoning of the burly slaves and her order to beat him to death. But the good friar saved her.

Going to the prison to inform her that her life had been spared, the priest begged her to marry. The Quintrala laughed. Why have a husband? Could she not have lovers she despised? But a husband she would have to respect—and how could she? However, she finally yielded to the importunities of the one man for whom she had affection and she agreed to marry anyone he might designate. She also agreed to a year of exile on her estate in La Ligua and promised to work hard physically during the period of her repentance.

She did retire to her estate and married, as she had promised, but very soon she wrought the degeneration of her husband and, as a Chilean historian has said, converted the spouse into an accomplice.

In the country her morals became worse, if that was possible, since she degenerated into a pervert. Tradition has it that during this period she made a determined effort to seduce the padre who had saved her life, but again she failed. Out of her own feudalistic acres she now had full play for her sadistic activities. Without any reason, she tortured her slaves, flogging them into insensibility, killing not a few. When, unable to bear more, the slaves fled in terror from the estate, she had them hunted down by the law and returned to her, whereupon she subjected them to such torture that no one was tempted to run away again.

She found a voluptuous pleasure in the sight of pain. After

her slaves had worked to exhaustion through the day, it gave her pleasure to make them sleep in stocks at night. She enjoyed the effect on these miserable dependents of separating husbands from wives, and children from their parents without cause. Her depravity was now so complete that she forced her slaves, without regard to age or sex, to go about stripped naked. Her conduct became known to the parish priest of La Ligua, who brought charges against her, and four years before her death she was again brought to trial and again escaped the penalty of her monstrous deeds through the influence of the family.

In her sumptuous house in Santiago once stood an image of the Crucified Christ, "El Cristo de la Agonía," noted because of its ineffably sad expression. It is famous in the church history of Chile, partly because in the terrible earthquake of May 1647, when scarcely any statue was left standing in Santiago and the church of the image came down in ruins, all that happened to "El Cristo de la Agonía" was that the crown of thorns was forced down over the neck. To this day, on the anniversary of the disaster, this image is borne through the streets of the city. It also figures in the bizarre story of the Quintrala.

Tradition has it that this famous image in her house once aroused her ire. On one occasion, as the story goes, when she was cruelly flogging her slaves in its presence, the image turned upon her an expression of indignation and reproval. According to another version, the image turned upon her when she appeared before it naked. At any rate, she summoned the servants and ordered the image removed. "I won't have anyone making long faces at me in my own house," she is reported to have said.

And so her days passed in licentiousness, cruelties and crimes until at last she realized that her end was near. The meticulous care with which she made provisions in her will gives no remote indication of insanity. Her mind was keen and practical as she put her affairs in order. As the end approached, she turned to the church she had defied, and to the one man for

whom she had some affection, her first confessor, the eloquent friar, who was far away. She sent him a message:
"Wherever you are, do not let go unheeded the plea of a dying woman who has need of you to ask God's mercy. They
say three months of life is left to me. You will arrive in
time."

This done, she made one of the most amazing wills in history. She left money for 25,000 masses for the repose of her
soul, and she left minute instructions as to her funeral. She
wished the services to be held in the old church of St. Augustine. Did she now regret the banishing from her house of the
image of the Crucified Christ? She left money for its annual
pilgrimage through the streets of Santiago for many years to
come.

Her old confessor responded to her summons and reached
Santiago in time to close the green eyes forever and to offer a
prayer for her forgiveness. The funeral services were imposing but the effect was spoiled because the slaves she had tortured assembled in the street outside the church to protest.

All this was some centuries ago, but in the very old church
of St. Augustine may still be seen the image of the Crucified
Christ she had ordered from her presence.

This is the story that came to me because, on the festive
occasion of a wedding on her old estate, I had heard the rich
tones of the bell she had given to the chapel.

2

Another strange story I often heard when men lighted
their cigars after dinner and fell into a storytelling mood is
concerned with a man, not a woman, but it also deals with
crime. It dates from the days when the First World War was
in incubation. In that conflict there was a division among the
Chileans on the issue, and no little bitterness was engendered.
The German Embassy, naturally and properly, was militantly
active for the fatherland, and no member of the staff was more

haughty and arrogant in method than the counselor, Guillermo Beckert.

One day the embassy building went up in flames, and when the Ambassador, Baron von Bodmann, appeared on the scene, he found the safe had been robbed, and in one room he discovered the charred remains of a man. While the features were burned beyond recognition, the Ambassador concluded from the counselor's wedding ring on a finger of the corpse, and a remnant of the counselor's clothing, that the dead man was Beckert.

That day the porter of the embassy, a Chilean worker named Tapia, was missing, and everyone assumed that he had robbed the safe, murdered the patriotic counselor, and made his escape. Was money the only object of the crime? Among the letters found in the house of Beckert not a few threatened him with death because of the fight he was making to align Chile with the Central Powers.

The Chilean Government was distressed. The German Ambassador was openly saying that Chile would have to answer for the crime of a Chilean workman. And, while Beckert was not a lovable man, but, on the contrary, unpopular because of his arrogant manner, the emotional reaction of the Chileans was one of bitterness against the assassin and of sympathy for the victim of the foul murder. The funeral, attended by a vast number, was impressive, and nothing about it was so impressive as the emotional and eloquent oration of Baron von Bodmann, paying tribute to the sterling virtues of the great patriot who had sacrificed his noble life for the fatherland.

A little later a dentist belatedly came forward with a report on the dead man he had attended, to the effect that the teeth of the charred remains were those of the little Chilean porter whom the public had thought guilty. No one was so much impressed as the Ambassador.

Then, about this time, a man appeared who had seen the noble Beckert and recognized him despite his disguise as he was about to take a train for the south. No longer could it be doubted that the murdered man was the Chilean porter and the murderer the great patriot embalmed so beautifully in the funeral oration of the German Ambassador. And when the murderer was caught as he was about to cross the border into Argentina, the case was closed.

And then the truth emerged. Beckert had given meticulous care to his preparations for the crime. He planned to steal the money, kill the porter, exchange clothes with the murdered man, and place his own wedding ring on the dead man's finger, convinced that no one would doubt that he himself was dead. To create the impression that he had died because of his devotion to his country, so tenderly dwelled upon by the Ambassador in his oration, he himself had written the threatening letters and planted them where they would be found. But he had not thought of the dentist's means of identification and had not doubted the perfection of his disguise until accosted on the street after the murder.

He was taken back to Santiago, tried for murder, and executed. Throughout this ordeal he maintained his haughty, arrogant manner, severely sober and uncomplaining. Only once between his conviction and execution was he seen to smile. When he was told of the Ambassador's glowing tribute to his unselfish patriotism in the funeral oration, a sardonic grin momentarily relieved the gloom of his countenance. The Ambassador did not repeat his tribute at the actual funeral of the counselor.

3

I have often heard Chileans chuckle over Chile's experience with another foreigner. This tale they rolled upon their tongues with gusto. Not many years before my time in Chile, the Military Attaché of Argentina, Juan Perón, conceived a scheme for getting the defense plans of Chile by bribing a Chilean army officer. Perón was never able to understand the Chilean people and the patriotism of its army. A bit fearful, however, of complications in forwarding the scheme, he returned to his own country and gave orders to his deputy to carry out the details. The Chilean officer approached pretended to take the wicked proposition under advisement and promptly reported to his superior officers. He was instructed to simulate an agreement and to arrange a meeting for the exchange of papers and money in a specified house, in a room opening on another room with a transom over the connecting door. At the moment of the exchange, the man concealed in the other room with a camera at the transom took a picture of the scene.

With this positive proof of the briber's guilt, he was unceremoniously thrown out of the country by Arturo Alessandri Palma, then President, who thereupon called the Argentine President on the telephone: "Hello, Mr. President," he said. "I have just been compelled to throw one of your men who tried to bribe one of our army officers for our secret defense plans out of the country. Now, Mr. President, we have no plans that are so secret, and if, at any time, you have a curiosity to see them and will let me know, I shall be glad to arrange it. That, Mr. President, will save you money and, more to the point, spare you embarrassment and the loss of dignity. Good-by."

The architect of this plan was the notorious Perón, and the successor on whom he imposed the burden of its consummation was a lieutenant colonel named Eduardo Lonardi. He had been on cordial terms with Perón, as a comrade, before the incident, but, on being ordered out of Chile, he bitterly resented the imposition upon him of carrying out a plan that was obnoxious to him; and when, years later, he led the movement that ended the regime of Perón in Argentina, it was thought that Lonardi enjoyed his revenge.

4

Chileans, with their rich sense of humor, are masters of the art of narrative in recalling amusing incidents. None, I am sure, more so than Arturo Alessandri Palma, whose reminiscences, drawn from personal relations with the great and near-great, were all the richer because of his wit, humor and satirical sketches of people and things. Though I cannot vouch for the truth of the story, I heard it many times, and it is not at all improbable since it fits in with his waggish fondness for mischief. Innumerable stories were told about him, some perhaps malicious, all amusing.

Chilean duels have usually been prevented through the intervention of seconds and mutual friends. The feeling in general is that duels are outdated and no longer impressive or even dramatic. The strategy through which Don Arturo once prevented an exchange of shots has a special flavor. Years ago, insults were exchanged between him and the father of a distinguished Liberal senator of my time in Chile, and a duel seemed inevitable. It was agreed that the duel should be fought far up in the mountains at the foot of the famous monument, the "Christ of the Andes." To reach the site it was necessary to have recourse to mules, and at the foot of the mountain a man kept mules to rent for the ascent. On the day agreed upon Don Arturo reached the "Christ of the Andes" on a mule and waited for his opponent. Minutes passed, even hours, and the opponent did not appear. At length, disgusted by the seeming timidity of the enemy, Don Arturo descended the mountain and announced to all and sundry that he had appeared at the stated hour and place but that his enemy had failed to meet him.

There was a reason: Don Arturo had appeared early and rented all the mules available for the day! When his opponent reached the foot of the mountain there was not a mule to be had and to ascend on foot was utterly impossible. Don Arturo made no secret of his strategy, and everyone laughed over the discomfiture of his foe—for whom he had a liking. Don

Arturo's chuckle finally brought an echo from his opponent, and the duel died in the general laughter.

5

During my time in Chile the Chileans roared with laughter over another duel that actually occurred. Two distinguished senators, whose names I spare, one a Radical and the other a Socialist, engaged in repartee on the floor of the Senate that went beyond the amenities of a drawing room. One was a physician, and a good one, and the other a highly reputable lawyer. When the lawyer implied that the doctor was a "quack"—which was not true—and the doctor replied that the lawyer was something worse—which was untrue—a challenge followed. Since both were liked and respected and the political party of neither wished to lose one of its ornaments, the friends of both became hectically busy trying to reconcile the furious men. They met, as usual, in the Union Club for the negotiations, but neither principal would yield an inch; each was grimly determined to shoot it out.

Failing in their attempt to reach an agreement, the mutual friends appealed to the police to prevent the duel, even if they had to take the principals into custody. The officers went forth in search of the duelists. As they approached the house of one he saw them, jumped out a back window, and made his escape; when close to the house of the other they were seen by him, and he, having taken the precaution to have a car handy on a side street, hurried out the back way and, reaching his car, was on his way when the police were hammering on the front door. They met on the "field of honor" and shots were exchanged; no one was hurt. One of the duelists insisted he had heard the bullet whiz by his head, but the Chileans just chuckled, and I am afraid they would have chuckled had one been hit. I knew both duelists. The Chilean chuckle is a safety valve.

X

The "Lion of Tarapacá"

My references to Arturo Alessandri Palma call for a more detailed story about one of the most interesting personalities I have ever known. Long before I saw Chile, I was fairly familiar with the dramatic career of this consummate politician and statesman who had twice been President of the Republic and was to be president of the Senate in his eightieth year. His career in Congress after having served as President of the Republic was similar to that of John Quincy Adams in the United States, and the fighting qualities of one were duplicated in the other. When in Paris, en route from Spain to Chile, the United Press correspondent informed me that Alessandri was in the city, and he asked permission to arrange a meeting. At that time there was no love lost between the government of Aguirre Cerda and Alessandri, and I had visions of headlines in Santiago papers announcing that I had been in "conference" with one of the leaders of the opposition before presenting my credentials to the President. Therefore, though I was keen to meet Alessandri, I was forced to decline. I do not know that he knew of my declination and resented it or not, but on his return to Chile before I met him, I had reason to believe that he was unfriendly. While the mass of the people were sympathetic toward the Loyalists in the Spanish war, his government was favorable to the rebels, and I suspected that the Spanish propagandists, because of my sympathy with the legal constitutional government, implied that I was something of a "communist."

I met the old lion for the first time at a reception in the apartment of Miguel Cruchaga, former Ambassador to the United States, Germany and Brazil, Don Arturo's Foreign Minister, a distinguished statesman and a foremost layman of the Catholic Church. I literally stumbled upon the former President in the crowd, and, from the startled expression on his face, it flashed upon me that he was shocked that his host was on visiting terms with one so "red" as to prefer democracy to Fascism. Later I found him at a reception in the beautiful country home of friends near Santiago. Shaking his finger at me, he said, "I am a great admirer of your country, but you do not like me." Since nothing was more remote from the fact, I told him so; and a few days later he sent me the huge volume of the proceedings of the Pan-American Congress, held in Santiago when he was President, containing his brilliant, militantly democratic speech. On a vacant space at the top of the first page of the speech he had written in ink that the speech was proof of his pro-democratic feelings, something I had not doubted. It was so characteristic of Alessandri that I extracted the many pages of the speech and had them bound in leather with gold lettering denoting the contents. Some time later, when he was a guest at my house and was looking over the books in my library, I took this slender volume out and passed it to him, asking if he had ever seen the book. He was astonished and not displeased, and thereafter he never doubted my friendly attitude toward him and became one of my closest and most cherished friends.

2

Knowing his fame as a fighter, with his finger ever on the trigger, I was surprised when I first met Alessandri at Cruchaga's to find before me a man of barely medium height, stoutly built but not fat, with shoulders broad and heavy and a bit bowed from bending over a desk. The years of constant combat had not whitened his hair. His face denoted grim strength. It was round, the lips full and firm; his eyes were keen and penetrating, and I found later that they could beam with whimsy or flash with wrath. The texture of his skin was rough, the color ruddy. His voice was strong and flexible—the voice of a natural orator.

Often I was to see him pounding the pavement with a heavy walking stick in the Parque Forestal across from my residence. He was always accompanied by his secretary and a huge dog to which he was devoted, and the dog was passionately fond of him. I never was comfortable in Alessandri's apartment with the dog stretched out in the room fixing a watchful eye upon me every instant, as though prepared to spring if he detected a hostile gesture toward his beloved master. One day when I extended an invitation to Don Arturo to visit the United States he replied quite seriously, "I am sorry. My dog is too old to travel and I cannot leave him." I am sure he meant it.

He lived with his son, Fernando, also a senator, in a modest apartment in the center of the city at 56 Calle Phillips, the windows of which looked out on the historic Plaza de Armas. In the living room hung a portrait of him wearing the presidential sash, and on the tables were inscribed photographs of numerous world celebrities. He always sat in his favorite highbacked chair, across which was draped a woolen robe which he spread over his knees if the weather was cool. His dining room was small, but he had never been inclined to elaborate entertaining. His workroom, in which could usually be heard the clicking of a typewriter, was small and cosy, a huge table taking up a large part of the space. It was handsomely carved. The walls were lined with books and pamphlets, the table usually covered with manuscript.

One day he led me to the window looking down on the Plaza de Armas and pointed to a large tree. "It was under that tree that I was arrested when I was a boy and thrown into jail," he said, with a proud grin. It was during the troubled days of the Balmaceda regime, and the young Alessandri, not of age but even then a stout partisan, came into possession of some leaflets against the regime, and he was caught passing them out to loungers in the plaza. When his father secured his release, he was made to promise that thereafter he would let politics alone, but he never was to let it alone to his dying day.

Among the photographs on the table in the living room he called my attention to one with the figures of three men, Alessandri, Archbishop Errázuriz, and another he did not identify. "That," he said, "is an historic picture since it depicts the scene of the final settlement in the separation of church and state"—for which he, more than any other, was responsible, though he was a Catholic. When the details of the separation had been worked out, largely with the much loved Archbishop, a great figure in Chilean church history, he called on Alessandri for at least a postponement. He opposed the separation as a matter of dogma, and though he was almost reconciled to the inevitable, he feared the effect, among the unreconciled, on his reputation and prestige as the head of the Chilean church. But when he was told that the negotiations had been going on in Rome and that Cardinal Gasparri, also loath to agree, had been reconciled to the necessity, the plea for postponement was withdrawn. Alessandri, who liked and admired the good Archbishop, admitted that his reluctance to hurt him might have persuaded him to postpone, if the Arch-bishop had persisted in his plea.

3

For years, Don Arturo had played a major role in the strengthening of democracy and in legalizing human rights. He was so much a "radical" in the early part of his career that, like all liberals of all time, he was described by the re-actionaries as a "red." Dubbed in those days "the Lion of Tarapacá"—the province he represented in Congress—he was to retain the description with pride throughout his life.

When first elected President, the Republic was living under the outmoded Constitution which gave the executive scarcely any power to govern. It created a purely parliamentary gov-ernment. This brought on a head-on collision between Ales-sandri and an obstreperous Congress, and when his foes were able to defeat his policies by refusing appropriations to carry forward presidential plans, he resigned. Leaving the Moneda one evening, he appeared at the American Embassy, where he was received, not as a refugee but as a guest, and the next day Ambassador Collier personally drove him toward the Ar-gentine border. The record shows that in these troubles he had the entire sympathy of the government in Washington. He crossed the border into Argentina and set sail for Italy, where he remained until conditions at home became so chaotic that he was summoned back to resume his functions.

His place in Chilean history is fixed by his sponsorship of social legislation which went beyond that of any other country in the Western Hemisphere until the days of Franklin D. Roosevelt. He fought a violent battle for social reforms and human rights, and no succeeding government has dared set these laws aside. He was also a pioneer in South America in the struggle for women's rights. It was he who gave women the vote in municipal elections, and this was the breach through which the Chilean women marched to full electoral equality with men.

His remarkable popularity with the masses was due in large measure to the battles he had fought for social justice. This popularity always astonished me. On the convocation of Congress, when the Salon of Honor in the capitol was packed with parliamentarians and the galleries were filled, his reception on entering sometimes surpassed that given the actual President on his entrance. He had enough human vanity to delight in these popular demonstrations. Often, on leaving the capitol on these occasions, he would cross the street to the park, packed with spectators, and the populace shouted greetings and cheered. On one occasion when I was a *padrino* at the wedding of Joe Cussens in Viña del Mar, and, in accordance with Chilean custom, I was standing with the bridegroom and the bride's mother at the church entrance to greet invited guests, I was startled by a loud burst of applause. I assumed the bride was arriving, though I had never heard of a similar demonstration. A moment later, the mystery was solved—Don Arturo, pounding the pavement with his cane, came into view.

4

It was interesting to observe the reaction of the crowd when he appeared as a speaker on a platform. He was a natural orator. His emotional temperament made him one. His voice was strong, his delivery vigorous, his language virile and picturesque, and his parenthetical asides, rich in wit, humor or sarcasm, delighted the audience. He was a master of give-and-take in debate, and woe to the heckler who sought to confuse him, since he would be pulverized with a biting sentence. His speeches, never florid, *said* something in a downright manner. He conveyed the impression that he spoke only because he really had something to say, and he said it bluntly and with force. One year he gave a series of lectures on the political history of the country, and these were as meticulously prepared as the chapters of an historian's book. Even these lectures, however, were sprinkled with improvisations. I attended one, arriving as he was entering the hall, and he accompanied me to my seat; referring to my presence, he amazed me with a rapid and accurate review of my books.

One year we asked him to be the speaker at the Chile-American Institute on the Fourth of July, and his intimate familiarity with the formative days of the North American Republic was startling. It was the only occasion I heard him read his speech, and at the conclusion he inscribed the last page and gave me the manuscript. He not only knew the facts of our history, but he had caught the tone and spirit.

5

When close to eighty, he entered the congressional election of 1949 as a candidate for the Senate and waged a campaign that would have challenged the strength of robust youth. "Though aged, he was so iron of limb, none of the youth could cope with him," and after one of his victories, I quoted that verse, written about John Quincy Adams, intending a compliment. He scowled and growled. Woe to the person who suggested that he was old. One year I heard him deliver a commencement address at Santiago College; it was almost an hour in length. The ceremony was in the open air on the grounds and the time toward evening. With the lowering of the sun, a cool breeze sprang up and blew upon the elevation where Don Arturo sat at the end of his address. He was overheated and susceptible to colds. Miss Mason, president of the college, urged him to put on his overcoat. He frowned upon her disapprovingly. I, seated beside him, rose and held up his coat for him. He looked daggers, but succumbed. "They will say I am an old man," he grumbled. He was then in his seventy-eighth year.

6

My family and I lunched at his apartment several times. Though of the third generation of his family in Chile, he remained Italian in temperament and he liked Italian food. He served cocktails, but I noticed that he merely put his lips to his glass, for he never was a drinker or smoker, though I have heard amusing tales of the young Lothario he was in his youth. His family relationships when I knew him were beautiful. He had five sons, all distinguished in law, medicine, politics or finance, and he was very proud of his "boys." He was pleased when I told him that his greatest distinction was in the production of such a progeny. On one occasion, an opponent in debate said, "According to the law of heredity, where the children are very intelligent, as is the case with Señor Alessandri, it is because the father is not." The old lion replied, "Because of my deep love for my children, I accept the offense to me, but let it be put on record that in the case of your lordship, the intelligent one was your father."

Never have I known a more fascinating conversationalist and raconteur. Seated in his favorite chair, with the robe over his knees, and in fine fettle, it was a delight to hear him in a reminiscent mood. His word etchings of public figures in both Europe and Chile were vivid and his talk sparkled with witticisms, and, now and then, with acid comments on men and events. Not a few of his recollections were racy. Even in conversation, he was energetic, and his eyes sparkled. I imagine old Dr. Samuel Johnson must have presented such a picture during his talks with Boswell and Mrs. Thrale.

7

One day I took an American friend to call on him, and, as usual, he was as sparkling as champagne; he held forth for an hour and a half on the war and some of the Axis leaders.

He had met Ribbentrop in Germany just before the invasion of Poland, and he was amazed by the German's incredible lack of imagination. When Don Arturo suggested that the invasion of Poland might bring the United States into the war, the Chancellor was contemptuous. He did not think there was any danger. "But," said the Chilean, "in the last war the injection of two and a half million fresh American troops into the struggle turned the tide." Ribbentrop smiled condescendingly. "The war will be ended before the Americans can get over," he said. "But," Don Arturo continued, "have you considered the fact that the next war will be mechanical and that the United States is the greatest industrial nation in the world?" The Chancellor repeated that the war would be over before the American factories could prepare. "Then too," continued Alessandri, "the English—they are bulldogs and never let go." The great Ribbentrop smiled pityingly and said that "the English are tea drinkers and week-enders and do not want to fight."

More interesting was his conversation with Mussolini and Ciano. For the latter he had contempt. "When I saw Mussolini just before the war," he said, he had been shocked by his deterioration since he saw him first in 1925. "I told him that from my conversations with military men and with men in the street, it was evident that the Italian people did not want a war." Unaccustomed to hearing unpleasant truths, the Duce showed resentment and, with a scowl, replied, "The Italian people will do what I say."

En route to Italy from France, Alessandri had talked with Herriot and was asked to assure Mussolini that there was no difference between Italy and France that could not be settled amicably. Since Alessandri was of Italian blood and was known to Mussolini, it was thought the assurance might be taken seriously. "But," said Alessandri, with a shrug, "they evidently looked upon me as a French agent."

I was about to give him the version of a British diplomat's wife of the feud between Anthony Eden and Mussolini when he anticipated me with Mussolini's version, as the latter gave it to him. When Eden made his official visit to Rome he was met at the airport by Italian officials in business suits—no tails or toppers—and, according to Mussolini's story, Eden expressed his displeasure. Later he protested to Mussolini, who replied that the staff of the British Embassy who had met the plane were similarly attired. The atmosphere was cold, and, according to Mussolini, Eden banged the table with his fist and said that England would not permit Italy to go into Abyssinia, and Mussolini slapped the table and said Italy was not consulting England—and good-by. Since Mussolini was not famed for veracity, part of this must be discounted, as Don Arturo said, with a smile.

Apropos of Mussolini's notoriously lecherous nature, Don Arturo, with a chuckle, told of attending a social function in Rome when the Duce, conversing with him, said that women were very inferior to men. This was overheard by several beautiful women and was not appreciated. Some functionary, an old man overloaded with decorations, said to Alessandri in an undertone that Mussolini was very fond of women. Whereupon Alessandri asked the Duce to reconcile his poor opinion of women with his marked partiality for them. The old functionary plucked Alessandri by the sleeve and, in trembling undertones, warned, "Don't—that is a dangerous subject."

Illuminating, too, is Alessandri's story of his conversation with Mussolini on Fascism. This entered into the conversation when the Duce asked why Alessandri "permitted" the Popular Front to take over in Chile on the expiration of his second term. "It was elected," said Alessandri, "and I believe in democracy." "What would you do," asked the Duce, "if the Masons got the government in Chile?" "If they had a majority in an election, I would do nothing" was the reply. Mussolini seemed dumfounded. "We had better drop the discussion," he said.

I was interested in Don Arturo's conclusion that the King of Italy was largely responsible for the state of the country due to the war. "I know Humberto, the Crown Prince," he said, "having entertained him during his South American tour when I was President. When in Italy I was entertained by him in his palace. I told him I was positive that the Italian people were against war. As I was leaving, the Prince tapped me on the shoulder and said, 'Don't worry. My father will never sign a declaration of war.' Within two months he signed."

These stories give an idea of Alessandri in a reminiscent mood; and also illustrate his political ideology.

8

During part of the period of my association with Don Arturo we sometimes found ourselves in sharp disagreement. He had no in-between colors for men or events. They were either white or black. These differences had no effect on our relations. When Sumner Welles made his Boston speech, the infuriated Alessandri gave the press a violent denunciation. Not long afterward when I spoke of Welles as an admirer of his, I was surprised by his emotion. "When anything is said that implies an attack on Chile, I see red," he said. "I am sorry about that letter. I wish you would tell Sumner Welles that I am sorry and that when I wrote that letter I was in a high fever."

He did have a violent temper when aroused, as one American ambassador during his Presidency can testify. Accompanied by Miguel Cruchaga, the astute and even-tempered Foreign Minister, the Ambassador had gone to the Moneda to discuss a controversial matter involving an American corporation, and when he seemed to lay down the law, Alessandri flew into a rage and attacked the diplomat in language so undiplomatic that Cruchaga became alarmed and yanked the Ambassador from the room with the observation that "the atmosphere is not right for a discussion." I have heard that when aroused Alessandri disclosed a most extensive vocabulary of profanity, though in my conversations with him, covering thirteen years, I never heard him utter a profane word.

One day he told me that he had known General Queipo de Llano, the rebel officer in the Spanish war whose famous radio talks were sulphurous with profanity. The General was in Paris in exile from the dictatorship of Primo de Rivera, and his profanity then matched that of his radio discourses years later. This reference to profanity recalled to Don Arturo the story in John Gunther's book, *Inside Latin-America,* in which he was pictured on one occasion as so unrestrainedly profane that the girl secretary fled from the room. He chuckled over the story but said it had no basis.

Another illustration of his hot temper when aroused: soon after entering on his first administration, an insolent youth insulted him at the entrance to the Moneda, and Alessandri slapped him. A reproachful friend asked the President what had happened. "Nothing" was the reply. "You see, I forgot this presidential sash I have been wearing a very short time and instead remembered my dignity as a man. Because of this momentary and very justifiable lapse I slapped a lad in the plaza of the palace under the stern gaze of Portales"—the leading statesman of the nineteenth century.

The very brilliant and clever weekly magazine of political satire, *Topaze,* edited and illustrated by Jorge Delano, familiarly known as "Coke," found in Don Arturo a rich subject for its barbs. Once it ran a cartoon that Don Arturo thought offensive to presidential dignity, and, in a conversation with friends, he said as much. These friends, without consulting him, had the issue withdrawn. Learning of the incident, Don Arturo telephoned Delano. "Pardon me, Coke," he said. "This was a mistake of functionaries. You know me, man— I am very violent and sometimes say the wrong thing. It is my bad luck that these overzealous colleagues do not put reasonable orders into effect but instead enforce the unjust ones that only represent the natural unburdening of a misunderstood man."

During his long career, *Topaze* published hundreds of cartoons of Alessandri. A favorite story that concerns Don Arturo involves a cartoon poking fun at him for making a call on a distinguished Chinese physician visiting Santiago. The *Topaze* cartoon showed Alessandri in consultation with the Chinese on the state of his health, with the physician's finding in the caption: "Throat firm—lungs velly good—heart velly big—head bad—there is no cure for him." The following day the President's military attaché called on Delano. "Delano," he said, "His Excellency has asked me to offer his congratulations on the cartoon." It was enough that his heart had been found "velly big."

9

In the field of international relations Alessandri was a force for good. Even as a deputy at the turn of the century he contributed greatly to the ratification of the treaties that settled certain boundary disputes with Argentina. During his first administration he submitted the Tacna-Arica dispute with Peru to the arbitration of the United States. During his second administration, when Bolivia and Paraguay were slaughtering their people in battle, he did not hesitate to intervene in the Chaco dispute. This he did first by direct personal correspondence with President Justo of Argentina and then by drawing other American nations into the mediation which stopped hostilities, and the commission named was able to get the acceptance of the peace treaty of 1933.

He was always direct, sometimes disconcertingly so, in his methods. Once, when he was a candidate for the Senate, he heard a fantastic story that my embassy was intervening in behalf of his opponent, and he appeared at my house to ask for the facts. I assured him of the absurdity of the tale. "I was sure of it," he said, "but I wanted to get it from your own lips." Had all politicians been as open and direct, many misunderstandings could have been prevented.

The strength of Don Arturo was in his warm human qualities and his psychological insight. His enemies found it hard to withstand his persuasive personality and found it wise to avoid him. Carlos Reyes, distinguished journalist, illustrates with a story. During a hot controversy over the dismissal of two ministers, their party friends decided to make a bitter protest and denunciation to Alessandri, then President. The problem was to find an emissary who would not succumb to "the seduction of Don Arturo's charm," and the choice fell on one of his most bitter enemies. To the latter's amazement, he was greeted with a warm embrace. "But, man, what a pleasure to see you," Don Arturo began. "Before you tell me about your problem I want to tell you some of my youthful memories. Just today I was thinking of your father. We were close friends. He was an illustrious citizen and, besides, a great poet. Many years ago—don't ask me how many—he wrote me a stirring poem in which he very warmly described my affection for the people." At this point he began thumbing through a small mountain of manuscript until he found the poem, and then he read it emotionally to the son, his enemy. The emissary was powerfully moved. He forgot his mission and the warning he had received, and without mentioning the object of his visit, he left Don Arturo with an affectionate farewell.

He was, I think, the most consummate politician in South America in his heyday, a genius in political propaganda, familiar with political psychology. His tentacles reached into every segment of political life. He could pull the wires that brought results with uncanny cleverness. He never awaited the bugle call to action but prepared for it in advance. On the stump he was a master. He fought always with a battle-ax, never with a ping-pong paddle.

As a constructive statesman, few in South America made such a record. The part he played in the making of the Constitution of Chile was pre-eminent. His social legislation was sound enough to withstand successfully all the years that have followed its enactment. He was at once a champion of human rights and a defender of the rights of property. He merely thought that where a conflict between the two occurred, human rights came first.

During the long years of ultraconservatism, based on the psychology of feudalism, the masses of the people had little contact with candidates. It must have been startling when, in his first congressional campaign, Don Arturo, wrapped in a cloak, was found traversing the highways, riding in a wagon, on a horse or on foot, pausing to converse with the peasant and the artisan. He spoke in factories and mines, to the stokers, the oilers, shaking grimy, oil-soaked hands. It was in these early days that he won the respect of the masses.

10

He seemed robust almost to the end. Two weeks before his death, when he was presiding at a special session of the Senate, I was impressed by the weariness stamped on his face when in repose. One day he dismissed his car, saying he wished some exercise. Feeling ill on his walk, he stopped at the house of a friend and asked the maid for a glass of water. She left the room to fetch it. Don Arturo took up a book as she left. When she returned, Don Arturo was dead, the book still in his hand. It was the death he would have preferred.

I was notified, and within half an hour I drove to his apartment. As we turned into the narrow, winding street where he had lived, we found it literally packed with silent men and women. The police had difficulty making way for my car.

He lay in state in the Salon of Honor at the capitol while an endless stream of every segment of society filed by for a last look at the features of the man whose career was now history. Half a million people lined the streets and roads to the cemetery, President González Videla walking the entire distance at the head of the procession.

I have known a number of really remarkable men, and among them Don Arturo ranks high. I have described him at some length, not only because he was one of my staunchest friends in Chile through almost fourteen years but also because of my admiration and affection for him as a man.

XI

Communist Plots and Alarms

The war was over, the pro-Nazi newspapers were closed, but with the defeat of the Right segment of totalitarianism, that of the Left marched into the breach with confidence and some arrogance. During the first phase of the war, before Hitler marched into Russia, the Chilean communists were as vicious toward the United States as were the Nazis, but when Russia was under fire they shifted overnight and became our friends for the duration. Because of their perfect discipline and centralized command they were, at times, effective in preventing strikes that would have seriously reduced the production of war material that the United States in part was pouring into Russia for the common defense, but when the war was over, almost to the day, the dog went back to its vomit, and they took up the anti-Yankee slogans their Nazi cousins had just abandoned. They had been represented in the San Francisco Conference, and their leader had signed the Charter of the United Nations, but, quite soon, this act of his was to undermine his position in the party.

The first premonitions of their policy came during the celebrations of the victory over the Axis, when they tried to create the impression that the United States and Britain had played but a minor part in the war and that Stalin and the Russians had achieved the victory. I was not in Chile some years later when the Russian communists killed the Stalin myth by showing that he had blundered gravely, militarily, and was a liability instead of an asset in the defense of Russia. The stout, magnificent defense of Stalingrad, however, had made a deep impression on the mind and imagination of the man in the street. Had not everyone thrilled to Neruda's poem, "Stalingrad"? But Stalin had little to do with that.

Meanwhile the communist infiltration into labor syndicates was being used to create unrest and to inspire revolutionary strikes, as much designed to overthrow democracy in Chile as the conspiracies of the Nazis during the war. Our erstwhile ally, to whose defense we had contributed both money and ammunition, food and ships, had become our most bitter enemy overnight.

2

Their political arrogance began in the presidential campaign over the election of President Ríos's successor. It was interesting to observe the political maneuvering of the politicians, especially of the Right, over the nomination of their candidate. A convention had been called in the hope that the Conservative, Liberal, and Agrarian-Labor parties would be able to unite on one candidate. The convention reminded me of the Democratic National Convention in Madison Square Garden in New York in 1924, since the hope for a united front was wrecked on the rocks of clashing personal ambitions. The Conservatives were reasonably united behind the candidacy of Senator Cruz Coke; the Agrarian-Laborites behind that of Senator Larraín; the Doctrinary Radicals supported Senator Alfredo Duhalde; but the Liberals went into the convention with three candidates, the venerable Arturo Alessandri Palma, José Maza and Senator Bulnes, all able men, but since all were determined fighters, the possibility of a unification on one seemed impossible. In the balloting, Cruz Coke led but fell far short of enough votes for nomination. Twice a day, morning and afternoon, the delegates met for six ballots each session, with scarcely any change in allegiance. After some days of futile effort, each candidate was given a run for four ballots, but none could poll the 65 per cent required, since the followers of the other candidates voted blank. At times the choice seemed to lie between Cruz Coke and Larraín, with the former always leading and the other second on the poll. No one was willing to withdraw for the sake of harmony. Occasionally the contest became bitter. Alessandri, an old man, when entering the Capitol was surrounded by fanatic young followers of Cruz Coke and insulted. The old veteran threatened to withdraw from the convention, but all the candidates repudiated the silly act of the juveniles. The bitterness intensified, but the Chileans' love of fun cushioned the collisions. The public was amazed by this drama of ineptitude. "The doctors say that Cruz Coke is a politician, and the politicians insist that he is a doctor"—and the people laughed. "There are two difficulties about Alessandri: one is that he may die and the other is that he may not." In truth it was his advanced age that eliminated the old fighter.

And so the convention adjourned for a week to permit the finding of a formula for harmony. In the interval, Duhalde accepted the nomination of the Radical insurgents in the wisest utterance of this time. Anarchy, he warned, is an enemy of democracy; the Radicals had not always supported their own President, and this had weakened confidence in their sense of responsibility; the divergencies of the Rightists were contributing to the triumph of the extremists—such was his assertion. He alone among the candidates openly attacked the communists.

Finally two nominees emerged, the Conservatives sponsoring Cruz Coke, the Liberals and Doctrinary Radicals nominating Fernando Alessandri, son of the former President, who accepted reluctantly. The Rightists were thus split in two.

Meanwhile, the Radicals, in coalition with the communists, nominated Gabriel González Videla, and while his opponents of the Right were quarreling among themselves, he gaily fared forth on his first campaign tour, accompanied by Contreras Labarca, the communist leader. Thus the Popular Front which had faded out under Ríos was revived.

Unhappily, but not unexpectedly, the communist campaigners all but elbowed the Radicals off the platform and engaged in furious denunciations of the United States in the presence of the embarrassed candidate. Deputy César Godoy, an extremist, later to join the Communist party, was soon attacking my embassy with the false charge that it was intriguing against González Videla—a communist trick.

Now grown arrogant, the communists were out in the open. Just before the election, the *Siglo,* the communist organ, was giving instructions, military fashion, to the faithful. Under the caption "Orders of the Day," the "militants" were instructed to "go out into the street" on election day. The Minister of the Interior called this to the attention of the army, charged with maintaining order and protecting the polls. The election was orderly. González Videla won by a plurality, and this plurality corresponded precisely with the communist vote.

Having fallen short of a majority, Congress had the legal right to elect either of the two highest on the poll, and constitutionally it could have elected Cruz Coke, but it wisely gave the election to the man with the plurality. In two interviews with González Videla, one in his apartment in the Plaza Bulnes and the other in my house, he said that since the communists had given him his plurality he would be obliged to place three communists in his ministry. I got the impression he did not think they would stay long.

3

Even so, these were the gaudy days of Chilean communism. Chile had established diplomatic relations with Russia when it was an ally of the democracies. Arturo Alessandri Palma, who had instructed Cruchaga to open negotiations with Russia in 1932, strongly opposed negotiations in 1944. I had heard he had implied that the United States had brought pressure on the Chilean Government to establish diplomatic relations. At a luncheon in the country he had told me that he himself had refused to express an opinion. If any pressure was brought it did not come from my embassy. I had never mentioned the subject in conversation with the Foreign Minister, and all I knew was what I had read in the newspapers. If there was any opposition to the establishment of diplomatic relations with Russia it was not articulate.

Recognition having been accorded, the communists immediately made plans to convert the reception of Dmitri Zhukov, the Russian Ambassador, into a great communist demonstration. Plans were made to line the road from the airport to the city with shouting men waving banners. A committee approached Fernández, then Foreign Minister, with the novel request that he personally greet the Ambassador at the airport, but when he asked if the Russian Foreign Minister would welcome the Chilean Ambassador at the airport, the request was dropped.

Later I was shown a telegram from the Chilean Ambassador in Russia disclosing the rankest kind of discourtesy on his arrival in Moscow. None of his baggage had arrived from Berlin, and he descended from the plane with a handbag only. Not a single minor functionary of the Foreign Office was there to greet him, and the Ambassador waited, unattended at the airport, for almost two hours. When Fernández spoke sharply to Zhukov about the clearly intended insult, he seemed stunned and he promised to seek an explanation, but if one ever came I heard nothing of it.

4

Zhukov was met at the airport by the protocol officer of the Foreign Office, as is true on the arrival of any envoy. Going to the chancellery across the street from the Carrera Hotel, where Zhukov was lodged, on the morning he presented his credentials, I found the ornate state coaches drawn up in front of the hotel and mounted *carabineros* congesting the street. This was the usual scene. But now there was something different and strange. A wagon filled with fish near the entrance to the hotel was surrounded by clamoring housewives of the very poor, since the fish were being given away. One explanation was that the driver of the truck had gone to sea for fish, intending to sell below the price in the shops, but that permission had been refused; and, in anger, he had decided to give the fish away. Others suspected that the communists had hoped to draw a throng of the very poor and ragged near the Carrera on the assumption that they would follow the Ambassador's ornate coach to the Moneda, creating the impression of a touching welcome from the poor. But that hope, if such it was, was dashed.

A few days later Zhukov made his protocol call upon me at my house. He was a tall, slender man, with a pleasant face and a modest and natural manner. He spoke English with a trace of a foreign accent. He frankly admitted his ignorance of the political setup in Chile, though he did smile over the number of presidential nominees. His ignorance of democratic processes was manifest in his assumption that Duhalde, Acting President pending the election, would undoubtedly become President. When I asked his reason he seemed astonished at my naïveté. "He is in office now, is he not?" he asked triumphantly.

Explaining that his primary purpose was to negotiate a commercial treaty, he professed fear that it might be impossible to make the necessary contacts in business circles because he was a communist. I suggested that if he concentrated on a commercial treaty, without interfering in the domestic affairs of Chile, he would probably be received well, but I warned him that if he failed, it would be due to his party. He asked why. I gave him a hasty sketch of communist activities and warned him that he would be held responsible for unpleasant incidents in no way due to him.

When I returned his call at the Carrera I was met at the elevator by a dapper young fellow whom I took to be an attaché of his embassy and warmly shook his hand, but a little later, when sandwiches were served with wine, this elegant young man did the serving. Zhukov apologized for not serving vodka. "All my vodka was stolen on the way," he said with a grin.

Apropos of the divergencies among the ministers of the five powers in Paris at the time, he ascribed them to fear that Russia wanted war, and he said, "The Russian people never want war. They do not like fighting. They do not like controversy even among themselves. A novelist has described Russia in the person of a big crude peasant who was being pushed around and insulted by another man. The peasant kept on protesting that he did not want trouble, but he was only pushed around more. Then the peasant was struck on the cheek, and he struck his tormentor down. Hitler should have read that story."

Zhukov's wife was friendly, and amusing, and spoke English, which she had mastered at the University of Moscow. Her manner was disarming. She asked my daughter whether invitations to a reception should be by card or through notices in the papers and was warned that the latter method would swamp the house. Very feminine, she asked how she could subscribe to the *Ladies' Home Journal*. The Zhukovs were well liked by all their colleagues. Frequently I was asked what I was "doing about the Zhukovs," since the inquirer liked them and would have liked to have them for lunch or dinner but was afraid of a misinterpretation of this natural act. Being in the same boat, I could not advise him. I saw the Ambassador therefore only at large receptions or cocktail parties, where I enjoyed chatting and joking with him, for he had a sense of humor. In truth, his personality was so pleasing that there was a popular impression that he had been sent as a "front" and the actual active ambassador was some minor member of his staff. The one who figured largely in these conjectures was the Public Relations Attaché, a little fellow with a sinister squint who had been an active member of the Cheka. The gossips were sure he sent reports to Moscow over the head of his chief and was spying on the Ambassador. Whenever I chatted with Zhukov at cocktail parties, this slimy little man invariably made a beeline toward us and stood close, with ears cocked and flapping. Others were sure the actual ambassador, there to spy on his chief, was the chauffeur, for could he not report secretly to Moscow whom his chief had called upon and how long he had stayed?

The Zhukov staff, with servants, guards, teachers for the children, occupied two full floors of the Carrera, but soon he took a large house in a fashionable neighborhood, and the entire entourage moved in. It was there, on the anniversary of the Soviet, that I had an illuminating insight into the Soviets' concept of democracy and a "classless state."

5

In most capitals the Russian diplomats seek the most palatial quarters available and splurge without stint. The *rotos* gasped when, in presenting his credentials, Zhukov appeared, resplendent in fashionable attire, wearing a high silk hat, but the incident on the national holiday was unique in my experience. Naturally, the entire Diplomatic Corps attended the reception, and I went with my daughter. On entering the hall, we looked around for the Ambassador and his wife in a receiving line, but they were nowhere to be seen. There was, however, a receiving line of the minor officials of the staff and their wives, and to these we made our identity known. When asked to accompany one of these upstairs, we assumed that the real reception was above, but the halls there were deserted. We were led down a narrow hall to a door where a big Russian sentinel stood guard. A whispered conversation with the Russian, and the guard knocked a signal on the door. The door opened a crack, revealing another Russian guard. Another whispered conversation in Russian, the door opened, and we were almost thrust into the room.

The room was small, and a long table, laden with food and drink, almost filled it, and there at the table sat the host and hostess, President González Videla, who had just been inducted into office, and his wife, one or two army officers and, across the table, former President Alessandri looking like a sheep-killing dog caught in the act. The scene was so startling that I forgot my protocol obligation to greet the new President at the far end of the table, and my daughter, who knew the President's wife, admitted later that she had been so flabbergasted that she had looked directly at the Señora without a nod of recognition. I owed my presence there to my seniority in the Diplomatic Corps.

The reason for this unique arrangement was clear. Communist "democracy" in a "classless state" did not think it proper for a chief of state to mingle with other guests at a diplomatic reception, as was the custom in all other embassies.

6

The appointment of three communists in the ministry had created a bad impression abroad. When, almost immediately, a strike in the copper mines, clearly of communist inspiration, reached disturbing proportions, the impression deepened. But it was not until October 1947 that the purely revolutionary program of the communists could no longer be doubted. Chile was then threatened with a major disaster when the coal miners at Lota announced a strike unless their demands were met. These miners, inadequately paid and improperly housed, had legitimate reasons for complaint, and, at the beginning, they had the sympathy of many conservative citizens. González Videla summoned the mine owners and secured concessions that exceeded what was asked by the miners, and this was announced the day before the strike was to begin. Even so, the communists, aiming at revolution, demanded that the strike should proceed. There had been some trouble between the communist miners and the socialists because of the former's terroristic methods. Learning of the concessions made, the noncommunist miners wished to resume work, but the communists objected violently, threatening the others.

This strike presented a grave peril, both political and economic, to the government. Chile's stockpile of coal would be exhausted in a week or ten days, and then the industrial life of the nation would be paralyzed. The railroads, using coal for fuel, would be motionless, and food for the copper miners in the north would be cut off; public utilities, such as light, would be shut down; thousands of workers would be thrown into the street without money to buy food; and the government would suffer seriously through the loss of revenue.

That day, summoned to the Moneda through the family entrance to avoid the press and prevent alarm, I was received by the President. Often excitable in a fight, the man who came in, in a dark gray business suit, was coldly calm. He said the government had positive proof of the subversive nature of the strike. A Yugoslav general had mysteriously appeared in Chile who was believed to have brought instructions from Moscow, and the Minister of Yugoslavia had been given his passport. To maintain order at the mines, military forces would be used, and Admiral Hoffman, a fine naval officer of sound judgment, would be in charge.

But the very life of Chilean democracy was at stake. Coal would be needed to prevent a dangerous economic collapse, and there was no place to get it but from the United States.

The President asked for a regular shipment of a stipulated amount throughout the crisis to keep public utilities and factories in operation and to prevent unemployment on a large scale. Knowing the crisis was serious, I was confident that my country would not let Chile down.

The next day, Vergara Donoso, the very able Minister of Foreign Affairs, reporting to me on the gloomy outlook at the mines, had been aroused by the sensational editorials in a New York and a Washington paper attacking the Chilean Government for maintaining some semblance of order at the mines with armed forces. These, he said, "based on gross ignorance of the facts," were being repeated by press associations to Chile and were having a bad effect. He asked me if I thought the cause of democratic law and order was being served by such effusions. *El Mercurio,* a conservative paper, severely criticized an editorial in the New York paper. Was it impossible, asked the minister, to convince the North American people that Chile was not a dictatorship or Fascist state but was one of the two bastions of democracy in South America? I told him I had often wondered myself.

Meanwhile, order was being maintained at the mines by the armed forces. No one was being pushed around. There was not a single incident. Finally, on October 18, the miners announced their acceptance of the concessions granted and their willingness to resume work. That night a large force entered the mines. The next morning a similar force was on hand to replace the night shift, but at the entrance to the mines they found armed communists refusing them admittance. More alarming, none of the men on the night shift inside the mines were permitted to come out. Later it was learned that the communists entering the night before had carried arms concealed on their persons, and they threatened anyone who took up pick or shovel or attempted to leave.

Fearing that the equipment of the mines was being crippled, Admiral Hoffman asked for fifty volunteers among the men to enter the mines and ascertain what was going on. A brilliant young officer, who had recently been graduated with honors from the military academy, offered to lead, and fifty privates offered themselves. Inside, they were confronted with armed communists who tried to betray them into firing, since martyrs could be used to heat the blood of resentment. But the soldiers did not budge nor pull a trigger. The young officer courageously approached the little band of communist leaders and actually persuaded them to go outside for a parley, and when they emerged they were taken into custody.

These men laid down the law as to their conditions for resuming work: the armed forces had to be withdrawn; the state of emergency had to be declared off; the communist leaders and agitators had to be released; in brief, the government had to abdicate to anarchy. These demands were instantly refused.

It was then that the revolutionary reason for the low production in the mines was found. Under the coercion of the communists, no more coal for a stockpile against emergencies could be produced than would last ten days. In the houses of the leaders was found enough accumulated food to last two months. All this implied a long-meditated plan for a communist revolution.

The men arrested were sent to a small, isolated town where they could be kept under close observation. They were free to walk around the little town and were in no sense "confined," but soon some newspapers in the United States began complaining that these harmless and well-meaning "martyrs" were in a concentration camp and were being treated atrociously.

It is significant that when work was resumed there was a marked increase in production—even with the depleted force.

7

This marked the end of the patience of González Videla. The actions of his communist ministers had proved to him the falseness of the idea that the Communist party was a Chilean party interested in Chilean progress. Taking their orders from Moscow, they had been using their official positions to undermine Chilean economy and they were dismissed in a violent quarrel and ordered from the Moneda. The President was through, not only with communist ministers but with communist nations. One day I was told he was in a state of rage, threatening to break relations with Russia, and that some of his advisers were trying to calm him down. But that afternoon I was summoned to the Moneda by the Foreign Minister and informed that Chile was breaking relations with Russia and Czechoslovakia. I was prepared to hear of the break with Russia but a bit startled to learn that the new Czech minister was getting his passport as well. If Washington was a bit doubtful about the break with Czechoslovakia it was soon satisfied that González Videla had acted wisely.

Thus Chile had broken with all the communist nations, and the Chilean President became more hated by communists than the head of any other nation in the world.

8

With the masks torn off, the communists injected themselves into all strikes and street demonstrations to convert them to their ends. When bus fares went up a bit because of the increased cost of gasoline, and students demonstrated, the communists elbowed them aside and took over, and some busses were overturned and one was burned. During this affair a young man, unknown to me, came to me with the story that he, a stranger, could not get to a hotel because of demonstrations at the entrance. I had just passed the Carrera and the Crillon and no demonstrations were near either, but the stranger modestly asked the use of my car to get to a hotel. I advised him that it would be safer to take a taxi. The appearance of my car in the neighborhood of a communist demonstration would almost certainly have meant an incident, and I wondered if the visit of the stranger had been inspired.

Because of the communist color of these demonstrations, Congress gave the President extraordinary powers.

Fortunately, at this time and throughout these troubles, Admiral Holger was Minister of the Interior and he could be trusted to deal with subversive elements wisely. No other man in Chile could have been more reassuring. A fine naval officer, in direct line of promotion to the command of the fleet—his supreme ambition—he had sacrificed himself for his country. He was fair and just in his estimate of men and events, pleasantly free from flamboyancy and bluster. He impressed Washington as a superior officer and gentleman when negotiating for the purchase of two cruisers from us. I had assured President Truman that his word was as good as a Rockefeller bond.

9

But the communists were tireless and they sprang up when least expected. One night when we were at dinner at the embassy the butler called my daughter from the table to tell her that a group of communists had hurled rocks through the windows of the front salon and through the windows of my wife's room. Strangely enough we had not heard the crash, since we were at another end of the house. We learned that a number of men and women across the street had apparently been waiting on the corner for a bus, as some really were. At a word from their leader, the communists among them hurled the rocks and fled. The *carabinero* at the gate summoned the police, and two patrol cars arrived within less than two minutes, but, under standing instructions, officers guarding an embassy or legation were to fire under such circumstances. Had our guard fired, he might have killed or wounded a woman waiting for a bus, but he was nevertheless taken into custody and dismissed. I appealed to the President in his behalf and found him sympathetic, but the chief of the *carabineros,* one of the finest police organizations anywhere, was adamant.

Discipline came first with his men, and there could be no exceptions. I was able to get the dismissed officer another job.

There was always a faint possibility of an attack on the Embassy Residence, what with the communist paper attacking me with fantastic falsehoods day by day. Was I not "dictating to Chile"? Converting it into a "Yankee colony"? These silly accusations were not confined to their paper but were scribbled on the walls in the city. We never had the slightest fear. True, for weeks when the trial of the Rosenbergs for treason was dragging along, anonymous telephone calls at the office, the Residence and at our summer place gave warning that should anything happen to the Rosenbergs I would be "taken care of." Since I had no connection with the Rosenberg case, we paid no attention to these threats, but the Chilean police treated them more seriously. We were puzzled when an officer came to the house to say that no one would be admitted to the grounds without identification after dark, to request that all the servants be in by ten o'clock and that we ourselves not leave the house at night. Sybil was warned against walking in the park across the street in the late afternoon. The police no doubt had received warnings of which we were ignorant. Occasionally we found the guard at the gate increased and supposed that the Secret Service had heard something we had not heard.

A few days before the execution of the Rosenbergs the police gave special attention not only to the Residence but to the chancellery as well. It was then that the police insisted that for a few days I permit a Secret Service man in civilian clothes to accompany me in the car, and for two days he sat in front with Pepe, but, in riding through the streets as usual, I did not see a frown and certainly not a hostile gesture. We were prepared for a demonstration in front of the house on the day of the execution, but since nothing of the sort occurred in any capital, we may assume that Moscow had advised against it.

None of us believed that communist leaders would sanction a physical attack on a diplomat, but this could not safely be assumed where the mentally unbalanced were involved. The mentally sick were not rare among refugees who had suffered the tortures of Nazi concentration camps. One day, in my absence, one of these called at the chancellery and was received by the counselor. He nonchalantly announced that he intended to kill me and displayed a gun, at the same time commenting that he was "prepared." He was eased out of the building and regarded as a crank, since the staff did not take him seriously. But when, on the following day, this man, standing in the street in front of the chancellery, with a *carabinero* near by, threw a stone through the window of a colleague's diplomatic car in the belief that the car was mine, he did not seem so harmless. He was arrested, but the next day released since he could not pay his fine, and the laughter of my staff was sour. Carlos Hall, the counselor, protested to the authorities, and the man, who had been one of the victims of Nazi persecution, was put on a plane and sent out of the country.

A few months before, another mentally sick refugee entered the office of Hans von Becker, the Austrian Minister, and killed him. His mind had been destroyed in one of Hitler's torture camps, and he had been assigned, in the distribution of displaced persons, to Chile. Without a job himself, his wife had taken employment in the minister's family to care for the children, and the man, in his muddled state, thought Von Becker responsible for his wife's refusal to give up her job. Such cases impressed upon me the slovenly manner in which the displaced persons were investigated, with no attention given to their mental condition.

We of the embassy had a tragic experience with one of these unhappy people with broken minds. One of them, sent to Chile, applied to our consulate for a visa to go to the United States to join his wife, but under the McCarran Act, which made thousands of enemies, he was refused. He made numerous calls at the consulate pleading for a visa, which was constantly refused. One day he appeared again, to be again refused, and he grimly said that unless given the visa neither he nor the consul would leave the room alive. The consul, Camden McLane, alone with an insane man, should have given him a visa and notified the Chilean authorities, but he always adhered meticulously to the rules. Nervously noting that the visitor was toying playfully with a bomb he had taken from a satchel, the consul, to gain time, said he would telephone the Attorney General in Washington and ask him to make an exception to the rule. He actually put in the call, expecting the usual long delay, but to his horror the call went through at once and he found himself connected with the Attorney General; he shuddered to think what that official would say of his amazing request. In the midst of the spluttering in Washington, he discourteously broke the connection. He could not explain himself in the presence of the man toying with the bomb. Turning a smiling face on the applicant, he said permission had been given and that he would have to leave the room to get the necessary papers.

Meanwhile word flashed through the chancellery, on the floor below, that the consul was in danger, and the police were notified. They arrived almost instantly and were in the hall outside the consul's private office. Carlos Hall, knowing that the moment they tried to enter, the deranged man would throw the bomb and probably kill the vice-consul, who had entered when the consul left, held the police back. Unhappily, when the consul left the room the man caught a glimpse of the uniforms of the police in the hall, and he was in the act of throwing the bomb when the vice-consul, by leaps and bounds, made his escape. The explosion damaged the room and smashed the windows, and the unhappy man sprang through the broken glass and hurtled to his instant death nine floors below.

These two incidents had nothing to do with communism; they were both the poisoned fruit of Fascism.

The strength of the communists, such as it is in Chile, is

not in their numbers. They are dangerous because they are militantly led and are tireless in activities that amount to fanaticism. Their members, zealously adhering to their cause, form a solid block and follow instructions to the letter. They have infiltrated into labor syndicates, where, though in most cases only a minority group, they sometimes impose their will by the violence of their methods and through a demagogy that conceals their purpose. They were outlawed as a party, but not individually disfranchised to any extent. Thus their votes become important in close elections, and noncommunist parties tend to cultivate them for their support. Even so, the press of the United States had an exaggerated idea of the possibility of the communists taking over in Chile. These make a loud noise because they shout in unison.

We may now take a rest from the communists and politics and seek fresh air in visiting some of the *fundos* and places of relaxation near Santiago.

XII

Country Life Near Santiago

Communist intrigues did not greatly disturb the even tenor of our way, even in Santiago, and then, too, one could occasionally turn one's back on the tumultuous politicians and find refreshment for the spirit in the country near by. Some country places and great *fundos* are within easy driving distance of the city. My first invitation to a country house came from a lady of an old family who was continuing the philanthropic work of her father. Her place at Pirque has both charm and beauty, and there she stays every spring and summer until the rains come in the fall. The large grounds are enclosed by a stone fence that is mellowed and stained by time and weather. These grounds are wooded, with winding roads and paths running through them, past a lily pond and tennis court to the river in the rear. From there one looks down into a delightful fecund valley where the grapes are grown for the wine, and over to a low range of hills in the distance. The house, an old colonial, is large, with all the rooms on the ground floor.

I had just arrived from Madrid, and in this house I had the feeling of being miraculously transferred back to the palace of the Duke of Montellano, with its Zuloaga portrait of the mother of the present duchess and the Boldini portrait of the duchess dowager in her youth, since here in this house at Pirque I found on the walls Zuloaga's portraits of my hostess and her daughter and Boldini's portrait of the lady of the house.

My hostess, of course, knew Zuloaga, whom I knew, and the old Count Romanones, through so many years the minister of the King. The count had been my neighbor in Madrid. When I also learned that the mistress at Pirque was a friend of the old Duchess of Montellano's, the feeling of being back in Madrid was accentuated. She also knew the brother of the old duchess, the Marqués de Villavieja, who had been an expert on the polo pony and had helped introduce the game into Spain. Although now well into old age, he was still a dandy and prone to be a bit boastful. His autobiography, *Life Has Been Good,* written when he had became a bit childish, had amused the Madrilenians, and here, near Santiago, I caught an echo of their chuckles when my hostess remarked that "it reads like the boastings of a groom."

She was an old lady when I knew her, gracious in manner, bubbling with vivacity, possessing wit and humor, and she carried her years gracefully. On Sundays a group of old friends lunched at the house in Pirque and played bridge through the afternoon. Intelligently interested, as so many Chilean women are, in politics, she looked upon the endless game with a tolerant cynicism, and her improvised portraits of the leaders were vivid, as penetrating as a portrait by Sargent and immensely amusing.

2

More interesting, perhaps, to the tourist, and illuminative of Chilean country life, are two great *fundos* within easy driving distance of the capital. Near by is the great 96,000-acre *fundo* of Chacabuco, to which I was drawn soon after my arrival because of its color and significance in Chilean history, for it was on its grounds that the battle was fought which went far toward the liberation of the colony from Spanish rule. It was now owned by the Petrinovich family, and I was indebted to the Yugoslav Minister for an invitation to see it. We drove out on a warm Sunday in June. The owner, courteous and keenly intelligent, was an interesting talker, and his charming wife was gracious and amusing.

From my host I learned something of the history of the place. The first owner was Martínez Vergara, a rich Spaniard, but in 1767 he gave the property to the Jesuits, who had arrived from Spain. The Jesuits made the most of its fertility, raising wheat and making wine from the grapes of the vineyard. When they were expelled from the country in 1767, the property was put up for sale at auction, and it went to Alberto Díaz for a price equivalent in our time to one thousand dollars, and his family held it until 1916, when it was purchased by the Petrinovich family.

The first day we lunched on the veranda of the long one-story residence. With the birds singing and the breeze whispering in the trees, the effect could not have been much different from that which the Jesuits knew. Facing the long house, across the lawn, is another long, one-story building that could have been used by the Jesuits' servants.

Close to the house—almost against it—is a fascinating old church. Here are two large paintings brought over by the Jesuits from Spain. Tradition has it that O'Higgins and San Martín prayed before the large canvas depicting the scene of the crucifixion the night before the historic battle. The church was built of adobe mud and straw, and the marvel is that it has withstood the earthquakes of centuries, though the walls are more than a yard thick. There is a legend that the Jesuits, on their expulsion, buried a great sum of gold—the old story of the "hidden treasure." A few years ago a servant, digging under the floor of the church to make improvements, ran excitedly to the owner with the news that he had uncovered a large iron box and another of marble. Here, at last, was the treasure! A further investigation disclosed that the boxes contained the bones of former owners.

On that first visit, after lunch, we made a tour of the estate near the house, walking under a very wide grape arbor extending the equivalent of two city blocks. It was under this arbor that O'Higgins, San Martín and their officers celebrated with food and wine. We meandered over the grounds, plucking and eating oranges from the trees, and then visited the modern open-air barn or shed which sheltered the sheep imported from England. There were 13,000 sheep on the place, most of them grazing in the mountains in the background, but in the pasture we found many, including a baby lamb whose mother had died at its birth and which had been nursed through the first days on a bottle. Our drive took us over a great field where 14,000 olive trees had just been planted. These were not expected to produce for seven years, and I was told that there are 50,000 olive trees yielding on the estate. Here were wheat, olives, oranges, lemons, peaches, sheep, cattle, horses, many fine imported animals and acres of vineyards for the wine—a colossal business, with North American machinery in use. In compliance with the law, there was a school on the *fundo* with five teachers. I was shown two bathhouses for the employees, with hot and cold water; one was for the use of the men, the other for the women.

Later, when I was again a guest at Chacabuco, I mustered the courage to climb to the top of the rounded hill which looks down on the scene of the decisive battle. The hill is steep and slippery, and I would have abandoned the climb had not two women of the *fundo,* going ahead, ascended with the ease of mountain goats and put me to shame. There, on top, where plans have long been made for the erection of a monument, the battlefield is laid out like a map before the eyes. I was told that chance and courage achieved the victory. San Martín was at his headquarters in the mountains. O'Higgins was not to attack the enemy of four thousand until joined by General Solar of the Argentinians. But on coming unexpectedly upon the enemy, with Solar nowhere in sight, O'Higgins attacked and was repulsed; he attacked again, to be repulsed a second time; and he was engaged in his third attack when Solar appeared, catching the enemy on the flank, and the Spaniards broke and fled. It appears that, in the mountains, Solar, marching to join O'Higgins, found himself on a height, with no possibility of descent; he was forced to seek other egress, and time was lost. The incident resulted in a feud between the Chilean hero and Solar, and I was shown the spot near the house where the quarrel took place and a duel was narrowly averted. This controversy continues to some extent even to this day, although the Chileans are so generous to San Martín that on one occasion, in the Salon of Honor in the capitol, I attended an anniversary celebration in tribute to him, when the Argentine Ambassador and the Chileans exhausted their vocabulary of adulation on San Martín, referring to him without qualification as the "liberator of Chile"; O'Higgins was hardly mentioned. At the close, as we were leaving, Alessandri, who had presided, invited me to join a cocktail party in another room. I assumed an attitude of enlightenment and observed that I had evidently been under the misapprehension that O'Higgins had played a minor part in the liberation. The old man scowled. Recalling that when Vice-President Wallace, speaking in Washington and enumerating the liberators of South America, did not mention O'Higgins, Alessandri had bitterly protested, I rather enjoyed the opportunity to prod him a bit. I once heard a retired Chilean army officer, a partisan of O'Higgins, passionately protesting against the tradition built up that O'Higgins played a minor part in the battle. In his fury he insisted that the tradition is based largely on the bronze figure of San Martín in the

Plaza Bulnes astride a rearing horse and triumphantly waving his sword. However, there is glory enough for both.

Descending the hill, I was glad to get into a car to visit the cave of Pachacamaco. We rode over ground thickly sprinkled with volcanic rocks. No one knows the story of this natural temple or whether there is a story, though human bones have been found in it.

It was now evening, and as we returned to the house, the *fundo* seemed transformed by the beauty of a mystic twilight.

That night, after a hearty dinner, we sat down before the open fireplace and talked until bedtime. Our rooms were in the old part of the house where O'Higgins had slept. These rooms had high ceilings, iron-barred windows and fireplaces in which cheerful fires were blazing. The next morning an old servant appeared with a large pitcher of orange juice, bacon and eggs, toast and coffee.

It was a memorable visit to a great, historic *fundo* seldom visited by casual American tourists.

3

One boundary of Chacabuco sets it off by a short distance from another *fundo,* that of San Vicente, which also borders on the town of Los Andes. This famous *fundo* should be of special interest to North Americans. The father of the manager during my time in Chile, Hugo Jordan, was trained in farming at the Agricultural College of Iowa; Hugo himself had received his training there; and he had sent his two sons to the same school.

This *fundo* embraces 74,000 acres. The house, almost two centuries old, has thirty rooms. The large narrow dining room, accommodating twenty guests, is none too large, since visitors are constantly trooping in. My first impression of the estate was of big barns, lofty silos, and cowboys training on breaking in ponies.

That which impressed me most at San Vicente was the treatment of the workers, and especially the children. The workers are exceptionally well housed in strong weather-proof buildings of cement, with porches and shower baths. Each worker, in addition to his wages, receives his ration, his house, grazing privileges for his animals, the loan of *fundo* horses for work on his allotted ground. The *fundo* at this time gave grazing to many of the workers' animals. The corn and potatoes they raise on the ground assigned them bring them some revenue from their sale.

However, it was the care of the workers' children that impressed me most of all. Mrs. Jordan, a lovely woman of character and resourcefulness, who died during my stay in Chile, supervised this phase of the work in addition to managing the chicken farm and dairy. Conspicuous among the provisions for the children, of whom there were more than two hundred, was the arrangement for their education. Under Chilean law, *fundos* with a certain number of employees are forced to maintain schools up to and including the second grade. San Vicente had them up to and including the fifth. Cheerful schoolrooms were provided, and for the teachers there was an attractive vine-clad house. There were seven teachers, two of them professors.

Every second week the children visited the doctor for an inspection, and, at frequent intervals, doctors and nurses examined their teeth and lungs and tested their blood. Before this preventive measure was set up, thirteen children had died, but there was no infant mortality afterward. In the industrial building the girls were trained in sewing, knitting, in making clothes, curtains and bed covers, and all they made was theirs.

The Jordans were progressive, sympathetic toward the workers and in favor of social reforms that were within reason, but this did not prevent the communist agitators from trying to insinuate themselves into the confidence of the workers in the hope of engaging them in revolutionary strikes, but up until the time I left Chile they had made no impression.

We were fortunate enough to see San Vicente *en fête*. It

was on the occasion of the wedding of Teresa, daughter of the house, to Peter Blake, a very fine young North American boy. The large house was packed with friends of the couple's, and we were guests of Señor Caballero at his pleasant house, "Santa Rosa," a charming place with a veranda on all sides and with orange trees in the patio.

After changing our clothes, we drove back to San Vicente for the civil ceremony, at which I was a witness for the bridegroom. The papers having been signed, the guests, Chilean fashion, embraced all around. I found the custom altogether delightful so far as the women were concerned, but was never able to embrace men with nonchalance or with any degree of grace or conviction. After an elaborate dinner of innumerable dishes, we drove back to "Santa Rosa" for the night.

In the morning we returned to San Vicente for the religious ceremony. The house is two centuries old, but the little church is older, having preceded the house by half a century. It is small but mellow with the memories of the many generations that have come and gone. Since only a fraction of the guests could be crowded into the church, the doors were kept open, and chairs were placed on the lawn facing the door and reaching back into the grounds. When the religious ceremony, performed by my friend, Father Weigel, was over, two hundred guests sat down to an elaborate luncheon under the trees.

And then, after the toasts, the lid was off, and the entertainment became hilarious. Wine flowed freely to drown inhibitions, sentimental songs were sung, and a clever mimic from Santiago created a tumult by imitating Hitler and Arturo Alessandri making speeches. His imitation of Don Arturo was superb. Then the party broke up into couples, and soon everyone was dancing the cueca on the lawn under the spreading branches of the forest trees, while the workers of the *fundo,* who had similarly wined and dined, gathered at the edge of the crowd clapping their hands and shouting encouragement to the dancers. It was a scene from the past.

4

We made occasional visits to "Las Palmas," a *fundo* near Quilpue, owned by Amos Neuberger, a New York businessman who regularly escaped his home town's wintry blasts during January and February by spending that time on his country place in Chile. This estate had 33,000 acres, part of which were wooded but most under profitable cultivation. An old woman would always open the gate from the highway, and we would drive quite a long distance before the residence came into view. The house is a large, Spanish-style dwelling, with the usual patio, though it bears some resemblance to the plantation house in the South at home.

As we drew near the house, Pepe was alarmed when twenty or more dogs, of a blue-gray, small German breed, surrounded the car barking a rapturous welcome and miraculously escaping the wheels. We always went for lunch, and for cocktails we were taken to a small room converted into a bar patterned after those of old provincial taverns in England, with amusing mottoes and prints on the walls. Lunch was served on the grounds under the greenery of the trees, where we had a refreshing, scented breeze. Lunch over, we found comfortable chairs and cigars and talked the afternoon away.

"Las Palmas" might better be called "Hospitality Hall," since friends and friends of friends scarcely known to the host were constantly descending upon it for week ends and holidays, and some of the visits threatened to last forever. At intervals, some priests appeared to minister to the religious needs of the workers and remained after their mission was over, held by the warmth of the welcome of their non-Catholic host.

Not far from "Las Palmas" in a region known as Viña del Sol is the home of Señor Puelma, once consul-general in New York. He amused himself by sculpturing and, being an ardent admirer of Lincoln's, he made an excellent bust of the Emancipator, to be placed on a pedestal on the grounds. On one of our visits to "Las Palmas" we joined the people of the *fundo* for lunch at Puelma's house. During the cocktail hour we caught the tempting odor of lamb roasting on the grounds over a wood fire. We ate in the old house of the owner, which had been abandoned as a residence after the completion of a new one. A very wide, low window opened from the dining room upon the grounds, and there at the open window a group of *huasos* in picturesque costumes and wearing forty-gallon hats stood and entertained us with the music of their guitars and with singing through the meal.

5

But to escape the politics and cocktails of Santiago, it is not necessary to await an invitation to a *fundo*. An easy escape is offered at Santo Domingo on the coast, reached by a smooth, paved road over level country. The road passes through a rich agricultural region, with great green pastures and fields under cultivation. This is Chile at its best. En route, we passed through the historic town of Talagante, associated with the wicked Quintrala. This drive unrolls a panorama of much charm and beauty. On our first visit to this region we enjoyed the hospitality of the little tavern of Tejas Verdes, built in Spanish style, where the meals were excellent, with seafood dripping from the sea. There we once had a two-day vacation in comfortable surroundings, and at night we were lulled to sleep by the murmur of a stream, beyond the window, rushing to the sea.

Santo Domingo is just beyond, on the far side of a bridge whose railing was always lined with boys and men fishing. Some years ago, an Italian immigrant came to love this region, which reminded him of Italy, and he bought, as a speculation, the ground that now embraces Santo Domingo for six million pesos. A simple man, he nevertheless had a sense of beauty, and he planted many trees where none had been before and refused to sell an inch of ground until some years after the trees were grown. Now the shade is there, and all about, on ground rising from the sea and facing a long sandy beach, very attractive villas with gardens have been built. The houses are individualistic, reflecting the taste of the builder, and there is charm in the absence of monotony in architecture. At the time of our first visit these houses were going up, and the hammering of the workmen made a merry sound. During the first phase we found a heavy chain across the road at the entrance to the village to exclude the merely curious, but this was soon removed. The flower beds along the driveways mingle their fragrance with the scent of the sea. Golfers going down from Santiago lunch on tasty meals at the Club Hotel by the course, and some stay over in its pleasant rooms for a rest, in an atmosphere of serenity, with beauty peering in at the windows. On Sundays tourists may drive down from Santiago in an hour and a half through a perfectly beautiful countryside.

Driving from Santo Domingo to Cartagena, one passes through San Antonio, a busy port where much of the copper is loaded for export. It is a typical port town, the streets alive with dock workers in their work clothes. It is in no sense a resort town.

But just beyond is Cartagena, the favorite playground in summer of the crowds from the capital. On Sundays and holidays excursion trains carry thousands to the sea. Facing the beach are scores of hotels and pensions, and on the rising ground behind are the houses of the residents. As one drives along the beach road, the scene suggests a picture post card of an Italian seaside resort.

Here is the summer villa of the widow of Blasco-Ibáñez, the Spanish novelist. When Mussolini's army wrecked his villa at Mentone in France and destroyed his library after his death, his widow returned to Chile, her native land. Though I never saw her in the villa in Cartagena, I have had some delicious *paella* feasts of her own making in her town house in Santiago. I had met her in October 1933, when we stood together on the balcony of the city hall in Valencia watching the procession bearing the ashes of Blasco-Ibáñez home after his long exile.

One need not go far from Santiago, which buzzes with politics and gossip, for a change and relaxation, since the near-by countryside acts on the fagging spirit like a tonic.

Before returning to the capital, if we wish a fairly well-rounded idea of Chile, we must now make a hasty visit to a number of Chilean cities, most of them unseen by the tourists, though all of them interesting and important, commercially, industrially, culturally and politically.

XIII

Rambles in Chilean Cities

We landed in Valparaiso in 1939, and from that city we
sailed for home in 1953. During the interval, when we had
summer places in the vicinity, we visited this second city of
Chile many times. Something of the romance of the far-off
days of the adventurers and buccaneers clings to the hills that
form the background for the business section of the town.
Long before the ports of New York or Boston existed, that
of Valparaiso was known to the world and had been written
into history. As early as 1528, one of Diego de Almagro's
officers sailing south from Peru on a voyage of exploration,
found a hamlet there, and he thought the region so pleasant
that he called it the "Valley of Paradise"; and Valdivia, having his choice of land from the King, selected this region for

some of his holdings. In the glamorous days of Elizabeth I, who smiled on pirates and buccaneers, Sir Francis Drake made an unpleasant visit to the little town of perhaps fifteen families, and Sir Richard Hawkins, less intent on booty than on fame and beauty, followed his example. Then the Virgin Queen—if she was a virgin—died, and the golden days of the buccaneers on the Pacific were over. But the British kept on coming for purposes of trade, and they have left their imprint on the tone and temper of the town.

To see the city at its most picturesque, one should see it first at night. Then, with the hill sparkling with twinkling lights against the darkness of the night, the scene is one of extraordinary charm and color. On this steep hill, built on shelves or terraces, live many of the inhabitants in comfortable middle-class chalets, but there too are many of the hovels of the poor. If one were venturesome enough to ascend the steep incline on foot, treading the narrow walks paved with slabs of rose-colored stone, one would become confused by the labyrinth of narrow streets. Better to use the *ascensores*—little cars drawn up almost perpendicularly by chains; although the ascent by motorcar might be more comfortable for the nervous. I have sometimes gone up at night, and because of the narrow, winding roads this is not without a thrill. Yet the inhabitants of this city of almost a quarter of a million do not seem to mind.

To me, the attraction of the city is down below in the business section between the hill and the sea. This region must evoke nostalgic memories of provincial towns in England to the British traders who have poured into the town since the days of the buccaneers and have given it a distinctly British tone. One feels at a glance that Valparaiso is a solid town of substantial traders, industrialists and financiers, who, while clever in business, have their rigid rule of ethics. Having arrived early, they have been able to plant a piece of England there. The tone of the shops is little different from that of those in English provincial cities. Walking along the rather narrow business street of banks, trust and insurance companies behind staid stone or brick walls, one is especially reminded of England.

Many persons belonging to the prosperous English colony in business in Valparaiso live in Viña del Mar, since in that lovely town it is possible to have enclosed English gardens. These commuters go back and forth along the busy, clamorous highway by the seashore.

Though one thinks of Valparaiso as a place of trade, it has had an appeal for artists for generations. Somerscale, the world-famous painter of marine scenes, once lived in Valparaiso and taught painting in an English school, and here he painted not a few of his pictures of the southern Pacific Coast that are to be seen in the art galleries of Europe. Then, too, Whistler sojourned here for a time, and it was in this city that he painted his "Nocturne in Blue and Gold."

On the outskirts of the city is the Naval Academy, which functioned before we had one at Annapolis, and the spirit of the navy permeates the town. The officers have their club in the city and another set delightfully in a wooded grove near town which is favored in the summer. The personnel of the Chilean Navy do not suffer when compared with the naval personnel of any other country in the world. I have it on the authority of one of the best of our officers that in professional skill they are most superior, and they are gentlemen in the true meaning of the word.

During my tenure in Chile, I had the pleasure to present the club in town with a handsome portrait of Admiral Charles Wooster and to review his brilliant contribution to the definitive victory of Chile in the war for independence. He had made himself unpopular with the English because of his capture of many of their ships in the War of 1812. Happening to be in Chilean waters later, he entered the service of the patriots and ultimately became Commander of the Fleet, after Lord Cochrane, the great British seadog who had made an indelible impression on the training of the infant navy, had left. In one sea engagement with the Spaniards, Wooster made a major contribution to the victory by his masterful sea-manship and daring. Reinforcements for the hard-pressed land forces had to be sent in by sea, and the shore batteries of the enemy made it almost impossible for them to disembark. By maneuvering his flagship defiantly into the line of fire, he forced the astonished foe to concentrate its attention upon him; the Chileans were landed, and victory achieved. Chilean history has recorded that act of supreme daring, and the patriots of the time gave him credit and warm praise, but I know of nothing but this portrait I presented to the navy to remind Chileans of a gallant friend.

Another Yankee associated with Valparaiso is William Wheelwright. It was he who built the first railroad in Chile, which I think was the first in South America, though it was built with English money. Wheelwright was a business genius, a man of daring and vision. It was he who organized the Pacific Steam Navigation Company, which has been operating for more than a century between Chilean and European ports. He introduced steam navigation into Chilean waters. Needing coal for fuel, he had much to do with the development of the coal industry. He managed his affairs for years from Valparaiso, and the Chileans still pay tribute to his genius.

2

Unhappily, a sad page in the history of Chilean-American relations was written in Valparaiso. An American ship, the S.S. *Baltimore,* was in the harbor, and the men, on shore leave, were involved in a street brawl with young Chileans. No doubt the responsibility was divided. After a thorough, honest investigation, the court recommended the imprisonment of one North American and three Chileans. Unfortunately, our minister, Patrick Egan, an Irishman of flamboyant patriotism, reported the incident to Washington in no judicial spirit. James G. Blaine, Secretary of State, accepted his version and transmitted it to President Harrison, who sent a message to Congress asking authority to use force. In the end, Chile paid

$75,000 to the United States, but since the eagle was still flapping its wings, more had to be done, and the Chileans were asked to salute our ship—an unnecessary wounding of the sensibilities of a justly proud people.

Sixty-five years have come and gone, but the resentment has not entirely died out, and our enemies still use the story of the *Baltimore* to create prejudice against us in a crisis. The Nazis used it during the war, and the communists since.

Such incidents—the landing of the marines in Nicaragua and other foolish acts of our adolescence, when Dollar Diplomacy was in full flower—have rendered no service to the friendly relations among nations anywhere in South America.

3

Conspicuous in the plaza in Valparaiso stands the monument to Arturo Prat, the great naval hero of the nation. This young man, a graduate of the Naval Academy, was practicing law when the War of the Pacific recalled him to duty as the captain of the Chilean ship *Esmeralda*. With Chile at war with both Peru and Bolivia, over both of which she prevailed, young Prat was assigned to the blockading of the port of Iquique with his worn-out wooden ship and another equally unfit.

It was a gloomy morning, enveloped in mist. In the distance, Prat sighted two iron-clad Peruvian warships bearing down upon him. There could be but one issue to a battle with the odds so overwhelmingly with the foe, but young Prat did not think of flight—had that been possible. Summoning his men about him, he described the prospect frankly. "Men," he said, "the odds are unequal. Our flag has never yet been hauled down before an enemy, and I hope it will not be today. While I live that flag shall fly, and if I die, my officers will do their duty." With that, he threw his cap in the air and shouted, "Viva Chile!"

The battle began, the impossibility of victory apparent. The shots from the *Esmeralda* struck, but bounced from the sides of the iron-clad enemy vessels. The boilers of the two old Chilean ships were rusty and worn out. In a contest of ship against ship, defeat was inevitable; then man against man, since superhuman bravery and the spirit of sacrifice offered the only hope.

Prat stood on the bridge. He ordered the bugler to sound the attack. His ship, rotted by water and presenting a sorry picture, seemed to respond to the spirit of its commander. The unfurled Chilean flag was waving in the wind with proud gaiety. A volley from the enemy ship fell upon the deck of the *Esmeralda,* and it was stained by the blood of the wounded and the dead. The maneuvering of the superannuated vessel to get it out of range was impossible. Another shot from the enemy pierced the rotten wooden side of the ship, springing a dangerous leak. The ship took fire. No time now to extinguish the fire or attend to the leak. But Prat fought on. Three hours of an uneven battle, and though the ship was burning and leaking, the Chilean flag still fluttered in the breeze.

Admiral Grau, the Peruvian commander, marveling and admiring the superhuman valor of his foe, eager to end an uneven struggle, now ordered his men to ram the *Esmeralda* amidships and to fire point-blank.

Some of Prat's men died from the shock, but he miraculously escaped. His deck was strewn with the dying and the dead, but the flag still flew. As the Peruvian ship made contact, Prat determined to board the enemy vessel and challenge its officers and crew for the mastery of the ship. "Board her, boys," he shouted. It was the last order he was to give. His words were lost in the confusion, but two sailors responded, and the Chileans were making for the conning tower when the Peruvians opened fire at close range. The three men fell; Prat was the last to die.

Inspired by the heroism of Prat, Lieutenant Serrano took command, and the struggle continued, the Chileans grimly facing the foe and selling their lives dearly. The bugler died;

another took his place. But the *Esmeralda* was now sinking rapidly. One gun, however, was still above water. A young midshipman fired it in final defiance as the ship plunged beneath the surface of the sea. The last scene of this Homeric struggle against impossible odds showed the Chilean flag flying at the mainmast as the ship went down. The flag had not been lowered to the foe.

From that hour, Prat has been the great hero of his people. The monument in the plaza commemorating his valor is a constant reminder to succeeding generations, and to this day the Chilean flag has never been lowered to a foe. With ships of all nations appearing in the waters of the harbor, their officers and crew invariably lay wreaths and pay homage to one of the bravest seamen in all the tide of time. On many occasions I have accompanied the officers of our warships to the monument to stand at salute in silence as a tribute to Chilean valor.

4

Quite as old as Valparaiso, but with different traditions, is Concepción. I had my first view of this city on the opening of an exhibit of South American paintings collected by a philanthropist of my country to whom I have referred. Taking Cecil Lyon of my staff along, we planned to go in the comfortable role of tourists. There would be no formalities, no official functions. We would attend the opening of the exhibit, and then, fancy-free, we would meander about the town. I knew something of the city's stirring history. Valdivia had made it his military base in his war with the Araucanians, and, near by, he was to suffer torture and death. For years it had challenged the political pre-eminence of Santiago and for a time it was the seat of government. During the swaying fortunes in the fight between Valdivia and the Indians, it had been all but exterminated; and it had contended fearlessly, through many generations, with nature, since devastating earthquakes and tidal waves had at times all but wiped it out. Standing on the deck of H.M.S. *Beagle* in 1835, Charles Darwin had witnessed the terrible quake of that year and had found it "the most awful and yet interesting spectacle" he had ever seen. In 1938 another earthquake took a dreadful toll of human lives and a disastrous destruction of property, and on my first visit I found reminders of it. A great column at the entrance to the cathedral was split and in danger of falling.

5

Near the city, Valdivia fought a desperate battle with the Indians, and some fantastic stories about it have survived the years. It was said, and so reported by Valdivia to the King, that in the darkest hour of the battle the Spaniards had been saved from extermination by a miracle. From a fallen meteor was seen to emerge the Holy Virgin, who prevailed on the savages to abandon the struggle, and, though unfamiliar with our religion, they thereupon gave up the fight and retired. Valdivia, who was not given to illusions, was so impressed by what he thought he had seen that he called the spot "Virgen de las Nieves"—Concepción.

However, anyone with a taste for the bizarre may make his choice between this pleasant story and another to the effect that when the pressure on the whites became unbearable, and defeat seemed certain, an army of stalwart men wearing helmets such as were worn by the legions of Caesar suddenly emerged from the deep forest, to the rear of the savages, and put them to flight. They then disappeared into the wooded wilderness as mysteriously as they had come. After this miracle, so tradition says, war equipment such as was used in the days of Caesar was found scattered on the ground.

This legend was so thoroughly accepted by the credulous, and the lovers of romance were so sure that somewhere in the forest would be found the "City of the Caesars," that for years expeditions actually went in search of the magic city, but they found nothing at all; and when I visited the museum in Concepción I did not find any of the belongings of Caesar on display.

6

One travels from Santiago to Concepción in a comfortable Pullman coach and may look out the windows on the fertile fields and pastures thickly dotted with the grazing cattle and sheep of the Central Valley, which is noted for the depth of its black soil. On leaving the train we found that our plan for a quiet survey of the city had gone awry. There on the platform were the *intendente* (governor) of the province, the general in command of the garrison, the president of the university, the *alcalde* (mayor) of the city and reporters. We were caught in a tangle of official functions.

The setting of the city on the right bank of the Bío-Bío River, surrounded by the wooded hills of velvet green, is beautiful. On this, our first visit, we accepted the hospitality of the British Consul, Cooper, in his pleasant old colonial house. But our hope of avoiding official entertainment was blasted, and the first night the mayor gave a large official dinner for me, and, with the usual prolonged service and the speeches, it was after midnight when we returned to the Cooper home, taking the mayor with us. Awakened by our movements, the consul, old in years, appeared in his pajamas to act as host, and, thus clad, he sat with us before a blazing fire until almost three in the morning.

Proud of the reputation of the textile mill operated by the Grace Company near the city, we went on a visit of inspection and then drove on to Lota, the seat of the coal mines not far away. A goodly part of these mines extend a long distance under the sea. As a mining town, Lota has unique features. The country and the hills about are wooded, and the little town is saturated with the scent of the woods. There is a little park or playground where the children of the miners romp.

The grim, ugly aspect of the average coal-mining town is less noticeable here, though we found the housing of the miners far from adequate.

7

While Concepción is primarily a bustling business and industrial city, it has its intellectual and cultural side because of the university, which is set in a natural amphitheater. The air is delicious with the odor of the pine and eucalyptus groves on the surrounding hills. The thoroughly modern buildings are architecturally pleasing, and even the School of Dentistry, seen from the outside, might be taken for a museum of art. The schools of philosophy, medicine, industrial chemistry, law and pedagogy, which are perfectly equipped and staffed by able professors, are quite superior. Benjamin Subercaseaux, frequently critical of his country, concludes that "never has so much scientific training been seen in the land or so many professors brought together in such well-equipped buildings."

The remarkable progress of this institution may be ascribed in large part to the brilliant president, Enrique Molina, a man of national prestige, who is much appreciated in my country because of his penetrating and eminently fair book on the United States. I saw him most frequently when, during a political crisis, he was made Minister of Education. When the crisis passed, he returned joyfully to the work he loved best. Though he is advanced in years, it is not apparent in his appearance or in the youthful spirit of experimentation which has kept him alert. One day when I presented the university with a large number of scientific books, he delighted me with his spontaneous response in the most beautiful English.

If our Cultural Institute in Concepción is conspicuously thriving, it is due in large measure to the generous co-operation of the university.

8

My most memorable visit to Concepción was on the occasion of the formal opening of the great steel mill, made possible through the financial aid of the Export-Import Bank in Washington, with the approval of my government. That day it seemed all Chile had assembled to cheer the onward march. Just outside the mill, before the ceremonies began, the bishop of Concepción blessed the undertaking. Then, to give an exotic touch, a child was christened, with the president acting as the godfather, since the child was the seventh son, and tradition prescribed this as his duty. There was much laughing and cheering. We then went inside, where a thousand people sat down at a banquet and I made one of the four speeches. In the evening a dance was held at the new Concepción Club, and President González Videla held up the dance by his tardy arrival—probably for the first time in his life.

Although Concepción is already an industrial city, the steel mill should multiply the smaller shops and factories and make it the Pittsburgh of Chile.

9

And now, Valdivia. It is a distinctly German town where the pro-Nazi element was strongest during the war. I liked these cities with a German population because they are clean and orderly, but it would not have been advisable to visit Valdivia during the war. After the war, I remarked to a functionary in the Foreign Office that I liked German cooking and was going to Valdivia for pigs' knuckles and sauerkraut and the best beer in Chile outside Limache. A few days later I was surprised when this officer asked me pointedly when I was going to Valdivia. Taking Philip Thayer, the Cultural Attaché, with me, we found quarters in the old German hotel, the Schuster, which possessed a homey atmosphere. One day

Thayer pointed out a man in the lobby and commented that he had seen this person everywhere we had gone. We thought nothing of it until this mystery man approached us at the railroad station as we were leaving and introduced himself as a member of the Secret Service, ordered by President Ríos not to let me out of his sight. It was an unnecessary precaution after the war was over. We were treated with marked courtesy. The officers of the garrison gave a dinner for us, and the atmosphere was cordial. We visited the shoe factory of Señor Rudloff, whose grandfather had established the factory ninety-odd years before. This factory, equipped with North American and German machinery, manufactures the best shoes in South America. We were welcomed to the work room by a pretty girl employee with some flowers and a charming little speech, and later that evening we had tea at the home of Rudloff and his amiable wife.

That night we looked out the window on a typical south Chilean rainstorm—the heavens seemed to open and let down a veritable flood. Between December and April southern Chile is delightful, but from April until December it is noted for torrential rains and high winds. It was my first experience with the deluge. Each drop seemed enough to fill a cup, and the rain was so heavy that we could scarcely see across the street as a fierce wind blew the rain against our windows. But the next morning the sun was shining brightly.

It was then that we had our most memorable experience—a long trip in the army launch of the general of the garrison up the Bío-Bío to the farm of a German family who serve luscious lunches on reasonable notice. The *intendente,* the general and Rudloff were along as hosts, and we were scarcely seated when refreshments appeared to help pass the time. The house of the farmer was a little way back from the river, and between the house and the water was a lovely lawn shaded by primeval forest trees. There the table was set, and we had roast duck with sage dressing. On the return trip all inhibitions had broken down, and when the Chileans began to sing their sentimental songs, the Americans responded with theirs. That journey up the Bío-Bío is one of my most pleasant memories of Chile.

But I had not had my pigs' knuckles and sauerkraut. Could not the manager of the German hotel satisfy our plebeian craving? Pigs' knuckles—yes. But sauerkraut—he did not know. At length, by canvassing private houses, enough sauerkraut was found, and the visit to Valdivia was a success.

10

Thence on to Temuco, the center of an important agricultural region, founded in the latter half of the nineteenth century and still suggesting a pushing frontier town with growing pains. This impression was accentuated by the appearance of many Indians in the streets and stores, since the Indian settlement is in the immediate neighborhood. These Indians sauntered along the street with no apparent destination. Given land by the government and protected against exploitation by a law prohibiting its sale without governmental approval, the Indians prefer renting the land to the whites to cultivating it themselves. Driving from Temuco to the fishing camp of a friend, we passed through the Indian reservation, and it was amusing but a little sad to see the Indians lounging in idleness watching the white men plowing their fields.

But it is different with the Indian women, who are industrious. They knit and weave, making beautiful rugs and blankets, and one finds them in the shops bartering their handiwork for merchandise. They are always solemn and silent, often picturesquely dressed. At the Temuco Club we were shown an exhibit of paintings of Indians by Celia Leyton that impressed me as remarkable revelations of character and emotions, and the artist told us interesting stories about some of the men and women she had painted.

The residents of Temuco are all white, largely of German blood. The town throbs with activity, like a young man in a hurry. We visited the banks, shops, factories, all hectically busy. With railroads and wagon roads leading in all directions, trade is drawn from the big estates in the neighborhood. Cattle are featured on many of these *fundos,* and Temuco is a thriving cattle market.

Visitors are overwhelmed by the hospitality of the people. The *intendente* and the two newspapers had us to cocktail parties, and the first night the Rotarians gave me a banquet. My curiosity was aroused at the dinner by the presence of a solitary woman beside me. After some men had spoken, she followed with such scintillating cleverness, in such beautiful English, that I inquired her status and learned that she was the principal of a very large girls' high school, and that when visitors were entertained she was often called upon to give the occasion some glamour and brilliance. It was my first contact with Ana Figueroa, who, later, was to represent Chile in the United Nations.

One day we had eight engagements. We visited an agricultural school where young men were trained in the technique of modern farming and an industrial school where others were being trained in mechanics. Here we were shown into a very large room with modern machinery where young men were enthusiastically at work at the anvils and forges. It seemed to me a foreshadowing of the industrial Chile of the not-distant future. One of the young men left his forge to make a speech of welcome and to present me with two book ends, the heads of Indian chiefs in bronze.

Later I was to visit Temuco several times to attend agricultural fairs and the formal dedication of a health center, or clinic, one of the contributions of the good-neighbor policy.

10

I had seen Osorno within a month after my arrival in Chile and it was to remain a favorite city of mine. Founded during the first years of the conquest, it was wiped out by the

Indians in 1600 and later rebuilt. Here German efficiency shows in the cleanliness and orderliness of the town. My most memorable visit was on the second anniversary of the Chile-American Cultural Institute in 1950. Because of the predominance of Germans it had not occurred to the embassy to undertake setting up an institute there, and we were astonished to learn that the Osornians themselves, under the inspiration and direction of Dr. Heriberto Espinoza, a physician, had established one. When it was thriving, at the end of the second year, I joined in the celebration, taking Sybil and Patricia and Ned Fahs, my Cultural Attaché, along.

We had scarcely settled in an excellent new hotel when a group of young girls from a convent school appeared with flowers and a charming little speech of welcome. Some time before, I had been able to render some slight service to the school, and three of the nuns followed the girls with an expression of appreciation. Our greatest surprise and delight came at the distribution of prizes at the institute to those who had excelled in English, and we noted, as the winners' names were called, that all were of German origin.

An elaborate program for our entertainment had been prepared. Most delightful was a long drive to a *fundo* cared for by a huge, hearty man who boasted that he was a *huaso*. A party of Osornian men and women went along. We drove a long way over a hard-bottom road, and every turn of the wheels revealed strange new vistas of charm and beauty. About halfway to the *fundo,* we stopped at an old tavern, then unoccupied, with literally breath-taking beauty all about. Though isolated, this area was rich in what it had to offer. And what serenity! A cathedral quiet but for the chirping of birds of many varieties, the rustling of the leaves of the forest, the gurgling of water in some hidden stream.

Driving on, we came to an agricultural experiment station and talked with the technicians in charge. The Chileans had found that in a given pasture space in Argentina four cattle could be fed, and in the same space in Chile but two. This was ascribed to some deficiency in the pasturage, and these men, all specialists, were experimenting to find that on which cattle would thrive best. Here was Chilean agriculture on the march.

Finally we reached the *fundo,* where our host was waiting with chilled cocktails ready, for it was a warm day. After a delicious lunch, we were taken to see a captive puma in a cage, and then through delightful scenery to where we could get a perfect view of a neighboring lake with the sun sparkling on the water.

The next day we were driven to the fantastic hotel of Puyehue in the heart of the country. Once we pulled off from the highway to see a picturesque waterfall, a miniature Niagara. The day was damp and chilly, and we surveyed the scene from the windows of an old tavern, on the casements of which were carved the initials of generations of lovers. Aside from the waterfall, the rolling country about and the wooded hillsides were worth the journey.

The hotel of Puyehue is a great mass of masonry, concrete and stone, built in the heart of the country and awaiting the completion of the paved highway between Santiago and Buenos Aires, which is to pass directly by. In the summer season—December to March—the tourists will find it a merry spot. Here one may row on the lake beside the hotel, or fish or swim in crystal-clear water, play golf, or tennis, or canter about the countryside on horseback. The building suggests a large feudal castle. The rooms or suites offer everything one needs of luxury or comfort, and the service is of the best. In the summer the halls ring with laughter from the suites where guests are entertaining friends with cocktails before lunch or dinner. At one time it was the custom to have costume balls, but these were abandoned when the guests ruined so many spreads and sheets in making their improvised costumes.

I had known the manager when he was the consul of the Spanish Republic in Hendaye in France, and he suggested a motorboat trip on the large lake to one of the numerous islands where an Austrian family, in flight from Nazi persecution, had found a home and now offered luncheons if notice were given in advance. So we all piled into a large motorboat, which plowed the clear water at great speed. We passed a number of heavily wooded islands without human habitation that promised something of the romance of mystery. How lonesome they seemed, and how beautiful! These green islands set in the lake were gems, and the views from the boat entrancing.

On the island, occupied solely by the Austrian family, lunch was served on the grounds facing the lake, in the shade of giant trees, in the branches of which a thousand birds were singing rapturously. We were given an epicurean luncheon, in an intimate, homey atmosphere, the mother and daughter serving, while the old grandmother, who had wandered far in search of the freedom she had found and had seen much she would rather have missed, entertained us with the story of her Odyssey, chuckling the while and glossing over the sad parts of the narrative.

The second morning we drove back to Osorno for a farewell dinner with Dr. Espinoza and his family. We had arranged for him to visit the hospitals, health and medical centers, and medical schools in the United States, and he was looking forward with zest to his visit. One day, soon after we left, he took a small plane to make a professional visit. The wreckage of the plane was found in the sea, but his body was not recovered. It is the one dark shadow on memories of a delightful visit to Osorno.

No one can pretend to know Chile who has not seen these cities, to which may well be added Talca and La Serena.

We have now described Chilean cities, learned something of Chilean politics, much, I hope, about men, but the reader, having heard of the charm, beauty, vivacity and intelligence of the Chilean women may naturally expect something about them. So now we shall join the ladies.

XIV

The Women of Chile

Since rumor has bruited it abroad that Chilean women are beautiful, charming and vivacious, it would be absurd to ignore them in any book about their country. Of course, not all these women would "launch a thousand ships and light the topless towers of Ilium," but the reputation of Chilean women rests on a firm foundation.

Two hundred years ago, the grandfather of Lord Byron, visiting Chile, was especially fascinated by the women. This may account for the rumor, recorded by Stephen Crissold, an English writer, that the author of "Don Juan" once thought of buying "a principality" in Chile and settling down there. It probably was enough for the romantic poet, who loved women, to read in his forebear's narrative of his travels in

Chile that "the women are remarkably handsome." They have not changed, though their appeal has been altered to fit the times. These women are minutely described by the poet's grandfather. Long black hair with four plaits behind, twisted around a bodkin and crowned with flowers; their shifts "all over lace," colored golden or silver; their waistcoats tight, their petticoats open in front and the end of an embroidered garter "hanging below the petticoat," and "their breasts and shoulders very naked." Lest one get the impression that these ladies of the higher circles were immodest, it must be added that such was their keen sense of the proprieties when in public, that the veil they wore concealed one eye, and if the other, peering out, sparkled with the triumph of conquest, who could blame them?

In the two centuries that have intervened since the grandfather of Byron wrote, fashion has altered styles in dress, but the women of the two centuries are "sisters under the skin." The tourists at the turn of the century in search of women to bear out their reputation for elegance and beauty could easily have found them driving in fine open carriages, shaded by their lace parasols, elegantly attired, during the fashionable procession in the park, but today they must be sought in their homes or on formal occasions.

The tourist, thinking of Chile as of Spanish origin and expecting Spanish coloring, is surprised to find that the Spanish type—dark complexion, coal-black hair and brown eyes—is no longer so predominant. He is astonished to see so many blondes, and gradually it dawns upon him that Chile is not so much a Spanish country as some of its neighbors. This is because of the mixture of races, which makes for beauty. The very large German, English, Scotch, Irish, Dutch and Scandinavian elements, intermarrying with the Chileans of Spanish origin, have made a race of women distinctly Chilean.

Chile's reputation for beautiful and charming women rests mostly on the middle and upper social strata, and it is from among these that many European diplomats have found their wives.

Chilean women are generally lovers of the out of doors and are physically active. They play tennis and golf, swim, fish, and many hunt, drive their own cars. They are also graceful equestriennes, and make a lovely, colorful picture in the Paper Chase. Through these activities most retain their slenderness. They have perfect taste in dress and know how best to show off their charms. In this they are individualists, not blind conformists.

However, the fame of Chilean women does not rest solely on their physical attraction. Beauty is also of the spirit and the manner. These women are very much alive. Much of the impression of beauty comes from their charm, their animation and vivacity, their keen intelligence, their sprightly conversation, their graceful carriage. In their familiarity with literature, both classic and contemporary, they are superior to the men, though, with the cunning of their sex, they conceal their sense of superiority. But they have no inhibitions in debating politics with their lords and masters. In politics they impressed me as more robust partisans than the men. They were eager and active politically before they were granted the national franchise, since they had had their initiation in municipal elections before. They were given the right to vote in national elections during my time in Chile, after they had carried on their campaign persistently but without the rowdyism that marked the struggle for women's rights in England. It never would have occurred to them to imitate their English sisters in beating Asquith over the head with umbrellas. They used a better and more subtle weapon—their persuasive charm—and they partly smiled themselves to the ballot box. There was no commotion.

But once granted the franchise, they took it seriously, forming their own opinions, independent of fathers, husbands or lovers. Politics rests to a large degree on intuition and here they have an advantage over the men.

Politically, the women of the aristocracy seem largely to align themselves with the Conservatives and not a few with the Liberals; those of the middle class with the Radicals, though some are Liberals; a large per cent of the working class support the Socialists, though some of these prefer the Radicals. I personally knew of none who were communists, but of course there were many. In the heat of their political discussions they actually seemed less motivated by emotions than by logic, and most understood the issues. Though many are active canvassers in campaigns they have not made much use of their feminine allure. I doubt that many, or any, would go so far as the lively Duchess of Devonshire, who bought with a kiss a vote for Charles James Fox from a butcher—though they are still young in the game.

I would not give the impression that they are "blue stockings," with no sentiment. Deep down, I am sure, most of them are romantics. Indeed, some are incorrigible flirts and masters of the art. When André Maurois, the brilliant French biographer of Shelley, Byron, Disraeli and George Sand, was in Santiago to lecture, preferably on literary subjects, the one request from women was for his lecture on love.

Having an abundance of domestic help, the household duties of the women of the middle class and aristocracy are light. Some begin the day at the telephone exchanging gossip with friends and arranging meetings. The morning often finds them canvassing the shops, at the hair-dressers and the beauty parlors. In the afternoon, tea; in the evening, parties, concerts or the cinema. Restlessly active, they keep abreast of current literature of the world, and the new novel that sets the tongues to wagging in Paris, London, Rome and New York is being discussed at the same time in Santiago.

And they are kindly and generous. When an old seamstress who had for years appeared periodically in the "big houses" to sew could no longer work because she had become senile, and her care fell to a niece who worked for a living and could not minister to the old woman's needs, the niece went to a woman who had formerly employed the old seamstress, and she was not dismissed merely with sympathetic words. Calling for her car and taking the niece along, the woman of the "big house" set forth in a search, far and wide, until she found a comfortable refuge for the old woman among some nuns and arranged for her maintenance.

2

Granted the franchise, the Chilean women plunged with positive glee into the political fray. On my arrival in Chile I was amazed to find that the mayor of Santiago was a woman. She was a very clever person and I knew her slightly.

I knew the mayor of Providencia far better. Providencia may be described as a borough of Santiago. It is an attractive section of the city, with tree-lined streets, where prosperous people have their homes. This sylvan section is much favored by many secretaries of the Diplomatic Corps. Alicia Cañas was the mayor when I arrived—a charming, keenly intelligent woman, politically clever, and thoroughly practical and businesslike, who made some notable improvements in her territory.

In the first two general elections after the women were enfranchised, a number of women were candidates for Congress and were elected. Most were women of ability, good judgment and a sense of responsibility, but one, elected to the Senate and more Perónist than democratic, was soon expelled.

Chilean women had been introduced into the foreign service long before this, when Gabriela Mistral, the Nobel Prize poet, was the cultural representative of some South American countries in the League of Nations at Geneva. Later, in recognition of the distinction she had given Chile, she was made a permanent consul, able to make her own assignment.

Chile's first woman representative in the United Nations was Amanda Labarca, internationally known as an intellectual, who was much appreciated in the United States, where she has lectured in colleges and universities. She is a woman of wide interests and stout convictions and she expresses them with force and eloquence. She had a chair on the faculty of the University of Chile.

She was succeeded in the United Nations by Ana Figueroa, the clever and eloquent woman I have described in a previous chapter.

The first woman who was to be chief of a diplomatic mission was Mrs. Olin Dows, whose marriage to the North American artist followed her retirement from the diplomatic service. A woman of intellectual and cultural distinction, with an attractive personality, she served Chile well at the Court of Holland.

Thus far but two women have been ministers in the government. Adriana Olguin de Baltra was Minister of Justice under Gonzalez Videla and Maria Teresa del Canto was made Minister of Education. Adriana de Baltra is an able lawyer and Maria Teresa del Canto had devoted her life to teaching.

So, in public or political life, Chilean women have played their part.

3

As for the professions, there have been women doctors in Chile since 1886, when Elisa Diaz got her degree from the University of Chile, though for years, despite their medical degrees from the university, the idea of a woman's being so familiar with the human anatomy was disturbing to the fastidious, and women doctors were described as "pharmacists." This strange feeling that women have no place in the science of healing comes directly from the old Spanish concept of women nurses, who, for centuries, were looked upon as being on a par with charwomen. The nurses, in consequence, were long recruited from the lowest segment of society and were so ignorant that no skilled physician or surgeon would tolerate them about. The need for scientifically trained nurses has been recognized in Chile, where nursing schools have been added to the universities. While the purpose is to raise the status of nurse to the dignity of a profession, some prejudice still persists among the very old fashioned. More than a century ago Florence Nightingale encountered the same prejudice and treated it with contempt. It discourages many young women who possess the necessary mentality and character to take up nursing, but the prejudice of the Middle Ages is fading out in Chile, where there now are excellent trained nurses, though not enough.

4

It is not surprising that in Chile, which forged ahead of the other South American nations in social legislation and institutions, the women have done distinguished work in the social-service field.

Let this be put down to Chile's credit: The first social-service school in South America was established in Chile in 1925.

This was the work of Luz Tocornal de Romero, wife of a prominent physician with whom the embassy had most pleasant relations. She had accompanied her husband to Boston, where he was working for his degree at Harvard, and since he was busy with his work, she enrolled at a social-service school and completed the course.

Another achievement to Chile's credit: The Escuela de Servicio Social of Chile was the first governmental institution of the kind on the continent.

One purpose of this school is to give young women an understanding of the pitiful plight of unfortunates, thereby making possible a sympathetic approach to their problem. The girls are trained to individualize each case through their studies in psychology. So much importance is attached to this that the applicant for admission is subjected to a rigid test determining her psychological fitness for the work. No one is admitted who does not have a *bachillerato* and does not meet the requirements in health and character. During the three-year course the students are trained in political economy, sociology and criminology. To impress them with their responsibilities, they are thoroughly grounded in the history of the nation's notable social evolution, and with the developments in medicine and hygiene throughout the world. Before receiving their diplomas, they have to submit to a rigid examination and present a satisfactory thesis.

Once in the field, as social workers, their duties are manifold. Where children are born out of wedlock, they try to get the union legally recognized; where the father of a family deserts, they try to persuade him to resume his responsibilities; and where abject poverty threatens to separate a mother from her children, they do what they can to keep the family together.

When the school at the University of Chile justified itself, a similar school was opened at the Catholic University, and here the response from the old wealthy families was generous, partly due to the fact that in scientifically carrying on the work for the needy it was acting in conformity with the religious teachings of the church. It is not unusual for young women of the leisure class to engage in some form of volunteer social work, and I know of one young woman on a *fundo* who set up a school on the farm to teach the peasant women fancy needlework and embroidery, which became so popular that women of neighboring *fundos* did the same. This young woman also undertook the marketing of their product.

Apropos of social service in Chile, no woman has a better record of achievement than Graciela Mandujano, whose work and purpose I observed for years. If she were tireless and efficient it was due to her very real sympathy for the poor and wretched. She had been trained in social service in the United States, and she spoke English so perfectly that a stranger would assume that she was English or American. She was an excellent organizer, most successful in public relations, and an effective speaker. She impressed North Americans when she lectured in the United States under the auspices of the American Association of University Women.

She had a passion for extending knowledge and, when teaching, it occurred to her that too little attention was being given to adult education. Being a practical woman, she carried this thought to the government, and out of this came the Instituto de Información Rural.

There was nothing sensational in its purpose. Here was a country that had enacted many liberal laws for the good of the common man, and yet, in the country districts, too few knew of these measures or how to make use of them. Graciela and her co-workers contacted the people of the hinterland, calling their attention to these laws and explaining how they might benefit from them.

But the institute offered opportunities for infinitely more. Pamphlets, written in simple language, with bits of Chilean history to awaken national pride, were printed for rural circulation. Poems and useful advice on home weaving, gardening, on bee culture, on health and sanitation were included. To make sure these pamphlets reached the people who might profit from them, Graciela appealed to the *carabineros* for a mailing list of *huasos,* peasants, small farmers, serious and sober people. The response was remarkable, and letters poured in to the institute from small children and tottering grandmothers asking advice on everything imaginable; each letter was answered individually.

This success suggested a plan for a more personal contact with the neglected people of the hinterland. A truck was found, and Graciela, with a few co-workers, rolled out into the heart of the country in search of people they hoped to interest and serve. When they came to a stream where there were trees, they camped out, cooked their meals, slept when necessary on the ground. When, drawn by curiosity, callers appeared, they were offered coffee and cigarettes. Pamphlets were distributed, books were given out, ailing babies were put right, mothers were advised on the better care of their children, and small farmers carried their problems to the little group, which included one person with a technical knowledge of farming.

When the truck finally moved on, the initial prejudice against the folks from the city, who had seemed so simple and direct, had warmed into friendship; and since the project had been supported by the government they had thought remote, indifferent or interfering, they now thought differently about it.

5

Many Chilean women are in business. These come from every segment of society, and in business they range from the old woman with a newsstand on the street to the successful operator of a real-estate business. Many of these come from very prosperous families, motivated partly by boredom and partly by a realistic concept of the changing world. Not a few train themselves for a profession or business. Many prepare for secretarial work, and some establish little businesses of their own. Some are drawn to giftshops and bookstores, where their friends can gather and rummage among the books while engaging in gossip. Some, more daring, bring in dresses from New York or Buenos Aires and do a brisk business in their homes. A few have been highly successful in real estate and rentals.

Just before I left Chile some resourceful young women found a way to make money almost under cover. Santiago, with almost a million and a half people going back and forth to work or on shopping expeditions, depends, on busses, which are usually crowded and uncomfortable. A few young girls conceived the idea of buying swift-moving, small busses, little larger than station wagons, which make better time and are more agreeable. They employ chauffeurs to drive them and make good profits on their investment without anyone's suspecting that they are "in business."

It was because so many Chilean women were in business that Mrs. Fraser Elliot, wife of the Canadian Ambassador, urged upon them the organization of the Zonta Club, which may be described as a women's Rotary. It meets at stated intervals for luncheons, news and views are exchanged, and someone usually speaks on a timely subject.

This brief discussion of Chilean women seemed to me necessary in any discussion of Chile, since they not only add to the country's charm but serve it in many ways. From the earliest days, when the indomitable Inés Suárez, the daring mistress of Valdivia, held the fort of Santa Lucía against the savages in the absence of her lover, the women of Chile have been conspicuous in the molding of its history.

XV

The Chilean Pen and Press

Four centuries ago Chile produced an epic poem of great beauty, power and emotional appeal. In the middle of the sixteenth century, Alonso de Ercilla arrived in Chile. The magnificence and beauty of the Araucanian forests fired his imagination, and the almost superhuman bravery of the natives made a profound impression on his fertile mind. In his immortal poem, *"La Araucana,"* he pays generous tribute to the native warriors who faced and fought the invaders with primitive weapons and who were often defeated but never dismayed. In virile verse the poet has told the story of the conquest with such fidelity to historic truth that it is an illuminating source for historians. The descriptions of the scenery are superb, and those of bloody battles have seldom been equalled in the whole range of literature. If the Chileans still salute the valor of these fierce antagonists, it is partly due to the pen of the poet. The Araucanians were noted for their natural eloquence, and some of the orations the poet puts into the mouths of the orators compare well with the best in literature.

Another poet of the sixteenth century was Pedro de Ona, whose poem, *"Arauco Domado,"* is rich in pages of great beauty. Brilliant, colorful and thrilling is his description of the tempest that tossed the Spanish fleet going from Coquimbo to Talcahuano.

Poems such as these were appearing in Chile and being read in Spain three centuries before the flowering of New England.

2

Most famous among the literary artists of our day is Gabriela Mistral, to whom the Nobel Committee gave the prize for literature a few years ago. She was not in Chile during my tenure there but I met her later in New York. She looks the distinguished person that she is. Her personality fills the room. Her strong features, dominated by bright, knowing, hazel eyes, denote her keen intelligence and a sense of humor. Her iron-gray hair is cut short. Her mouth is generous, her hands beautiful and eloquent in conversation, her voice low and rich with feeling; her conversation can be salty with irony. A militant liberal, a friend of the poor and lowly, she has a passionate sympathy for the underprivileged.

Her grandfather had gone down from the mountains to the plains and married "above his social station," and, after producing a flock of children, he vanished into the hills again. One of his sons, Jerónimo, became a teacher, married, and produced the future genius, but when she was a child of twelve, he, too, took flight from domestic responsibilities. He had imagination and some gift as a writer of verse.

Gabriela attended her sister's school and learned rapidly "everything but how to play," as Erna Fergusson says. Her fatherless home made her sensitive and she suffered as a child. Was it this early that, like Unamuno, she came to look upon life as a tragedy? It is not unusual among the Spanish mystics. Her first poem, written at the age of thirteen, reflects this sense of tragedy that runs through many of her later verses. The first volume of her selected poems bears the significant title *Desolation* and includes her "Sonnets of Death." These poems are thoughts on fire. She had been an admirer of D'Annunzio and his work, and perhaps this explains why she chose a pen name and called herself Gabriela. She died in New York in 1957.

She loved her country, not uncritically, was proud of its past, but she was primarily interested in lifting the submerged to the dignity of manhood through better living conditions and, above all, through the education of the children of the poor. On her return to Chile after a long absence, she was asked whom she especially wished to see. "I want to talk with the schoolteachers," she said.

3

Another Chilean poet of distinction, famous throughout South America and in Spain, is Pablo Neruda, who, unhappily, in recent years has subordinated his art to propaganda for Moscow. I met him first accidentally at the home of a friend in Paris in 1939, but since I shared the almost studied ignorance of my countrymen about South American literature, his name, when he was introduced, meant nothing to me. I saw before me a tall, strongly built man, smooth shaven, with strong features, whose conversation revealed the intellectual. Later, he and his wife called at my house in Santiago on a visa case, and I found him pleasant, interesting and amusing, and possessing considerable charm of manner. This was to be my last contact with him. I do not know whether at that time he had become a convert to Stalinism. During World War II, after Hitler's invasion of Russia, I heard him give a reading of his poem, "Stalingrad." It was during the days when we thrilled to the heroic resistance of that stubborn city, and the emotional reaction of the vast throng as Neruda read the stirring lines with passion was remarkable. When he became an active communist, his comrades were quick to take advantage by making Neruda a member of the Senate.

Thus Neruda the poet became submerged in Neruda the communist.

Among Chilean novelists of distinction, perhaps the most famous is Blest Gana, the only Chilean novelist of repute in the nineteenth century. During his notable diplomatic career in Paris, he numbered among his most intimate friends the celebrated correspondent of the London *Times,* the famous Blowitz, with whom he formed a close friendship. Gana was a fascinating conversationalist, immensely entertaining, and his stories of men and events, sparkling with wit, sweetened with whimsy, related with vivacity and charm, opened the doors of the famous salons of the French capital to him. Depressed by the deterioration of a large group of Chilean expatriates, he wrote his truly great novel, *Los Transplantados,* his master-piece. His *Martín Rivas* was almost as fine. The literary and artistic atmosphere of Paris profoundly affected his thinking and his literary style.

Another novelist of distinction was Orrego Luco, whose *Casa Grande* is a delightful satire on the pretentious social life in Santiago during the Victorian years. I met him but once at a dinner at the embassy, for he died soon afterward. His son was Chief of Protocol in the Foreign Office during a few years of my tenure.

But Augusto d'Halmar was still living and vigorous when I went to Chile. He was a powerfully built man with a magnificent head. He was a delightful raconteur, drawing on his memories of his long sojourns in Paris and Madrid and vividly sketching portraits of the great, often with no little acid in his paint. He knew not only the Paris of the salons, the writers and artists who had arrived, but also the unconventional quarters of Montmartre, so loved by Clemenceau, and the rollicking students' rooms in the garrets intrigued him more than the salons. In conversation he was a monologist, and his powerful voice drowned the voices of the others, but he was easily pardoned, for the resulting entertainment was lively. His wit could be wicked when he wished, since he had a caustic tongue. When a cultural institute made me an honorary member and he presided at the ceremony at the university and discussed my *Spanish Adventures of Washington Irving,* he sounded complimentary but I had an uneasy feeling that there were thorns among the roses. He had imagination and a superior creative faculty. Among his novels, the most popular is his *Smoke Dims the Mirror.*

Of the contemporary novelists during my residence in Chile, Eduardo Barrios is perhaps the foremost. There is nothing in his manner or appearance to suggest the Bohemian, since he could pass in a crowd as a successful business or professional man. He is an artist free from pose who lives and works in the country. I met him first at my own table when I gave a luncheon for John Dos Passos. None of his novels have been failures. His *Love-Smitten Boy* and *A Waster* are eclipsed by his audacious *Brother Ass,* which greatly extended his reputation while incurring the displeasure of a religious order. The scene of action is a monastery, and the plot develops the theory that it is not objectionable to commit a sin if the purpose is to discredit a pretender cloaked in the garments of sanctity.

In some ways, the most picturesque and original of present-day Chilean writers is Benjamin Subercaseaux, whose novel *Jemmy Button,* published in translation in London and New York, is a masterpiece that will survive. He is Bohemian in spirit, with none of the eccentricities of the tribe. Indeed, he is more suggestive of Savile Row. His strong, smooth-shaven face is handsome. He comes from a famous aristocratic family. In a drawing room or at a dinner table he is a charming conversationalist. His book known as *Chile: A Geographic Extravaganza* is delightful, rich in humor and philosophy.

Joaquín Edwards Bello, a favorite of mine, has written

fine novels, two dealing with Chileans in Paris and Madrid, and one outstanding novel interpreting the *roto*. Charm distinguishes everything he writes. Perhaps his novel, *Valparaiso,* re-creating that city as he knew it in his youth, is his best.

4

In the writing of history, Chileans have excelled. According to the *Encyclopaedia Britannica,* the greatest of all bibliographers is the Chilean José Toribio Medina. A lawyer by profession, a diplomat by chance, an historian by preference, he delved deep into dusty archives previously neglected in Europe. No one has so completely covered the discovery, the conquest, the exploration, the history and geography of the Americas. This was a labor of love. He set up his own printing press, from which poured a flood of books and pamphlets —his own and others. On the centennial of his birth, in 1952, the anniversary was celebrated by scholars and historians throughout the world.

Perhaps the stirring of the intellectual life of Chile was due to the advent of Andrés Bello, a Venezuelan by birth. A militant in the fight for independence in his own country, he had lived for twenty years in London as a diplomat, and during these years he read, wrote and taught. On his arrival in Chile he became the prime mover in the molding of the intellectual life of the nation. His was a major role in the founding of the University of Chile, of which he became the rector. Seeking service, he went to the Senate, and he was largely responsible for the promulgation of the civil code. He created a school of literary criticism. No one did so much toward awakening the intellectual life and molding the minds of youth along the line of intellectual and academic freedom.

Another historian of just renown is Vicuña-Mackenna, whose work is classic. Because he had imagination and the ability to create, in intimate detail, the life and atmosphere of other times, he aroused an interest in history in the young. He had a graceful style and, without sacrificing accuracy, gave to his work the fascination of fiction. He was undoubtedly a partisan in his interpretation of events, and men whose principles or actions did not meet with his approval fell foul of his pen. He was literally born in an atmosphere of history, for he first saw the light in the house of the Carreras, leaders in the Revolution. Having decided views, he could not avoid politics and, when involved in a liberal revolutionary movement, he was arrested and condemned to death. Miraculously escaping, he lived for some time in Chile without detection, posing as a French physician. Having admiration and affection for the Carreras, he put his feeling into perhaps his most distinguished book, *The Banishment of the Carreras*. Again involved in political troubles, he was arrested, imprisoned and deported. But everything was grist for his mill. Digging into the Archives in Seville, he discovered historical data of real value. On his return to Chile, he became the editor of *El Mercurio*. In 1875, the liberal and democratic forces nominated him for President, but liberalism at the time was at a low ebb and he was defeated. As an intellectual force he would have been distinguished in any country.

Among the historians, the Amunátegui brothers, Miguel Luis and Gregorio Victor, hold unassailable positions. Both were outstanding. Gregorio's *The Spanish Conquest, Notes for the History of Chile* and *The First Years of the Revolution in Chile* have permanent value. At one time, he was Minister of Foreign Affairs. Both brothers had died before I went to Chile. Miguel's son, Domingo Amunátegui, former rector of the University and then an old man, carried on the intellectual tradition of his people, and, when honored by the American Historical Society, I availed myself of the opportunity to pay homage to a distinguished family by giving a luncheon in his honor at the Embassy.

None among the historians surpasses Barros Arana, thought by many to be the most eminent of them all. Like others of his craft, he had strong political convictions, and an attack on the government sent him into exile, but he profited by collecting material in the archives of Europe. His *History of Chile* is a standard work. Like Bello, he served as rector of the university.

One of the most amazing men in Chile is the historian Francisco Encina, who finished the nineteenth volume of his *History of Chile* just before I left. I called upon him to congratulate him on the publication of his last volume when he was eighty-four years old and found him as chipper as a two-year-old colt. He had entertained Theodore Roosevelt on his farm near Santiago, and I asked him what he thought of our Teddy. He wrinkled his nose. "He was an imitation cowboy," he snorted.

Eugenio Pereira Salas, head of the history department at the University of Chile, has specialized in phases of the Chilean story, in Chilean culture, folklore and the relations between the United States and Chile. Important among his numerous books is one chronicling the story of North American ships in Chilean waters from 1788 to 1810; one on the origin of the musical art in Chile; and another on the influence of North America on the framing of the first Constitution. Well known and most favorably thought of in intellectual and artistic circles in the United States, he has lectured at the University of Chicago and a university in Washington, D. C. As President of the Chile-American Cultural Institute for some years, he has rendered a high service to both countries.

5

Such is the intellectual background of the Chilean press, which is free, independent and influential. In 1812 the great Carrera introduced the first printing press from the United States, on which was printed the first real newspaper, the *Aurora* of Valparaiso. The first distinguished journalist was its editor, Camilo Henríquez. Though not a model in conservatism, he lifted the standard in style and reasoning. Influenced by the French philosophers of the eighteenth century, he was a militant liberal and consequently a target for the barbs of the old aristocracy, but as a consistent champion of political liberty he served the nation well, and more than any other writer of his time he awakened the civic consciousness and pride of the people and made Chilean democracy articulate. Amunátegui describes him as "the most capable and intrepid thinker of the Chilean Revolution." The course he took did not make for opulence, and he lived and died in poverty, but the liberals and the intellectuals rallied around him. With the reactionaries attacking him as the "Apostle of Satan," Manuel José Gandarillas, son of an aristocratic family, worked with pride in his shop as a printer, and Manuel de Salas, one of the greatest of the intellectuals, who contributed greatly to the founding of the National Library and the Academy of Mathematics, wrote for the paper without pay. In the office of *El Mercurio* in Valparaiso, the publisher showed me a number of copies of *Aurora;* it was small in size but meaty.

During the early years of Chilean journalism, there was little reporting of local news. The papers were mostly editorial, dedicated to discussions of political and other controversial subjects.

Of the journalists of the first fifty years, few could approach Manuel Blanco Cuartín, who, for twenty years, was the editor of *El Mercurio* of Valparaiso. He brought to his work the highest ideals of his profession. His wide reading and love of literature was manifest in the purity of his style, the grace of his phrasing. He was a master of satire and irony, and, with the utmost suavity of manner, he could cut an opponent to pieces with a smile. He once engaged in a long duel of words with an Italian over Voltaire, and two pamphlets, "What Is Left of Voltaire" by the Italian and "What We Have Inherited from Voltaire" by Blanco, may still be seen. It was Blanco who founded the Chilean Academy.

Contemporary with him, but younger in years, was Zorobabel Rodríguez, who was as strongly conservative as the other was liberal. He founded *El Independiente* in 1864, to expound the philosophy of the conservatives, but his interest in social and political reforms was not appreciated by his party at the time. He wrote with force and grace. He found time to write a novel depicting the social life of the Chileans of his generation and, more important, a *Dictionary of Chileanisms,* a noteworthy work revealing his talent as a philologist.

These men suffice to show that Chilean journalism is rich in an inspiring tradition.

6

During my time in Chile I daily read *El Mercurio, El Diario Ilustrado* and *La Nación,* expressing diverse views of different schools of political thought. These, along with *La Union* and *El Mercurio* of Valparaiso, were the most important papers at the time.

El Mercurio of Santiago is one of the greatest newspapers in South America, ranking with *La Prensa* and *La Nación* of Buenos Aires. I came to think of *El Mercurio* as *The New York Times* of Chile because of its remarkably wide coverage of world news, the fairness of its presentation and the scholarly quality of its editorials. Though in my time he did not personally write for the paper, it was the embodiment of the taste and spirit of Agustín Edwards, the Ambassador, in whose family the paper has been for many years. He was a man of manifold activities, in all of which he was distinguished. His greatgrandfather reached Chile from England as a doctor on an English ship, and, falling in love with both the country and a Chilean girl, he left the ship, married the girl and settled down to the practice of his profession. His son, Agustín, had genius in business. He founded the Banco Edwards in 1867, and an insurance company; both still thrive. He made a fortune in copper.

The latter's son, also named Agustín, had an even more remarkable career. In his twenty-second year he began a political career as a member of the House of Deputies, and at twenty-five he was Minister of Foreign Affairs. During his long tenure as Ambassador in England, he presided over the Assembly of the League of Nations and took part in numerous international conferences. During his diplomatic career, he found time to write three valuable books on Chile in a charming and lively style. Meanwhile he was active in industrial and banking enterprises. Soon after his death, his portrait by László was hung on the wall of the Foreign Ministry. It was painted early in his life and shows a young man, slender, elegant and courtly in his ambassadorial uniform. I knew him after his retirement, when he was much heavier and in ill health. It was he who fashioned *El Mercurio* after his own taste and patterned it, I think, on the London *Times.*

Intellectual, cultured, scholarly, he insisted on the highest ethical and literary standards for his writers. He found them among men of culture and comprehension, some trained in statesmanship and diplomacy, with a clear understanding of the international scene; their expositions on foreign affairs were as prescient and penetrating as could be found anywhere. In later years the paper passed to Agustín III, an Eton and Oxford man, who shared his father's adherence to the high journalistic standards of the greatest English papers. At his death he was succeeded by his son, Agustín Edwards Eastman.

My first contact with a Chilean journalist was with a great writer on *El Mercurio,* Carlos Silva Vildósola, who replied to my initial speech at the luncheon of the Chile-American Society. His editorials were thoughtful and in good taste, never flippant or commonplace. There was virility and vitality in his words. Though a master of satire, he was usually generous and just.

Another member of the editorial staff who was an artist in words was Galvarino Gallardo Nieto, whose articles were often brilliant, dynamic and caustic. Still another, a dear friend of mine, was Felix Nieto, an accomplished diplomat, who wrote with clarity and understanding on international matters. He was greatly admired in Washington, where he was

Chilean Ambassador through the administration of González Videla.

Still another member of the staff was Rafael Maluenda, the editor-in-chief, who had been with the paper for a quarter of a century. His editorial work was forceful, with close-knit reasoning. I had a memorable evening with him at my home in New York after my retirement. His talk was stimulating, like his articles. He has many Latin characteristics in conversation—much gesticulation, with his facial expression changing to reflect the thought.

Throughout my stay in Chile, the general manager of *El Mercurio* was Guillermo Perez de Arce, the "grand old man of Chilean journalism," and he was still at his post carrying his fourscore years lightly when I left.

El Mercurio was partial to the Liberal party, though it did not conform blindly and followed an independent course.

El Diario Ilustrado was likewise excellent because of its wide and discriminating coverage of both domestic and international news. Its relation to the Conservative party was similar to that of *El Mercurio* to the Liberal. Luis Silva, the editor, whose friendship I enjoyed, had a legal background. I found his paper friendly to the United States, though this did not deter it from criticizing some of our policies. The president of the board during my time was Alejo Lira Infante, with whom we had the warmest personal relations. José Ramón Gutierrez, a former Minister of Foreign Affairs, wrote brilliant editorials on international problems, and Prieto, a humorist, enlivened the pages with amusing articles. The editorial page was strong, the editorials dignified, conservatively reasoned and forceful.

The embassy's relations with the *Diario Ilustrado* were unique—so friendly, despite occasional disagreements, that each year on our national holiday it gave a luncheon at the Union Club for my entire staff, attended by all the editors and executives; and on Chile's natal day the embassy returned the compliment. These luncheons invariably were gay, since the talk was uncensored and repartee gave spice to the occasion.

La Nación was known as the government organ, in that its policy shifted to reflect that of the government in power. A generation before, under the dynamic directorship of Carlos Dávila, *La Nación* became a journal of great influence, with a wide circulation. Dávila had distinguished himself as an intellectual before going to Washington as Ambassador. There he was much in demand for lectures in the universities. He was the head of the Organization of American States when death terminated a brilliant career.

At the time Dávila gave up the directorship of *La Nación* the paper declined in circulation and influence, but it had a marked revival during my stay in Chile. Conforming as it did to government policy, it was helpful in the clarification of governmental actions. Concerned primarily with Chilean politics, its coverage of foreign news was subordinated to domestic news.

During the war years the editor was Domingo Melfi, an intellectual whose office often resembled a literary salon where writers gathered for literary gossip.

Invariably, I turned first to the clever, sprightly column of Joaquín Edwards Bello, which was so charming and intimate in style, so penetrating in its observations and, at times, so caustic and devastating in its irony.

Another morning paper I read was *La Hora*. It made its first appearance in June 1935. Behind it at the beginning was more cleverness than money. It began as a modest enterprise but with intense doctrinaire enthusiasm, since its purpose was to co-ordinate all the political parties and elements of the Left for the presidential election of 1938. It had an impact from the beginning and went far toward the election of Aguirre Cerda through a Popular Front coalition. Since its principles closely conformed to those of the Radical party, the Radicals bought one third of the shares. The two men responsible for its initial success were Aníbal Jara and Manuel Muirhead. The former, a man of gargantuan size, with rough-hewn features, was forceful in polemics and his editorials were powerful. I knew him well and saw him occasionally later when he was the Chilean Ambassador in Washington during the first years of the Ibáñez administration. Muirhead was a pleasant man, less aggressive politically than Jara, and he was the director of the paper during my time. After their victory in 1938 the Radicals seemed to lose interest, and the paper suffered. When, independent of my government, I arranged for seven Chilean press men to work for two months on North American papers, *La Hora* was included along with the two *El Mercurios,* the *Ilustrado,* the *Imparcial* and *La Unión* of Valparaiso. The brother of Muirhead represented *La Hora.* His article on a press conference of Roosevelt's attracted the favorable notice of the President, who wrote me about it.

Another new paper, *El Debate,* was founded during my time in Chile. It was ably edited by Octavio Marfán and its philosophy was inspired in the principles of the Liberal Party.

In Valparaiso, *El Mercurio,* the sister paper of the one in Santiago and under the same ownership, is the oldest Spanish-language newspaper in South America, with a rich historical background. Its editor, Francisco Le Dantec, is a clever newspaperman with resourcefulness and a sense of humor. He was one of the young reporters I sent to the United States to work for two months on a paper there. He was assigned to the Boston *Globe,* where he made a fine impression.

La Unión, under the directorship of Alfredo Silva Carvallo, was and is noted for its courageous adherence to its principles. There were times when this courage was audacious, and for that reason all the more commendable. During the unfortunate visit of Perón, the Argentine dictator, he and his party assumed an attitude of supercilious condescension and hinted at the merging of Chile with Argentina under the benevolent government of the dictator. *La Unión* attacked him and his regime with brilliance and vigor. Silva was awarded the Cabot Prize for journalistic achievement a few years ago at Columbia University in New York.

Among the literary critics of the Chilean press two are conspicuously able. These are Ricardo Latcham and Hernán Díaz Arrieta, both professors at the university. These two critics have made literary criticism an art.

The culture and democracy of a nation may be gauged by its press. That of Chile is proudly free. Its personnel is of a high order. It is a staunch defender of the freedoms. I found the reporters dependable and honorable, and it was possible to talk with them off the record without fear of betrayal. In fourteen years I was never betrayed by one.

7

Among the magazines, it can be safely said that *Topaze*, as a periodical of political satire, is unsurpassed, if indeed, equaled, anywhere, and it has held that position for a generation. Its founder, and until recently its director, Jorge Delano, impressed me with his genius as an artist and satirist. He is one of the Delanos of the Roosevelt family who settled in Chile many years ago. Short but not dumpy, robustly built, his very pronounced features do not denote the humorist, since they give the impression of solemnity. He has told the story of the founding of the magazine in his immensely amusing autobiography. Beginning with inadequate capital, the dodgers announcing the first issue were printed on the back of an advertisement of some commercial product, which defrayed the cost, and they fluttered into the city from an airplane. It worked like magic, and three printings were necessary to meet the demand. To this day, *Topaze* has kept Chile roaring with laughter or indignation.

In its early days it fell foul of the government, since, contrary to tradition, it treated the President as a politician subject to criticism. These satires of the President and other politicians were not inspired by personal malice, since often "Coke," as Delano is affectionately called, had a personal admiration for many of his victims.

As a political cartoonist, "Coke" has few rivals. In poking fun at the politicians, exposing their fallacies, hypocrisies and failures, the words beneath the cartoon, put into the mouth of an uncouth, jeering *roto,* smack of the bitter wisdom of the London Cockney. These cartoons are an invaluable source for historians, since the comedy of the political history of the hour is a reflection of public opinion at the time. The collection of these cartoons by Ricardo Donoso, the scholarly director of the National Archives, re-creates the changing political scene through more than a generation. As sharp and stinging as the satire may be, the prodded politicians pretend to enjoy the wit, never miss the point, and laugh with the public, whatever their inner feeling may be. They usually pretend to an embarrassed delight in their own crucifixion.

The tumultuous and colorful career of President Arturo Alessandri Palma was a favorite subject for Delano's pen. Astounded by the audacity of the cartoons on the Chief of State, Alessandri was resentful, but in time he came to enjoy them.

Before I left Chile, Delano, while retaining an interest in the magazine, had retired, but under the new director, Gonzalo Orrego, the paper has lost none of its sparkle.

When invited to the United States as a guest, Delano spent some time in Hollywood, where he made a number of sketches of famous actors and actresses that were sold at a fair to raise money for the soldiers. Most of the monarchs of the screen were pleased, but Ronald Colman protested that he was made to appear too old. "Coke's" sketch of Charles Laughton as a fat man bearing no resemblance to a product of Savile Row rather shocked the actor, but he sent a note to Delano: "God forgive us, my wife says it is brilliant."

He worked rapidly. I sat for him once for a sketch for *El Diario Ilustrado,* and though he required not more than twenty minutes it was the best ever made of me. In recent years he has shown much talent as a portrait painter. He also finds time to act as a director of Chilean movies. A many-sided man, and every side artistic.

Among the numerous illustrated magazines, the best known

is *Zig-Zag,* which is quite similar in appearance and purpose to the *A.B.C.* of Madrid, which chronicles social events, with special emphasis on illustrations and feature articles on historical episodes and contemporary politics.

Nothing contributed so much to the embassy's understanding relations with the press as the trained newspapermen who served as press attachés. Since such relations were of the utmost importance during the war, special credit is due Lester Ziffren, whom I had known well in my Madrid days when he was with the United Press. Aside from being a master reporter, he was *simpático* to the Chilean press, and his close relations with it extended from the reporters to the editors and owners. He entertained them in his home in an atmosphere of informality and fraternity.

No position in an embassy can be more important than that of press or public-relations attaché. Noteworthy, too, among those who thus served during critical days was Dick Cushing, who later was to render valuable service in Havana.

XVI

The Road to Quillota: Summer Revels

When the wintry blasts, with snow and sleet, angrily attack the New Yorker, I can warmly recommend the Chilean summer for escape, since in December, January, February and March, the sun shines brilliantly, the nights are cool, and amusements are abundant. One thinks at once of Viña del Mar. It has been called the Biarritz of South America, though, familiar with both resorts, I found Viña more beautiful and with facilities for amusement equal to those of the French. When summer comes, the people of the *fundos,* who may have spent the spring in the country, leave their estates to enjoy the gaieties of the pleasant resort on the ocean. When one arrives by car in the morning and drives along the Avenue Valparaiso, the long street, with shops displaying finery in the windows, one is certain to feel the thrill of pleasurable anticipation on observing the promenaders—pretty women in gay flowered summer dresses, strolling with friends, some in truth in shorts and slacks, all gossiping animatedly over events in the Casino, perhaps, the night before, or the latest scandal, which may be malicious but is certain to be amusing. Throughout the summer months the town is crowded, the hotels filled, the pensions packed, but the experienced will have made reservations at hotels or have taken a furnished villa long before.

The more conservative Chilean families are apt to take quarters at the O'Higgins Hotel facing a small park or plaza, and it was there I preferred to lodge when in Viña, summer or winter, for even in winter, without the tumult and the shouting of the many in pursuit of pleasure, I found it attractive. The O'Higgins is a large hotel, excellently managed, with rooms of comfortable dimensions and sitting rooms adjoining the bedrooms if desired. The thick walls shut out the noise of the halls, when the night owls return in the wee hours from the Casino. The service is all that can be desired.

The tourists and the younger set are likely to prefer the Miramar, which I had seen being built on the edge of the sea one summer. No hotel could be more attractively situated. Directly on the water and resting on a rock foundation, it certainly is substantial. The cuisine is as nearly perfect as one could ask, since the restaurant is managed by two men who, in my Madrid days, had the best restaurant in that city. Being republicans, when Franco went in, they went out; and, establishing themselves in Paris, they were rapidly making their restaurant outstanding when Hitler went in, and they went out. Somehow they found their way to Chile, where the Nazi salute was neither fashionable nor imperative. Very often we would lunch at the Miramar, since one could look out of huge windows directly on the sea and across the water to a strip of land where tall trees swayed in the breeze. Then, too, the food was delicious—lobsters so famous that Buenos Aires would have taken them all if permitted, oysters small but tasty, crustaceans from Robinson Crusoe Island and congrio, a fish of great delicacy.

But the special feature of the Miramar is the very wide paved terrace reaching from the building to the sea, shut in by shrubbery and small trees in tubs. There, at teatime or at the cocktail hour, all chairs and tables are taken, and pretty women in gay colors, chatting and drinking beneath large striped sun shades, make a charming picture. Large rocks enclose a small portion of the sea for swimming. The pool is reached by going down a few steps from the terrace, where a small bar serves drinks to the swimmers.

At night many find their way to the Casino, a large edifice, which is much more attractive than the one I knew in Biarritz. If one wishes, extraordinarily good dinners may be had in one of the dining rooms. As the night advances, one may go to the upper floor to a night club, where entertainers furnish amusement, or one may dance, as most do. The gambling room is interesting. I never tried my luck, for I have never had any to try in games of chance, but it was intriguing to watch the expression on the faces of the players. The veterans, women as well as men, seemed nonchalant enough, since most could afford to lose, but sometimes it was apparent to me that some were playing in the hope of much needed gain. One night I watched an old woman, evidently in poor circumstances, as she tossed her chips on the table and saw them swept away. Women are among the greatest devotees, especially young women. I knew one who slept all day that she might play all night, and she was a nice girl with that one vice only. One year it was proposed to prohibit women from playing unless they could produce a written permit from their husbands. Clearly their lords and masters sought in this way to stop their losses, but the indignant clamor of the women, who rule Chile, forced the abandonment of the plan.

Facing the plaza, across from the O'Higgins, is the Viña Club, with a large garden where on summer nights the young and not so young are wont to dine and dance under the stars.

However, life in Viña is not all flirting, gambling, dining and dancing. Here is the Sports Club, where the polo players find their amusement, and under its auspices are the Sunday races on a fine course. From the grandstand one may watch the races or gossip with friends. Once a year comes the feature race, the Derby. There are great prizes for the winners, and huge sums of money are lost or won. The scene is animated, with the grandstand packed and with spectators parading back and forth between the stand and the track.

On the outskirts of Viña is a remarkable park, along with a large house that had been the owner's home when this was his *fundo*. The park is known as the Quinta Vergara and was bought by the town council from the family. Few tourists have ever heard of it. On entering the grounds one notices at first a long avenue of giant palm trees. But it is not the avenue of the palms that makes this park notable. Aside from the central clearing of the grounds, little hills and ravines have been left in their natural state, and, entering this thickly wooded section, one has the feeling of being in the wilderness, remote from humankind. After years of effort, trees from every climate and remote country have been planted. I once conducted through these grounds a group of congressmen from home who had an interest in horticulture, and they were astonished and delighted by the variety of trees from faraway places.

Within ten minutes of the town is Salitre Park, given to the city by a Chilean who had made his fortune in nitrate. Here, too, the hand of man has not marred the natural beauty. Driving through, one finds oneself on a narrow dirt road thrown into a cathedral twilight by the overarching of the great forest trees.

We will now retrace our steps to the town. One of the charms of Viña del Mar is in the beauty of the tree-lined streets and the varied architecture of the houses. Many have gardens of goodly dimensions shut in from the street by cement or brick walls or shrubbery, and over the walls flowers often overflow, within plucking distance of pedestrians on the sidewalk.

But to see the town spread out like a map, one must ascend the steep hill to the summer palace of the President of Chile. As we ride up the narrow, winding road we are startled by the unexpected appearance of a veritable medieval castle, patterned by the architect after the castles in Spain. Quite as startling as a novelty is a pretentious house by the ocean which is partly built over the sea, with one room looking down through a thick glass floor on the surging waters.

The summer palace of the President is set in extensive grounds, with charming walks and vistas, a tennis court and a long swimming pool fed with water piped from the sea. The house is dignified and impressive. Looking out the wide windows from inside the house, one gets the impression of being on an ocean liner, since the road below, between the house and the sea, cannot be seen. Numerous times I have attended luncheons and dinners on the terrace, which is the crowning attraction of the place. Dinners there in the light of a full moon, with the stars sparkling on the sea, are memorable.

One would go far to find a more picturesque drive than that from Viña to Concon. It winds around rocky heights on one side and the sea on the other, where huge volcanic rocks contend with the tides. All along this scenic highway are beaches, always gay with colorful umbrellas and with bathing beauties on the sands seeking a tan—perhaps. Unhappily, candidates, availing themselves of the rock surfaces on the hillside, use paint instead of chalk to blazon forth their names and virtues, and these remain through the years to remind the tourist that years before, some forgotten man was a candidate for the Senate. This abuse of a beautiful highway is an abomination and should be forbidden.

I have a special feeling for Viña del Mar because the municipality made me an honorary citizen in a formal ceremony. This was all the more flattering since nothing of the sort had been done since the Prince of Wales and the Duke of

Kent were made citizens during their visit. And yet we spent but two summers in Viña del Mar. After the social ordeal in Santiago we needed a change from people we met daily in the capital, and in Viña one encounters the same groups one sees constantly at dinners, luncheons and cocktails in the capital. One reaches a point where one relishes a cocktail when one craves it, and is eager to eat what one pleases and not whatever is offered, however delicious, and to lounge under trees in a steamer chair and read biographies, memoirs, novels and detective stories, with occasional excursions into Viña del Mar for lunch or dinner, or for tea or cocktails on the terrace of the Miramar, to gossip with a friend or to visit the excellent English colony library.

2

The war had forced us to abandon Zapallar as a summer retreat. I have often been fascinated and charmed by country roads leading through old towns. Many have written books about rivers, few about roads, which are so intimately identified with human life. The older they are, the richer they are in the romance of history. Nothing in the Roman Forum or the Coliseum evokes more vivid pictures of ancient Rome than the Appian Way. Time has passed that way and left its imprint.

At any rate, we came to love the road from Viña to Quillota. It delighted us because it was old, mellowed with history and went through a beautiful countryside, past well-ordered towns that have housed many generations, around verdant hills and past green pastures where the grazing cattle lift their heads to see us pass by. Cultivated fields, orchards and the vine offer luscious fruit and the juice of the grape. This road to Quillota has the serenity and dignity of its years.

I had first driven over this delightful road on the way to the Cavalry School in Quillota during our first summer. Thereafter we made the journey again to enjoy the feats of horsemanship and the remarkable Chilean horses, distinguished not only for their lines but for their extraordinarily high intelligence. They are easily trained and are as much attached to their masters as their masters are to them. Passing along the stables on our first visit, my attention was drawn to a horse looking out of one of the stalls. On reaching it, I found it as immobile as a statue and then learned that it was the famous horse that had thrilled thousands at Madison Square Garden in New York, where the Chilean teams were usually successful. This, then, was the celebrated "Chilena." When it met its death in an accident at the Garden, it was given a military funeral on Governors Island by the North American soldiers. When I saw it looking out of the stall on the familiar grounds, I had not yet heard that it had been taken back and mounted.

Chileans share the Englishmen's love of the horse. In my time in Chile there was another remarkable horse of the *carabineros*. Though in its twentieth year, it had remained young in spirit, retaining its zest for exhibitions of prowess. The most difficult jump in horsemanship contests is over very high rails, with a pool of water just beyond. Usually the horses are given a longish run as they approach the ordeal, but more than a few times I have seen them stop suddenly when they reached the jump, landing the rider over their heads into the pool, but finally they always made it. This gallant veteran of twenty scorned the run. It seemed to approach the ordeal slowly, with some deliberation—so slowly, in fact, that one was sure there would be no jump at all. Then, what seemed a miracle: as if by magic, the horse appeared to rise and float gracefully over the top with apparent ease. This timeless horse was named "Dax," and once I had the pleasure of pinning the ribbon of victory on its bridle. This was the horse always ridden by Colonel Lema in the Madison Square Garden contests.

During my time in Chile one of these horses made the highest jump ever made, taking the championship from Italy.

3

The town of Quillota has played a conspicuous part in Chilean history. It was near this town that Portales, the premier statesman of Chile, was murdered by some military officers. Longer than most towns, it clung to the old social customs, the dignified aristocratic traditions of the more courtly days. Joaquín Edwards Bello, whose column in *La Nación* I found charming, and who knew Quillota in his youth, wrote a beautiful, nostalgic article lamenting the recent change in the tone of the town. The houses face directly on the street, with gardens behind, and the atmosphere is Old Worldish.

Once we drove to Quillota for tea. I am afraid they are not specialists in the serving of tea in the restaurants there, but we may not have found the right place for the ceremony. Pepe drove us to an old hotel where we were told tea could be had. The age of the hostelry may be guessed from the stone at the entrance, worn deep with the feet of generations. We entered a court with a cobblestone pavement. Here, a very large palm tree, and in the center a murmuring fountain. Hanging about, a large number of bird cages; the birds, of many colors and varieties, were chirping merrily. The tea was bad, the toast was worse, but we found enough charm in the scene, with the rapturously singing birds and the murmur of the fountain.

We had become very partial to the road to Quillota when in 1946 our friend, Miguel Flores, kindly offered us his house on the edge of Limache, along this highway, and we accepted with joy. It was a new house, with all modern equipment, set within large grounds entered through a gate at the lodge. From the cupola of the gatehouse hung a rope, and the visitor, pulling it, rang a bell that summoned an attendant. Just behind the house was a well-wooded hill, immediately in front a beautiful swimming pool, and just beyond a large pergola from which one could look out over a rich valley to the town, though from the distance only the steeple of the church and the chimney of the brewery could be seen. Refreshing breezes on the warmest days fanned the pergola, where we had our meals. At night, when the air was chilly, we continued to cling to the pergola for our dinners, though toward the end we wore heavy coats and took blankets to warm our legs.

Some steps down from the house was a large vegetable garden, with peach and apple trees, and the friendly servants of our host brought us the fruit of the garden. In the morning our own staff plucked from the trees the famous large juicy peaches for our breakfast.

During the day we sat mostly in the pergola reading, listening to the chirping of the birds, the singing of crickets, enjoying the serene beauty of the valley spread before us. Patricia had been furnished with a horse and most days she rode about the countryside. One day she found herself on the grounds of an estate where a man on horseback smilingly asked whether she was one of his house guests. Noting her embarrassment, he hastened to add that his house was usually filled with guests and he really did not know all of them. Pat apologized for trespassing. "Not at all," said the man. "You may have the full run of the place. Ride here any time you wish." And that was typically Chilean too.

We were not much disturbed by callers, but Mr. Brett of the Macmillan Company of New York had written me that Kathleen Winsor, whose novel, *Forever Amber,* had created something of a sensation, was making a South American tour and would be in Chile. She and her husband, well known as a football star at the University of California, came to lunch and to spend the afternoon at Limache. She was a beautiful young woman, but I was impressed by her intelligence and her interest in the social and economic problems of the country. Never, she said, would she write another historical novel. She had read thirty memoirs, and on cards she had written notations on fashions, customs, weather, people—grueling work. Many have criticized her novel because she depicted an immoral or amoral society, but just how a re-creation of the time of Charles II can be written along puritanic lines and still be historically sound, no one has said. I thought her description of the epidemic a masterpiece of creative writing.

About this time, too, a group of beautiful girls from Hollywood, the Goldwyn Girls, making a tour of South America, paid us a visit at Limache. Our house was at the edge of the town and was reached in the last short stage over a dirt road that ended at our gate. While Limache proper was kept clean and orderly, the short dirt road to our place was neglected, and along the roadside grass and weeds had grown high. The day before the arrival of the cavalcade from Hollywood we were amused to find a small army of men at work mowing the weeds and grass and removing the debris. Hollywood had done it!

4

When, after two summers in Limache, the property was sold, we were forced to seek other quarters. We found a pleasant house with large grounds at Quilpue, fifteen minutes by car from Viña. For years Quilpue had been noted for the healing qualities of its pure air, found ideal for lung and heart ailments. Though but fifteen minutes from Viña, where fog and mist settles down almost every day until the sun puts it to flight at about ten o'clock, in Quilpue one looks up in the morning to fleckless blue skies, no fog or mist. This puzzled me, but the only explanation offered was that a hill between the two towns makes the difference, though the hill is not at all high.

The grounds were enclosed, and at night the gate was locked. The house was comfortable, the grounds filled with trees and flowers, and Quilpue, a bustling little city, was always animated and interesting. The scene at the railroad station when the many trains came in persuaded me that the station platform was a kind of *paseo,* since pretty young girls and ogling beaux were conspicuous on the promenade.

We lived on the grounds, having our lunch under the trees. A large swing, well shaded, was my favorite spot for reading. While shut in, we had no feeling of isolation, since adjoining our place was the Retiro Hotel, owned by the government, which was always filled. The grounds of this hostelry, with their winding walks and boxwood partitions almost a yard in width, were lovely for promenades. Across the narrow dirt road from our house was a small hotel run by refugees from Germany. There, in a large garden, literally filled with flowers, we had an occasional lunch. Then, too, we were entertained by the dogs of our place, two magnificent Irish setters and two small dachshunds. The affectionate relations between the setters and the little dogs were astonishing, and at night, when the air was chilly, the little ones always slept on the backs of the setters to keep warm.

With the sale of this house, also after two years, we were again forced to find other quarters, but we wished to remain on the road to Quillota. But, alas, there was no place to be had, and we spent the summer of 1950 in Viña del Mar, where we had a large brick house surrounded by an attractive garden. It was in the section favored by the English. The road in front was hard but unpaved, and the roomy houses set in beautiful gardens gave to this corner of Viña the impression of an English town.

5

The next summer we wanted to be back on the road to Quillota. Our consul-general in Valparaiso recommended a place in Villa Alemana, between Limache and Quilpue, though with some misgivings. "It is across the railroad tracks and beside an old abandoned quarry," he said apologetically. This had a dismal sound, but we visited the place, took to it instantly, and there we summered during our last three years.

The house in Villa Alemana was set in very large grounds enclosed by a brick wall six feet high. Of the two gates into the grounds the one we used, nearest the house, was forbidding from the outside, suggesting the grim entrance to a prison— all the more so because of the stern brick wall. I am sure that Kathryn Grayson and Howard Keel, the movie stars, thought this entrance grim when they made their wholly unintentional call. We had given a luncheon for them at the Miramar in Viña, and we had not been home more than an hour when our luncheon guests appeared. It was a comedy of errors. After the luncheon, the *intendente* of Valparaiso had given a cocktail party in their honor at a club in Villa Alemana. A dapper captain of the *carabineros,* who was a friend of mine, had been assigned as their escort. With the evident thought that the movie stars would not visit Villa Alemana without making a call on their Ambassador, and knowing nothing of the luncheon, the captain conducted them to their car after the cocktail party and entered with them. They supposed they were being taken back to Viña del Mar. When the car was stopped by the captain in front of the forbidding gate, which suggested a concentration camp, they were not sure whether they were being imprisoned or kidnaped. Kathryn Grayson asked where they were. "This is the place," said the captain. "Get out." Puzzled, if not alarmed, they got out, the gate was opened, and they found themselves in the garden facing their hosts of an hour before. They were flabbergasted, we were amused, everyone laughed, and we had another visit. Of the numerous movie stars I have seen, none has impressed me as more charming than Kathryn Grayson, our embarrassed visitor in Villa Alemana.

The forbidding appearance of the entrance near the house was deceptive. The house was comfortable and homey. In front, facing the garden, was a terrace leading down to a very wide grape arbor supported by cement columns and extending the length of almost two city blocks to the main gate, where the mailman rang by pulling a rope, and a servant went at a trot, followed or preceded by the dogs making the welkin ring. The vines of the arbor were heavy with huge grapes. We had tables, benches and steamer chairs under the arbor, and there we read and lounged throughout the day. After breakfast in the house we did not enter it again until after dark.

The "old abandoned quarry" contributed to our entertainment. Small boys played mountain climbing on its rugged sides. The day of our arrival we were amused to find a dozen goats lined up at attention at the top of the quarry, peering down with unashamed curiosity and evident displeasure upon us, and their periodic inspections left no doubt of their disapproval.

In none of our summer places did we receive such gracious attentions from the people and officials. The day of our arrival, my friend the captain of *carabineros* called to offer any service we might wish, and the mayor appeared with an official welcome. Since the place was on the outskirts of the town, the municipality installed arc lights around the wall.

Years before, the Germans, with an eye to beauty, had discovered the charm of the region and had settled there, giving the town its name, but the Italians had moved in, and there were two Italian clubs to which I was invited. The neighbors were friendly, and we were made to feel at home. Because of idle threats and the stoning of the Embassy Residence in Santiago by the communists, *carabineros* were assigned to patrol the walls, and after the condemnation of the Rosenbergs the number was increased.

The large grounds were thick with fruit trees—orange, lemon, peach, the juicy Chinese peach, plum, pomegranate, fig —and fruit for the table came freshly picked from the trees. An Italian and his wife, who tended the trees and their irrigation, lived in a neat little cottage on the grounds. Here, too, we had our dogs—two large ones and one small one which was extremely jealous of the larger ones and so devoted to us that when we left it stretched out on the terrace facing the door and refused to move or eat for two days. When the cool of the evening came this little codger would spring into my lap for warmth, and if the huge dogs approached it growled and snapped.

No matter how hot the day, when evening came the temperature dropped and a coat was necessary for comfort. It was when the sun went down that we would sit on the terrace and enjoy the sunset throwing weird lights on the stone hill of the quarry and watch the moon climbing in the sky. We made our usual excursions to Viña, returning laden with books, from the generous library of the British colony, which we read under the arbor.

One day the butler rushed to us in the garden with the startling announcement he had just heard on the radio that a baby had been born in the embassy garden. A young girl employed in a shoe factory was hurrying with her mother to the hospital, and, reaching the embassy, she told the *carabinero* on guard at the gate that she could go no farther. The officer took her into the garden to the lodge house, and there the baby was born. The newspapers ran lurid stories, with pictures of the lodge house. Patricia, my daughter, bought and gave the mother a complete outfit of clothing and asked the famous Marie Schultz of the Maternity Hospital to make weekly inspections of the child. "Well," said Marie, grinning, "we don't ordinarily do that, but it is not likely that many babies will be born in the embassy garden, so in this case I will." The mother named the child "America Patricia"; my secretary, Marcia Lindgren, being a Catholic, acted as godmother, and so it turned out well. I expected that *El Siglo,* the communist paper would insinuate that it was "not without reason" that the mother had the baby in my garden, but it was fairly decent, confining itself to the charge that we had "enticed" the girl to the garden to "force American citizenship upon a helpless child."

Many times through these three delightful summers I had to return to Santiago for a few days because of the negotiations of the Mutual Security Pact and the meeting of the Economic Council of the United Nations.

In recalling Chile, the remembrance of the road to Quillota through a beautiful countryside, where for seven years we summered, is vivid. The settlement of the country along this road so many years ago, the historical associations of its prosperous, well-ordered towns, the serene atmosphere of security and tradition, enter into its appeal. It is too bad that tourists, and especially those who appear with pen and pad to write their impressions of Chile, do not see this charming side of Chilean life.

XVII

Church and State

The separation of church and state in Chile was brought
about during the regime of Arturo Alessandri Palma without
any serious trouble, partly because of the toleration of the
venerable archbishop and partly because of the wisdom of
Cardinal Gasparri, the Foreign Minister of the Vatican. During my fourteen years, there was no indication of any clash
between the authorities of church and state. While the great
majority of the people are Catholics, the Constitution guarantees religious freedom and toleration, and other sects have
their churches. The English have their Church of England,
the other denominations have their Union Church and the
Jews their synagogue. The Catholics object only to attempts
from the outside to divert their people from their faith.

If I had had any doubt that Chile is a Catholic country it would have been wiped out on June 13, 1946, when I witnessed the emotional reception given the old archbishop, José Maria Caro, on his return from Rome after having had the cap of a cardinal put on his head by the Pope. The fact that he was Chile's first cardinal no doubt made the occasion all the more notable. He had been stricken with pneumonia in the Eternal City but had made a miraculous recovery.

Never have I seen such a popular demonstration of affection. The entire Diplomatic Corps joined the great multitude at the airport. The scene before the arrival of the plane was picturesque and colorful. The emotion of the crowd would have made it notable had there been nothing else, but there, with the dignitaries of church and state, were the *huasos,* the cowboys of the *fundos,* vivid in their gay *mantas,* seated proudly on their prancing horses, the scene all the more festive because of the gaiety of the colorful *mantas.*

When the cardinal descended from the plane the multitude roared its welcome home. He was hurried to an ornate carriage drawn by horses. Other carriages followed with the various functionaries, and, behind these, were men on horseback and on foot, and the procession moved slowly toward the cathedral.

The streets were packed. We were far back and a little late in reaching the cathedral, where we found a dangerous congestion. Our car was hemmed in by people and we were barely able to move even with the energetic assistance of the police. Even so, we would move a yard or so and then stop until the *carabineros* could force a passage. The crowd was in a friendly mood, laughing good-naturedly at our predicament.

Within the cathedral, built on the site of the first church in Santiago, we were impressed by the beauty of the scene. The figures of the saints were illuminated. Brilliant lights were thrown upon the altar. Flowers everywhere delighted the eye and gave their fragrance to the air. But even here the congestion was dangerous, and but for the quick action of some young men, a heavy marble figure on a pedestal would have crashed and injured those in the immediate vicinity.

Bishop Salinas delivered the sermon—one of moving eloquence—and then came the virile, vibrant voice of the cardinal, who was surrounded by the clergy. The *Te Deum* over, he moved up the aisle to greet the functionaries of state seated on a platform, and in the strong light thrown upon him, he seemed frail and ethereal, but he was smiling. The congestion at the door when we approached was threatening, and under the pressure of the crowd, the heavy door groaned in protest.

At length the cardinal reached his carriage. The people had now overflowed into the streets, and for blocks our car had difficulty making progress.

Having reached his house, the cardinal immediately drove to the country house of President Juan Antonio Ríos, who was dying, and for whose recovery the head of the church had asked prayers. This characteristic visit, so human and civilized, seemed an unspoken rebuke to the politicians fighting for the Presidency around the deathbed. Five years later I was to see a repetition of this tribute to Cardinal Caro.

2

The first two years of the 1950s in Chile were a bit boisterous, with the clacking of the poison-tipped tongues of contending politicians and with communist groups battling bravely to save the country from "Yankee bondage." Happily, there were gentler features to the Chilean scene. In January 1951, forty thousand people assembled in the National Stadium to pay homage to Cardinal Caro on the sixtieth anniversary of his induction into the priesthood. The Diplomatic Corps should have been represented on the occasion by my friend Monsignor Zanin, the nuncio, but on his insistence I was asked to speak in behalf of the corps. This was no doubt due to my warm personal friendship for the cardinal.

Church and State

Forty thousand looked down from the amphitheater upon an impressive pageant. In a large open space in the center of the field a platform had been constructed. A bugle sounded. Then, through the main gate into the grounds could be seen the red robe of the cardinal. Accompanied by a group of priests, he moved to the platform and ascended. From my seat among my colleagues I could see but could not hear; the spectacle was colorful, and with a touch of drama, when the priests who had accompanied the cardinal grouped themselves around the platform and from an underground passage on either side emerged a great number of monks and priests, who surrounded the frail little man. From the distance he seemed a mere speck.

Then into the field came a large wagon drawn by oxen and piled high with hay. It was surrounded by mounted *huasos* in their ornamental *mantas,* and with articles symbolical of the soil. These were joined by a detachment of the armed forces.

At length the cardinal descended from the platform in the center and, accompanied by the dignitaries of the church, walked to the amphitheater while forty thousand men, women and children cheered fervently. The eighty-four-year-old prelate carried his years gallantly, though, at length seated and in repose, he seemed tired, but not too tired to smile.

After almost an hour, Horacio Walker, Minister of Foreign Affairs, spoke, an amplifier carrying his words to the thousands so far away that their faces were but a blur. I followed with a tribute to the career which had begun humbly on a small farm and had been famous for its service to the poor, for its humane spirit of wisdom and toleration. In closing, it was my privilege to present to him, on behalf of the Diplomatic Corps, a magnificent silver plate bearing the signatures of all the ambassadors and ministers accredited to the Moneda.

Just before the last speaker finished, a deep purple twilight had fallen.

The scene was one of extraordinary beauty and not without a certain religious symbolism. The lights were then turned on, and the ceremony was over after almost three hours.

3

I formed both admiration and affection for Cardinal Caro from my first contact with him. Small, very slender and seemingly frail, he bore a strong resemblance to the Cardinal Gibbons I had known years before, since both, in their seeming frailty, appeared symbols of a soul. Both were tolerant, patriotic and politically wise. Half a century before, the doctors had given the young parish priest but a year or so to live, since he then had tuberculosis. As a lowly priest among the poor, he had gone about his ministrations cheerfully, as though pushing death aside. Somehow his life was spared, and now, at eighty-four, he was constantly in motion, sparing himself nothing. His voice rang out vibrantly in the great cathedral.

He invariably appeared at the crowded, jostling diplomatic receptions in high spirits, smiling and jesting. He stoutly refused suggestions that the church be used as an instrument in the struggle among political parties. When some would have had him snub Aguirre Cerda because he had been elected through the Popular Front coalition, he wisely sought the President's friendship, and the resulting relations of the two were beneficial to both the church and state.

Consequently he had the reverence of all political groups and classes. When accompanying Vice-President Wallace's car from the Military Club where he was lodged to the Moneda, my car was immediately behind that of the cardinal, and I witnessed a dramatic revelation of his popularity with the working class. I was startled by loud applause, and, looking for a reason, I saw that the cardinal's car was passing between rows of the labor syndicates, and the workers were giving him their tribute of affection because they felt he knew and understood their problems, since he himself was one of the people. The story is told that once when events vindicated his judgment on a controversial matter that could have aligned some elements against the clergy, he chuckled and said, "It was not for nothing that I was born a *huaso*." It seemed appropriate that in the assignment of his church in Rome it was in the section of the poor.

When he was in Rome to receive the cardinal's hat he narrowly escaped death. He had left Chile for Italy in the heat of the summer, and the cold and dampness in Rome had brought on pneumonia, which was serious at his age. When he was convalescing application was made to our military forces, still in Italy, for the use of a military plane to convey him as far as the United States, and his application was turned down. I learned of the incident through an article in the *Imparcial* appealing to me to intervene. I knew the refusal had come from some minor official who had no idea of the identity of the applicant, and I cabled Washington, which instantly ordered our military in Rome to grant permission, and a plane was placed at the cardinal's disposal. When I saw him first on his return to Chile and congratulated him on his safe arrival, he chuckled and said that I was responsible; he prodded me in the chest with his forefinger, a habit of his.

I think he won me first by his sense of humor. Despite the high dignity of his position it was possible to joke with him. I had observed that at luncheons and dinners he always took a cigar when cigars were passed, though I knew he did not smoke and took the cigar for some smoker in his office. Once when I was seated across the table from him I lighted a match and held it to him as he took the cigar. He was momentarily startled, and then he chuckled and spread his hands. Thereafter at public dinners or luncheons when cigars were passed I always took two, and, on leaving, I would go by him with a bored expression as though performing a routine, none-too-pleasant duty, and held out the second cigar, which he always took with a laugh. This routine became our standing joke.

He lived simply in the archbishop's palace, which had no

central heating, and if there was a fireplace I never saw it. I have sat in one of the rooms wrapped in a heavy overcoat and shivered, while the old cardinal in light dress seemed comfortable. Having lived in them since infancy, Chileans are used to cold houses. "These Chileans," explained a friend, "do not know what comfort is." But our ideas of comfort differ. I have found that Chileans often suffered from the warmth of the embassy.

4

Soon after reaching Chile I formed a close friendship with Father Gustave Weigel, S.J., a priest from home who had lectured at Catholic University, where he was popular with the students unaccustomed to humorous realism from their professors. He had a brilliant mind. His thinking was not on the surface but went deep. His eloquence was that of sober thought on fire. His popularity transcended religious lines that divided Catholics and Protestants. He was a prime favorite among the English and Americans. I found him hard to contact quickly, since he hurried from one engagement to another with such rapidity it was difficult to overtake him. He knew most phases of Chilean life intimately and I found him invaluable as a source of information about people and events. Nature had made him a clever diplomat.

During the war I heard him deliver a sermon, apropos of the times, that impressed me as extraordinary both in substance and phrasing. Since he has a delightful sense of humor and loves a joke, I was surprised to find, apropos of this sermon, that one of my jokes may have annoyed him. At the conclusion of the sermon, a number of people, all friends, were on the veranda of St. George College, where he had preached, and I approached him with the remark, made solemnly, that he had the most remarkable memory of any man I had ever known. He seemed puzzled. The audience drew closer. "Yes," I said gravely. "I followed your sermon closely and you did not deviate one word from the manuscript as I had handed it to you." The audience laughed. Some time later he told me I should not have said it. Astonished, I reminded him that everyone who heard had a sense of humor and knew I was joking. "Well," he said, "the British Ambassador heard it and the English have no sense of humor." I knew his remonstrance was another joke.

On the death of Roosevelt, the American colony and many of the British had a memorial meeting on the grounds of Santiago College, and Father Weigel was asked to deliver the oration. It was a masterpiece.

I thought it unfortunate for us that he should have been called home by his Order, since he not only served his church but his country too, and I had found him dependable in his interpretations of some phases of Chilean life. The communists had begun to intensify their activities, and he could well have been left on the firing line. He was sent to the Jesuit college at Woodstock, Maryland, where I found him on my return. Some of our enemies in Catholic countries try to create the impression that our priests are not superior, and since one example is worth a thousand arguments, priests like Father Weigel are the refutation.

5

Nothing has done so much to dissipate this false impression than the appearance in Chile in recent years of many young Maryknoll priests and those of the Order of Precious Blood from the United States. There was a theory centuries ago that the priesthood should hold itself aloof from the rank and file of the people, and there may have been a sound psychological reason that no longer exists. These young American priests go on the theory that there should be close personal contacts between the priest and the people.

These are keenly intelligent young men, very human in their contacts. I noticed that usually they were stationed in

regions of poverty and squalor, and that they did much to re-
deem the surroundings with a shovel and a broom. One group
built a small church with their own hands and greatly improved the appearance of the neighborhood.

More important and effective, they entered understandingly
into the lives of the underprivileged boys, mingling with them
in friendly fashion, entering into and directing their sports,
and thus winning their confidence and friendship. This was
something of a novelty in the experience of these youths. Soon
they were going without embarrassment to these cordial young
priests with their problems, and with the feeling that beneath
the priestly garb was an understanding of the problems of the
young. Picture the background: many of these boys lived in
squalor, with no visible prospect of improvement and with the
feeling that no one was interested in their welfare. They could
easily drift into a life of indolence and crime. These young
Yankee priests have heartened many and set them on the path
to a useful life. This was especially important since it was
among these drifting youths that the communists had made
inroads. These North American priests have met the communists on their favorite field of operation and have held the
enemy in check where they have not taken possession of the
field.

6

The work of Father Manning especially attracted my attention. He was attached to the official household of Bishop
Larraín in Talca. The community was overrun with parent-
less children ranging in age from six to seventeen, having no
homes, no shelter from the cold and rain, sleeping in doorways and under bridges. Utter neglect was preparing them for
lawless lives. The law had become an enemy to avoid. If there
was such a thing as the milk of human kindness they had not
seen it.

One bitter winter night a group of these, in sheer desperation, appealed to Father Manning, a Maryknoll priest, for shelter. No provision had been made for such a contingency, but the sympathetic priest could not refuse them refuge from the cold and rain, and he took them in.

That was the beginning of a remarkable experiment in Talca. The news spread among the waifs that there was someone who really cared, and they moved en masse upon the priest, who received them. Somehow he found places for them to sleep. No longer did they have to rummage in garbage barrels for food. He organized them into a City of Children and put them on their honor to observe the rules. Thus they organized their own court for the trial and punishment of the transgressor. They had their own judge, their own prosecutor, their own jury. Evidence was heard, verdicts were rendered, and the sentence was respected. One trial was interrupted by a culprit who rose to say he deserved punishment for committing an offense that might be taken as a reflection on Father Manning. A feeling of responsibility was created. Pride and self-respect had been awakened. In the summer Father Manning took them to a camp in the country near a body of water where they could fish, swim, cook their own meals and play games in which he took part. Soon trusted as a friend and benefactor, he was usually surrounded by these waifs he had taken from the doorways and the garbage barrels and set on the path to self-respecting manhood. His work became so famous that when boys of the street appeared in court after an arrest they were released to Father Manning. The plan of rehabilitation included the teaching of trades, and work was found for some on farms.

Twice I witnessed his appeal to children. An orphan's home had been established during the regime of President Ríos consisting of small cottages; to each was given the name of some country. I occasionally visited the one named after the United States and joined the children in Christmas dinners in their house. One day I offered them a party at the embassy. They cheered excitedly, but there were problems. Tranportation could easily be furnished, but how could one entertain thirty small children through an afternoon? I had heard that Father Manning was an expert in games of magic and I got him on the telephone. Would he make the trip from Talca and entertain the youngsters? He shouted his acceptance. The moment he appeared in the room with an air of jollity, he entered into the hearts of these children. They screamed their amazement and delight over his tricks of magic, laughed uproariously over his jokes, grouped themselves about him and plucked at his sleeve. The party was a grand success and we repeated it the next year, when Father Manning again gave it glamour.

7

His experiment in Talca was repeated on a larger scale in Santiago, but this was the work of a Chilean and included not only children who were shelterless but others as well. I had often heard people speaking with admiration of its creator, Father Alberto Hurtado, though I never met him. He was the nephew of the distinguished diplomat and statesman, Miguel Cruchaga, whose name is sprinkled through these pages. He was the first, certainly the foremost, to hear the imperative call to initiate action to prevent large numbers of children, sleeping under bridges and living on their wits, from degenerating into criminals outside the law. His ambitious project resulted in the organization of the Hogar de Cristo, which is a power for good.

Since Chile is a Catholic country where there is a separation of church and state, the visitor often asks if the system works without constant conflicts, and the answer is that it does.

It has seemed appropriate to take note, as I have, of the work of the Yankee priests in Chile, who, in rendering service to their faith, have reflected credit on their country.

XVIII

Cavalcade of World Celebrities

The popular impression in the United States that Chile is "so remote" is a manifest absurdity when one may fly from New York to Santiago in less than one day. The flood of visitors from North America was astonishing to me, since during my six years in Spain I saw comparatively few from home.

Winthrop Aldrich of the Chase National Bank headed the long procession of bankers, industrialists, businessmen and eminent educators from North America who came to lecture and observe. There was a colorful procession of generals, admirals and occasionally groups of congressmen and senators arriving in official planes. Among the generals were General John Hull, General George Brett and General Crittenberger; among the admirals, Halsey, Shafroth, Whiting and Train.

Unhappily, there were few writers and artists, thus giving the impression our enemies try to convey that ours is a purely materialistic nation with little cultural life. Among the leading novelists, only John Dos Passos appeared, and then only to pass through after a pilgrimage to Perón's Argentina. Quite a number of the celebrities of the screen visited Chile for pleasure. Douglas Fairbanks, Jr., was the only one of these who had a mission, since his visit was during the war, and his speech to the British colony was moving. He and his wife were guests at the embassy, and we found him serious and keenly alive to the significance of the war. Later Tyrone Power appeared, causing a flutter among his feminine admirers, and Bob Hope came to delight his followers with his wit and whimsey. Joan Fontaine called one day at the chancellery, and the girls in the office found excuses to trail through the reception room to see her, but when they found her wearing dark glasses that concealed her beautiful eyes they filed out muttering imprecations. Ruth Draper gave her impersonations at the Municipal Theater and later at my house after dinner.

The most fascinating to me was Jo Davidson, who came to make a bust of Aguirre Cerda for the gallery in Washington. I sat with him when he was at work on the bust and was astonished by the incredible rapidity with which he transformed a chunk of clay into a living likeness of his subject in one sitting, but his physical exhaustion at the end was a bit alarming. When, after several sittings, the bust was finished in clay, I exhibited it at the embassy and invited Chilean officials and the Diplomatic Corps to see it. A lady, given to ecstasies over works of art, who had never seen the President or me, swept up to the bust, registered delight and exclaimed, "What a perfect living likeness of the Ambassador!"

Jo Davidson, who was standing near pulling on his beard, remonstrated. "No, no, Madame. I am the Ambassador."

A bit confused, the lady lost herself in the crowd.

Davidson, more Gallic than the French, scintillated with

wit and humor. His mind and spirit had been molded during his many years in Paris.

One of our earliest visitors was Admiral Richard Byrd, returning from the South Pole. En route south, he had been
slightly injured in a storm, and he left his famous ship at
Puerto Montt and slipped into Santiago and to the embassy,
where he was our guest for several days. Since he planned to
slip away and join his ship before it arrived officially in
Valparaiso he became a problem, since he thought he could go
into town and shop without his presence being known. Somehow he escaped discovery, reached his ship and made his formal entry into Valparaiso. His visit interested the Chileans
later and he was cheered in the streets. Since he was a Virginian, with a marked admiration for beautiful women, I
gave him a dinner and ball, selecting the loveliest women—
not hard to find in Chile—and he danced that night until
dawn.

2

When informed from Washington that former President
Herbert Hoover would soon arrive on an official mission I
looked forward to the meeting with some trepidation since I
had been conspicuous as a critic of his administration and I
expected to meet a resentful man. Happily, I found him
mellowed by the years, friendly and pleasant. Prepared for a
possible snub, I drove to the airport to meet him, but when,
immediately on landing, he thanked me effusively for my treatment of his son when he was in Santiago, the ice was broken.

Though well into his seventies, the difficult air journey had
not tired him. His hair was white and he had aged much since
I had last seen him. I dined with his party that night at the
Carrera, and the next day I gave a luncheon in his honor with
thirty-two guests, including the Acting President of Chile,
and introduced him as the man "who had fed more starving

people than any other man in history." On his request, I attended his press conference. The communist newspaper had welcomed him with an insulting article describing him as "an ambassador of hunger." He assumed he would be questioned about it, and he asked my opinion of the reply he had in mind. He proposed to say that in the 1920s, when Russian children were dying of starvation like flies in autumn, he had headed a commission with ninety million dollars to furnish food, and that, on leaving Russia, he had been presented with a silver—or was it gold?—plaque with a fulsome expression of thanks and bearing the signatures of Stalin and all the hierarchy of Moscow. He would mention this and ask if he had been an emissary of hunger then. I thought the reply would be perfect if he said it with a smile. But such was his hatred of communism that instead of stopping then, he launched into a general denunciation of communism everywhere, and the longer he talked the madder he got, and the faster he swung his glasses by their cord. Later, when I drove him to the airport on his departure, he told me that the public-relations man with him had severely scolded him.

In August 1946 I drove to the airport to meet Admiral Halsey, one of the heroes of the war in the Pacific. I thought he looked the part history assigned him. Slender, and graceful in his bearing, his features were those of a fighting bulldog. His hair was iron gray. His most noticeable feature was his eyes, which were gray in color, cold, penetrating, except when he smiled, and then they beamed with good humor. His voice was strong, his manner simple, and he exuded charm. He was received by the high functionaries of state and given the military honors due his rank. Unhappily, there seemed to be no end to the round of entertainment for him, but only once did I notice that he was suffering from strain. When he placed a wreath on the monument of O'Higgins and had to stand at salute through the long national anthems, I noticed that his hand was shaking violently. Evidently embarrassed and assuming that I had noticed, he said at the close that this affliction was confined to stiff ceremonial occasions, and he supposed it was an aftermath of the tension in the Pacific war.

Among all the functions in his honor, I am sure he enjoyed most the simple buffet dinner at the home of Commander Weaver, my Naval Attaché. This was informal and charming, as all the Weaver parties were. Here he could relax and joke with the Chilean officers and their wives. One of the officers sat at the piano and played and sang the then famous song, "Halsey and Nimitz and Me," with the party joining in.

3

Two distinguished American visitors rendered a service to their country in war days. In the spring of 1943, in the midst of the war, Henry Wallace, Vice-President of the United States, visited Chile as a deputy of the idolized Roosevelt. To Chileans, in sympathy with our cause, he was the symbol of our leadership in the struggle for the preservation of democratic institutions, and this goes far to explain the tremendous enthusiasm that greeted him everywhere. But he had personal qualities that contributed to his popularity. At the airport, when he descended from the plane, his hair falling over his forehead, his suit sadly rumpled, the astonished crowd cheered. As we drove between solid ranks of men, women and children from the airport to the Military Club, where he was lodged as the guest of the government, he received a continuous ovation; and when he appeared on the balcony of the club and faced the great throng packed dangerously close together, the greeting had an emotional quality. From that moment, and throughout his visit, such ovations continued. A hundred thousand people listened to him at the stadium and cheered lustily; and at the Hípico race course, when he passed through the third-class section the reception was especially fervent. Part of this was inspired by his association with the United States, foremost in the struggle against Hitler; some to his association with Roosevelt; but much was due to his own personality and manner. The mass of the people, thinking of the United States as the most powerful of nations, was astonished by his simplicity. I noticed numerous incidents that brought gasps of astonishment. Passing through a factory under the ciceronage of state dignitaries, his attention was attracted to an intelligent workman at a machine, and he left his party to speak with the artisan. The latter, at first startled, was soon at ease as his visitor plied him with questions about the machine. The conversation lasted for some minutes while the dignitaries waited impatiently. That day I drove him to the country house of President Ríos for lunch, and whenever we came to a group of farm workers lined along the road, to satisfy their curiosity, Wallace had the car stopped so that he might engage them in conversation about their work. It required but a moment to put them at their ease when they found he was intelligently interested in farming.

I accompanied him in the President's private railroad car on the journey to the south. The train reached a tiny hamlet after midnight and stopped for water. I was awakened by the blare of horns and drums. Wallace had retired, but he appeared at the open window in his pajamas to thank the musicians and to shake their hands. This was an unscheduled incident. The musicians were not artists, and their instruments not the best, but their hearts were right, and I thought the incident touching.

I was surprised by the precautions taken by both my government and that of Chile, since, in addition to the Secret Service men sent from Washington to guard the Vice-President, those of Chile were added. An engine preceded the train as a precaution against some possible obstruction on the tracks. I was in the presidential coach with Wallace, occupying one of the two bedrooms, and I was amazed to find one of our Secret Service men staying up all night in the lounge on guard. However, these were war days when hates were hot.

We had taken the train after a memorable luncheon given by the Agricultural Society, the oldest in South America, on the estate of an old family, where a stone mansion suggesting a French château, once occupied by the owners, stood in grounds shaded by mighty forest trees of great age. President Ríos and other guests had arrived by special train. We lunched under the trees on a lawn of velvety green. Suddenly, through the forest aisles, came two antique wagons drawn by oxen and filled with beautiful girls in the gay costumes of long ago, with young men playing guitars, all singing sentimental songs of another generation. Immediately in front of our table a platform had been set up where the cueca was danced by experts in the art, a beautiful Chilean girl sang "Old Black Joe" with enough feeling to moisten eyes, and the popular entertainer Molinare sang his improvised satirical songs, with people in the audience his writhing victims. He was a genius of sorts and deservedly famous among the Chileans.

It was here that the Agricultural Society presented Wallace with a gold medal bearing his name and the inscription "Gentleman Farmer." I noticed the Vice-President squirm. In an undertone he said to me, "Beautiful—but can you imagine what my political enemies could do with that inscription?" He meant, of course, that at home the "gentleman farmer" is a dude farmer whose hands are never stained by the soil.

We reached Santiago a scant hour before my dinner for Wallace at the embassy, to which the President and the highest officials of Chile were invited. The most stubborn and yet amusing diplomatic problem that faced the embassy was the insistence of Wallace that he would wear a black tie at dinners, though the most rigid protocol prescribed a white tie at all dinners attended by the President. I exchanged a number of telegrams with Wallace en route begging him to comply, but he was adamant. The President had planned a dinner for him—but there was that damned black tie! At length Ríos decided to give a luncheon instead of a dinner, but in the end he joined his guest in kicking protocol out the window and he came to my dinner with a black tie.

The dinner at the embassy was to be followed by a reception, and the guests were arriving before we left the table. Again I was puzzled by the extraordinary precautions demanded by the Secret Service. Seven hundred outstanding people had been invited, but none were to be admitted to the grounds without producing their invitations at the gate, where police officers were stationed. At the door to the house a *carabinero* stood, with a Secret Service man just inside. The Secret Service men of both nations mingling with the others were indistinguishable from the guests. It seemed an absurd precaution until a little later a ranking American official attending an international conference in Geneva took his "taster" along as a precaution against poisoning. Perhaps we were entering the Period of the Great Fear when Wallace was visiting Chile.

The President's luncheon at his charming country place was free from protocol and delightfully informal. A rich Chilean soup, baked corn wrapped in corn husks, the incomparable Chilean lobster, delicious Chilean fruit with Chilean wines and French champagne—such the food and drink. After lunch, Wallace was presented with a beautifully carved saddle, a spirited horse was brought to the lawn and he was tauntingly invited to prove his prowess as an equestrian. With the company looking on, Wallace mounted the prancing horse easily and put it through its paces, to the amusement and delight of his audience.

It was a multiplicity of things like this that rendered signal service to the United States in war days, making new friends and warming the old ones.

4

It was just before this that another distinguished North American visitor made a notable contribution to a better understanding between the two peoples. For years our enemies, through ignorance or malice, had created the impression with many that ours is a godless land of unbelievers, given to the persecution of the Catholics. Very few realized that close to thirty-three million Americans are not merely Catholics but more meticulous in the performance of their religious duties than others of the faith in Spain and some South American countries. When war conditions made excursions to Europe all but impossible, great numbers of Chileans made their first visit to New York, and many of these, devout Catholics, expressed to me their astonishment when on attending mass at St. Patrick's Cathedral in New York they found it crowded with as many men as women.

It is not surprising, therefore, that the announcement that a North American cardinal was to visit Chile was sensational in some quarters. I was on vacation in Zapallar at the time of the arrival of Cardinal Dougherty of Philadelphia on the *Santa Lucía.* I had arranged with my friend Monsignor Aldo Laghi, the nuncio, to meet the cardinal in Valparaiso when he arrived and to return to Santiago and open the Embassy Residence for a luncheon in his honor. We drove the cardinal to his ceremonial call on President Aguirre Cerda at the summer palace in Viña del Mar. Since the President had been elected by a Popular Front coalition, I suspect the cardinal thought him something of a "red" and expected a very formal reception and cold courtesy. Instead, he found a very human person who received him warmly and offered the Presidential railroad car to convey him to Santiago on the morrow.

The next morning when I went to the station to meet the train, I found a large crowd assembled to see an American cardinal from the land of the unbelievers, as many thought. When he stepped from the coach a roar of applause greeted him. The government had ordered out four ornate state coaches to convey the cardinal and his party to the Carrera Hotel. Each coach was drawn by four horses, and mounted police rode, with drawn swords, on each side and in the rear. Crowds in the street cheered his progress. The old cardinal, with whom I rode, was as delighted with the pageantry as a small boy with his first pair of red-top boots.

The next day I had thirty persons to luncheon, including ministers of state and high-ranking ecclesiastics, among whom was Archbishop Caro, soon to be made the first cardinal of Chile. It was all the more pleasant because it developed that the cardinal and the future cardinal had been students in Rome at the same time. Among the diplomats invited was Sir Charles Orde, the British Ambassador. "I am glad you invited the British Ambassador," the Irish-American cardinal said to me. "It gave me an opportunity to tell him that my sympathy is with the English in their gallant fight for preservation."

Someone had told him that I had interrupted my vacation and opened the embassy for his entertainment, and the next day at the luncheon at the nuncio's he expressed his appreciation. I wrote Roosevelt that the cardinal had rendered a very great service in an interview with the press in which he disabused the minds of some confused Chileans as to the status and treatment of his church in the United States. He enjoyed his brief visit, despite his age and weight. I drove to Valparaiso to see him off.

5

During these years numerous Englishmen of distinction visited Santiago. Early in the war Lord Willingdon, erstwhile viceroy in India, headed a very large delegation of English industrialists and bankers on what appeared to be a purely economic mission having little to do with the war. The former viceroy was an old man, very tall and erect, and while his wife hovered about him in an effort to spare him as much as possible, she got no co-operation from him. I saw a great deal of the members of the mission, and it was soon clear that they were mostly of the Chamberlain segment of the Conservative party and not partisans of Churchill, then the idol of the English people and universally acclaimed. I was momentarily surprised that my expression of admiration for the man I had respected for years as orator and writer was received a bit coolly. I knew, of course, that the Conservatives had been dead set for many years against the advancement of Churchill to the post of Prime Minister. Just what Willingdon's feelings were I did not know, but in a conversation with him I thought his admiration for the great genius was a bit restrained. He conceded his brilliant leadership in the war, while admitting that he had differed widely with him on India. Then he added: "Just now he is the indispensable man, but in peacetime he would be impossible as Prime Minister."

"Why?" I asked.

"Because he is undependable," was the startling reply.

I wondered why in the piping days of peace when the Empire was flourishing like the green bay tree, without a shadow in the sky, he should be "undependable" but when the Empire was fighting for existence with its back to the wall this "undependable" man should become the "indispensable" man. But the viceroy did not elucidate.

He was a very interesting man, friendly and bubbling with fun, and at an intimate dinner at the British Embassy where the talk ranged from war and politics to books and plays, I got another impression of him.

None of his party had seen Charlie Chaplin's *The Dictator,* since it had been released after they left England, and while it had not yet been shown in Santiago I was permitted to show it after my dinner for Willingdon, and the entire mission was invited to see it. It did not seem funny to them. Bombs were falling on London, and Willingdon remarked that "Goering and Hitler are not comic figures with the English today."

I was impressed by the number of leading English statesmen who visited Chile at this time; all the more impressed because those of my country did not show an equal interest. Especially interesting to me was the visit of a distinguished leader of the Liberal party, Hore-Belisha, whose career I had followed from the time he was one of the coming young men in English politics. I had been interested too by his policy in the Ministry of War aimed at making the army a little more democratic. I was familiar with some of his speeches in the House of Commons. When he was in Santiago he called at the house, and I gave a dinner in his honor. His wife, a very clever woman who had but recently been released from a Nazi prison, was with him. He was a delightful conversationalist, and I found myself more in accord politically with his views than with those of the Willingdon mission.

Quite a different type of British statesman was Sir Samuel Hoare, then Lord Templewood, who also found his way to Santiago. I had some prejudice against him and Laval because of the agreement that gave consent to Mussolini's war on Abyssinia; then, too, he had been sent as Ambassador to Spain to deal with Franco, who was supporting the Axis to the full extent of his capacity, and I assumed that Hoare had been on friendly terms with the dictator. Thus are we deceived by superficial appearances. At a dinner for him at the British Embassy in Santiago, when I had a full hour with him alone, I got a different slant on his career. He talked frankly about his mission to Spain and his problem there. He said he had never seen Franco when he had not been flagrantly insulted, but the nature of his mission made it necessary for him to bear the insults in silence. I gathered that the major object of his mission was to prevent, if possible, the granting of permission to the German Army to cross Spain to Gibraltar. In this he succeeded, but whether this would have been probable had the terrain made possible the provisioning of the Germans may be doubted.

I had thought of Hoare as a rather heavy man with hanging jowls, but I found him slender, with the face of a student, an ascetic, his voice soft, his manner intimate and ingratiating. I have never had a more interesting conversation with any man. It was quite evident that there was no love lost between him and his American colleague, Carlton Hayes, who attacked Hoare in his book. The British diplomat found Hayes in complete accord with Franco.

It was clear to me that the English have a more intelligent

conception of the importance and significance of South America than we. Still another visitor was English statesman Lord Reading, whose position in the English ministry was similar to that of our Undersecretary of State. He was then serving under Anthony Eden. I had him to a luncheon. He interested me because he was the son of his brilliant father, the first Lord Reading, the statesman and one of the greatest trial lawyers in England in former years.

Another Englishman, once a Liberal member of the House of Commons but better known as the brilliant author of *The Second Empire* and *Palmerston,* spent a few days in Santiago. This was Philip Guedalla. He had no official mission but he called at the house. He was of medium height, robust but not heavy, his large round face almost somber, his manner serious, and though his conversation on English politics and world conditions was most interesting, it lacked the color and the sparkle of his written prose.

6

Frenchmen of world distinction in the cultural field frequently made visits to Santiago, and I was delighted to see one of my favorite biographers, with whose books I was familiar, for most of them were in my library at the embassy. This was André Maurois. I had read and reread his clever biography of Disraeli, his books on Shelley, Byron, and Châteaubriand. I had a delightful evening with him after dinner at the home of the Agustín Edwards. I was then working on my biography of Pierre Vergniaud, in my opinion the supreme orator of the French Revolution, with only Mirabeau as a rival, and I found Maurois interested in my project. On the publication of the book he reviewed it for *The New York Times.* I found him as scintillating and amusing as his brilliant books. A man of medium height and slender, he is easy and graceful in his manner, his bright eyes sparkling and revealing his keen sense of humor. He inscribed two of his books for me, and of one inscription I am rather proud: ". . . who, though a diplomat, still has a sense of humor."

Then, too, came Italian statesmen. When Chile resumed diplomatic relations with Italy after the war, with a friendly ambassador in its embassy negotiating for the settlement of a large Italian colony of farmers in Chile, two high officials of the Italian Government, Salvador Aldisio, Vice-President of the Senate, and Giuseppe Brusaco, the Under-Minister of Foreign Affairs, made a visit to Santiago. Though Mussolini had gracelessly dragged the peace-loving Italians into the war against democracy as the subordinate partner of Hitler, I knew that the sad adventure had not had the approval of the Italians, whom I like. I therefore gave a large luncheon for the Italian statesmen. Because the most distinguished Chilean of Italian blood was the former President, Arturo Alessandri Palma, I seated him across the table from me as co-host, with the visiting Italians on either side of him. I spoke briefly in praise of Italy's democratic trend and institutions, and Brusaco eloquently replied. Before leaving Chile, he sent me an inscribed copy of his beautiful speech at the luncheon.

7

Nor did royalty find Santiago too "remote" to reach. The Infanta Maria Christina, daughter of Alfonso XIII of Spain, appeared in the city quietly, and, after a few days, as quietly left. There was scarcely any publicity. I met her at a very small cocktail party in the Spanish Embassy. Tall, slender, graceful, vivacious, she bore a resemblance to her mother, the Queen, in her younger years. I found her conversation interesting but do not feel at liberty to record it. As I was going with her to the dining room, we passed a large painting of a gay scene in the royal palace in Madrid in the days when the monarchy was in full flower. With a shrug, she called my attention to it in passing. "And now!" she said.

Prince Bernhard von Lippe, consort of Queen Juliana of

Holland, spent several lively days in Santiago thoroughly enjoying the entertainment while sighing over the demands of
protocol and the tiring procession of formal functions. He is
described by Ilisabetta Cerruti, in her pleasant book, *Ambassador's Wife,* in his pre-marriage days in Berlin, as a "very
handsome young man who used to attract general attention by
virtue of his grave charm and distinguished manner." He was
a very masculine type, but not noticeably "handsome," and
his charm, as revealed in Santiago, was hardly a "grave
charm." On the contrary, it was quite gay. He told me an
amusing story of a state visit to a Scandinavian capital where
he was exhausted by the entertainment. Finding a short break,
he had thrown himself upon the bed in the palace where he
was lodged. Footsteps in the hall outside his door gave warning of the approach of a servant—or so he thought—and, in
irritation, he called out, "Well, what the devil is it now?" A
moment later he was shocked to find the King in the door-
way!

I have mentioned these many visits to point out the absurdity of the idea we Yankees have that Chile, with all its charm
and beauty, is remote.

XIX

"To Educate Is to Govern"

It is not incomprehensible to me that there was strong opposition to the technical education agreement I had negotiated with the Minister of Education, since it was mistakenly understood to be an attempt on our part to take over and revamp the educational system of Chile. Had such a thought been in our mind I would have advised Washington of its impertinence. The Chileans take pride in their educational system. Chile was the first country in South America to have a normal school for the training of professional teachers. Primary education is compulsory.

The Chilean system is patterned more on the French than on the North American model. The examination for admission to the teachers' corps is thorough and rigid. The elementary course in the schools includes the study of Spanish literature, history, geography, mathematics, music, manual training and art, with some home economics for the girls. As a rule the two sexes do not mingle in the same classroom until they reach the universities, where co-education is accepted.

The Liceo, the secondary school, covers six years and is more intensive and comprehensive than the pre-university high schools in the United States. The curriculum includes philosophy, literature, chemistry, logic, history, psychology, political economy, civics, biology.

Thus the graduates of the Liceo would be qualified to enter at least the sophomore year in the average North American college. In talking with these young people of the Liceo I was impressed by their maturity.

The fly in the ointment comes from the financial inability of the state to pay adequate salaries to well-trained teachers and to maintain properly the physical equipment of the schools. Many of the buildings are old and crowded. This, however, is quite as true in the United States.

In visiting many of the Chilean schools, I have been impressed by the young people's eagerness for learning. At one school featuring manual training I was astonished by the technical skill of the young students and their imagination and resourcefulness.

2

Foreigners stationed in Chile often inquire about private schools. Among those for girls, established eighty years ago, with North American teachers, is Santiago College. It has been famous for many years in neighboring nations. Beautifully situated in the refreshing greenery of Providencia, with its colorful gardens, its attractive campus, its impressive buildings, some vine covered, it is one of the show places for tourists. Elizabeth Mason, of Goucher College, Baltimore, was the principal during my fourteen years in Chile. Trained as a teacher, eminently qualified as an administrator, she has helped the school make steady progress. It maintains the most friendly relations with the government and enjoys the good will and support of the Chileans who comprise the greater part of the student body. This is drawn from both the aristocracy and the middle class in both Chile and surrounding countries. The school has been thoroughly established for generations in Chilean life, and I have seen old grandmothers, who had attended years before, at commencements to witness the graduation of their grandchildren. Consequently much sentiment attaches to the school.

3

Chile is predominantly a Catholic country, and many of the young girls attend the schools of the nuns. The French convent schools were long preferred by the aristocracy. During my first year in Chile a large group of nuns arrived from Philadelphia and founded the Villa Maria Academy. This was due in large measure to Monsignor Aldo Laghi. He had observed the brilliant success of a school in Lima conducted by the Sisters of the Immaculate Heart of Mary, whose mother house was near Philadelphia. The Lima school became famous under the direction of Mother Cornelia Higgins. The nuncio set his heart on having a similar school with American nuns in Santiago, and he succeeded in interesting the Sisters in opening a school in Chile. In the initial period Mother Cornelia was a tower of strength. She had initiative, resourcefulness, the qualities of dynamic leadership, and she was a master of administrative details and organization. From the moment of its founding the demand for admission was far beyond the capacity of the school, but as the demand increased the facilities were extended, and when I left Chile a thousand students were enrolled. I had delivered the first two commencement addresses, which gave the impression that I could manage to get students in, and I was constantly importuned by parents to have their children admitted!

The course of study at Villa Maria is patterned largely on the high-school course in the United States. Except in the study of Spanish and Chilean history, the teaching is in English. The school ranks so high in the esteem of the government that when Mother Cornelia left she was given the Order of Merit. Mother Geraldine, who succeeded her, carried on along the line of her predecessor with success. These nuns were very kind to me, and the school is one of my pleasant memories of Chile.

4

Among the private schools for boys, the Grange has been famous for many years. It prepares boys of English families for admission to English colleges and universities, and the training is along traditional English lines. Its excellent teaching has attracted many children and American students as well. Perhaps it can be described as a little Eton. The campus and buildings of the Grange are both adequate and attractive. The boys wear the school uniform, but even without this means of identification their carriage, bearing and manner would leave no doubt.

Until recently there was no North American school for Catholic boys. One was established in 1935 but it got off to a bad start, and Father Weigel, the American priest I mentioned earlier, arranged with Bishop O'Hara to interest some congregation. The Congregation of the Holy Cross, with headquarters at Notre Dame University, responded. In 1945 the reorganization of St. George began under the direction of Father William C. Havey, and on his resignation because of ill health, Father Alfred Send took over, arranged for a larger building and increased facilities. An attractive site was purchased and a large building erected. Under the direction of

Father Theodore Huard, with the assistance of fourteen members of the Congregation of the Holy Cross, the college has flourished.

St. George is a combination of grammar and high school. In the grammar school the instruction is in English and in the high school in Spanish. The boys wear natty gray uniforms, not much different from those of the boys of the Grange. The faculty is composed of thoroughly trained young teachers bubbling with enthusiasm. One bitterly cold day I attended the dedication of the new building and spoke with the Minister of Education.

5

We now come to the universities, of which Chile can be proud. The University of Chile was founded in 1738. The portraits of the rectors in the office of the president reflect the flowering of the Latin-American mind. Though the origin of the university goes back to 1738, it has undergone many fundamental changes to meet modern conditions and requirements. Andrés Bello, a man of the widest culture and scholarship, introduced the spirit of the academy into political life and founded the university of today. Men like Bello and Barros Arana, another rector, certainly made major contributions. During my time in Chile the rector was Juvenel Hernández, who was to serve for twenty years. In addition to his high standing in intellectual circles, he was politically prominent, like his greatest predecessors. He was frequently mentioned for the Presidency of the Republic. He was the Radical party's "scholar in politics." As a speaker he was both forceful and graceful, his speeches scholarly and in good taste.

The university is housed in a large stone structure on the Alameda in the heart of the city. Unhappily, there is no campus to soften the approach, and one enters directly from the street. Like so many public buildings in Santiago, it is in-

adequately heated, and once I spoke there wrapped in an overcoat, but the Chileans do not mind.

The dominant tone of the university is liberal. Because of
its continental reputation, students are drawn from all the
surrounding countries. In the schools of medicine and law the
most successful lawyers and physicians take time from their
practice for regular lectures. Until recently the preference of
young men was for the law, but many have shifted to engineering and architecture, since the legal profession is
crowded.

All the different schools of the university are not grouped
together in the main building but are scattered in several
buildings in the neighborhood.

6

The Catholic University, also on the Alameda, is an impressive stone building. It was founded in 1888, though this
calls for an explanation. The university of colonial days, the
San Felipe, was founded in 1756 but was suppressed almost
a century later in accordance with the Napoleonic idea that
the state should have a monopoly on education. When a plan
for a Catholic university was urged upon Don Mariano Casa-
nova, who had become archbishop, he accepted it and announced the founding of the university in June 1888. The
project might have failed but for two men of dynamic energy,
Larraín Ganderillas, the first rector, and Don Abdón Cifuentes,
who directed and taught in the law school later.

The first building was destroyed by fire within three years;
new quarters were found and were occupied until 1918,
when the present building was constructed. Despite discourage-
ments, the university has prospered.

In 1920 the direction of the university passed to Don
Carlos Casanueva, the new rector, and for thirty-two years
the story of the university may be written around this quiet

and yet energetic man. I met him soon after my arrival, when he invited me to speak, along with Miguel Cruchaga, the statesman, on the observance of the Pope's birthday. The reason for the invitation was that very similar appeals for peace had just been made by President Roosevelt and the Pope. After that I saw him many times. Small in stature, slight in figure, seemingly frail, his appearance was deceptive since he was tireless in his activities. He was very simple in his taste and dress. He was ideally fitted for developing the excellent relations now existing between the two universities. Very winsome in manner, unpretentious, modest, courteous, kindly, he impressed his personality on the community. He pressed forward with his work persistently but with so little clamor that his method was once described by a friend as that of "seemingly disorderly efficiency." Though almost eighty and not in good health, he never failed to appear at crowded receptions at the embassy. Worn down by labors and bowed by his age, he retired the year I left Chile, but his name is written indelibly in the history of the university.

7

Driving along the coast from Valparaiso to Viña del Mar, one's attention is drawn to an impressive building on a high hill off the highway, and one learns that it is the University of Santa Maria. The neo-Gothic building of stone is architecturally beautiful.

The story of this fine technical school is colorful. It came from the bequest of a picturesque and eccentric manipulator of the stock market in Paris, who, gambling in sugar, made and lost more than one fortune. This was Federico Santa Maria, a native of Valparaiso. Having lost a fortune, he set himself to master all the secrets of the sugar market until he could foresee the size and value of each year's crop, and, with this advantage, he mowed down all rivals and amassed another fortune. His methods were so daring that they were once denounced in the French Chamber of Deputies, but this was no embarrassment to him.

In later life, grown more eccentric, he is pictured as living drably, almost in an attic, in the Rue de l'Opéra in Paris. His work desk was his bed. To save the cost of stationery, he wrote some of his letters on the backs of old envelopes. Having no family to provide for and recalling the poverty of the very poor in his native city, he finally evolved a plan to build a university where young men of promise could be given technical training that would not only lift their status but render a real service to Chile.

Whether the idea germinated in his mind or was planted there by a distinguished friend I do not know, but he did consult Agustín Edwards, long Chilean Ambassador in London. It is difficult to understand the relations of the two men, one something of a miser living in garretlike quarters, and the other surrounded by luxury and a favorite in the most fashionable society in Europe. It is a reasonable assumption that it was Edwards who planted the idea in Santa Maria's mind of leaving a part of his fortune for the building of a technical school. At any rate, the money was bequeathed, and Agustín Edwards was made the executor to carry out the plan.

Impressed in his travels with the superiority of the technical schools of Germany, Edwards visited them all, studied their methods and arranged for teachers. Meanwhile, the money had been so invested that he had been able to construct the building without touching the principal. The university was named for the donor. Nineteen German professors and lecturers were engaged, and the finest German equipment was provided.

The unique feature was the provision that penniless young men of undoubted ability were to be given free tuition. So thorough is the training that, on graduation, the graduates are in demand by industrialists.

I was strongly attracted to this university because the greatest need of Chile is technical education and also because of my admiration for Agustín Edwards. Soon after his retirement from the embassy in London, he returned to Chile, an old and tired man in ill health. A very few days before his death he came to see me regarding the university. He asked my help in getting some North American professors. In a sense, the university is his monument. If it was the purse of Santa Maria that furnished the money, it was the brain of Edwards that actually made the university.

8

Another great university, that of Concepción, has been described in another chapter.

It is manifest that Chile has the keenest interest in education; that its public schools, despite financial handicaps, are excellent; that its four universities, staffed by able professors, both men and women, have a high standard of scholarship, and that among their rectors, past and present, are names that illuminate the cultural and intellectual history of Latin America.

When Aguirre Cerda said, "To educate is to govern," he described, in a few words, the Chilean feeling for education.

XX

Fruits of the Good-Neighbor Policy

The war was over, and Chile, which had meticulously adhered to the fundamental principles of its democratic institutions, continued its friendly relations with the United States.
Gabriel González Videla was now President. During his six-
year tenure he had but four ministers of foreign affairs.
There actually were five, but Raúl Juliet, the first, very soon
resigned to enter the House of Deputies.

The four ministers under González Videla were men of
ability and culture, with wide experience in public life and
with a comprehensive understanding of the significance of international events. All were friendly to the United States,
and their friendship was based not on "subserviency," as was
charged by the communists, but on understanding. The interests of Chile were stoutly guarded by them all.

The first minister, after the brief tenure of Juliet, was Vergara Donoso, a career diplomat long attached to the Foreign Office. He was not a politician and he had no political aspirations. Unmarried, he lived quietly, preferring evenings with his papers and books to the cocktail parties that must have been an abomination to the ministers. Short in stature, quiet and unpretentious in manner, frank and honest in negotiations, he enjoyed the confidence and admiration of the entire Diplomatic Corps. We were sorry when he was sent as Ambassador to Argentina, where, despite the provocations of the Perón regime, he upheld the dignity and defended the interest of his country. His life in Buenos Aires was not lived in a bed of roses.

He was succeeded by German Riesco, son of a former President. He was politically prominent, though not a member of the President's party. He was an able lawyer and businessman, and had spent some years in New York as the representative of a Chilean steamship company. He understood the North American people and their psychology. He had insight into international affairs. He and his clever wife were popular in social circles and much appreciated in diplomatic society. He was a gentleman in the true sense, always courteous and frank.

His successor was Horacio Walker, a member and sometimes leader of the Conservative party. His father had represented Chile as Ambassador to the United States, and Horacio was educated in Washington, where he got his degree in law. As a speaker, he was fluent, often eloquent, and when he accompanied the President on his official visit to Washington and New York, his speeches on numerous occasions made a most favorable impression. He was courteous in speech and manner and always frank, and my relations with him were most cordial. He and his wife were favorites in diplomatic circles.

On his resignation he was succeeded by Eduardo Irarrázaval, also a Conservative, and a man of fortune who divided his time between his town apartment and his beautiful country estate near Santiago. Having no political ambition, he was not easily swayed by the clamor of the street, and I formed a very high opinion of his principles, courage and official integrity. His moral courage was put to the test a number of times, and he never deviated one hairbreadth from the policy he thought right and in the interest of the country. The Diplomatic Corps found him and his vivacious wife socially delightful.

These were the men with whom I dealt most intimately during the regime of González Videla.

2

I felt there were ample reasons why Chile should have a friendly feeling for the United States since the good-neighbor policy was in full flower. From the moment they took office, Roosevelt and Cordell Hull determined on a radical revamping of our Latin-American policy. This was dramatically proclaimed in the conference at Montevideo in 1933, one of the epochal conferences in the history of hemispheric relations. It definitely put an end to intervention in the internal affairs of Latin-American nations and set the pattern for our economic collaboration with our southern neighbors. This purpose was strengthened in the conferences at Lima, Havana and Rio de Janeiro.

The Institute of Inter-American Affairs grew out of Resolution 30 in Rio in 1942 providing a hemispheric program concerning health and sanitation, food supply, education, transportation and strategic material, in order to mobilize the resources of the hemisphere for both war and peace. The institute was fortunate in having Nelson Rockefeller as its head, for he was eminently qualified by his intelligence, energy, enthusiasm and vision and his appreciation of the vital importance of South America to the United States.

The program of co-operation was signed in 1942 by General George C. Dunham, Director of the Division of Health and Sanitation, and Dr. Eugenio Suárez, the very able Director-General of the Chilean Public Health Service, a man of scientific knowledge and dependability. The work in Chile was under the supervision and direction of Dr. Theodore Gandy, a Virginian. He was perfectly qualified because he brought to it an enthusiastic appreciation of its value and a sympathetic understanding of the Chilean people and their needs.

The general impression in the United States that, in the work done, we furnished the money without the contribution of Chile is absurdly false. Thus, in the project of housing, Chile contributed seven times more than we, and on every project Chile did its part. The program included the building and equipping of health centers in regions where the very poor needed them most. These are monuments to the good-neighbor policy. Here children are given medical attention, vaccinated free, and public-health nurses make the rounds regularly, ministering to needs. Because of the success of these centers, the Chilean Government has set them up on its own throughout the country.

There were two major health problems. One was in the field of infant mortality. Children died because of the lack of proper sanitation, the absence of health education, the lack of vaccination in cases of preventable diseases. The other major problem was the prevention of the spread of tuberculosis. This scourge was due in large part to overcrowding in the homes of the very poor, the absence of case-finding facilities and the scarcity of hospital beds for isolation. To help here, the institute, with the co-operation of the Chilean Government, put up the fine tubercular hospital of Trudeau at a healthful spot on the plain of Maipo.

The result? The death rate from infant mortality dropped from 172.9 per thousand in 1943 to 128.6 in 1951; and deaths from tuberculosis dropped from 324.6 per thousand in 1943 to 127.7 in 1951. Now that an intelligent public interest centers on this work there should be a continuing reduction in the death rate from year to year. In this work Chile asked for nothing in which it was not ready to co-operate with money to the extent of its resources. With the impetus I think we gave, the Chilean Government is making great progress in protecting the health of the nation. By the end of 1952 the Chilean Health Service under Dr. Suárez had trained 717 technicians, including doctors, nurses, hospital administrators, sanitary engineers and inspectors and health educators.

The contributions of the good-neighbor policy to the betterment of conditions are utterly insignificant compared with the billions we are spending in arming allied nations for a war that may never come. Here is the field in which to fight communism in South America. The work of the Institute of Inter-American Affairs has now been taken over in part by the Point 4 Program and goes on, and any cutting of appropriations to "balance the budget" would be a grave blunder and would lower our prestige as a friend to a people so thoroughly appreciative of the help we have given.

The good-neighbor policy was not confined to assistance in fighting disease. During the war, and after, we made our contribution to the strengthening of the army, navy and air force for defense. In collaboration with Chile's Fomento Corporation, created to encourage the industrialization of the country, on which part of its future rests, the Export-Import Bank of Washington found the money for the financing of sound enterprises. In some poor retarded sections where the people suffered from the lack of proper sanitation, we aided the government in the building of sewerage systems. One of the most notable contributions of the good-neighbor policy was in the redemption, through proper sanitation, of the northern section of Santiago.

Here dwelled 200,000 people of moderate means and many poor, whose health was suffering from the lack of sewerage. The poor here, with their little patch of garden, could not raise vegetables for their tables because the irrigation was polluted. Though geographically favorable for factories, manufacturers would not build because of sanitary conditions. But the people of this section were of the best.

Thus in a practical attempt to interest the institute, an energetic, dynamic citizen, Mario Rojas Martínez, called a conference of local businessmen, educators and workers and raised money for the building of the sewer. It was not enough; but it was enough to justify a petition for help from the United States. Rojas made his application, an agreement on plans was made, our contribution in money was fixed, and the construction of the sewer was entrusted to the direction of the Institute of Inter-American Affairs. Under its supervision 224 kilometers of concrete pipe was laid, 200,000 people were served, 40,000 hectares of ground, before unfit for cultivation, were redeemed for the raising of vegetables.

Visiting congressmen from home often inquired if the contributions under the good-neighbor policy were appreciated. I had been present on the formal opening of health centers attended by crowds that certainly seemed pleased, but it was on the completion of the sewerage system described, that I had spectacular proof of this appreciation.

I was invited to attend the formal completion of the sewerage system and to speak. The demonstration came on a Sunday. I sat on the platform outdoors facing an impressive assemblage of the people of the community, who had come to express their thanks. There, lined up, were the schoolchildren and their teachers. Girls from the normal school were there to sing the national anthems of Chile and the United States. It seemed that all the people were festive, as on holiday. A runner from far-off Peñaflor appeared in the midst of the program bearing flowers. Speeches were made by businessmen of the section, by a teacher from the schools, by a high officer of the army and by a spokesman of the Chilean Government. My attention was called to a marble memorial, erected in the plaza, expressive of the appreciation of the people for our collaboration, and bearing the names of Roosevelt and the Chilean President. I thought I had positive proof of appreciation, but more was to follow.

Two years later, in connection with the celebration of the Fourth of July, the people of this section gave a luncheon in the barracks of an army regiment as a further expression of appreciation. I was invited. Here speeches were made in homage to the United States. A tiny girl made a charming little speech carried to the crowd by an amplifier and ended by presenting me with flowers for my wife.

The popular reaction to our assistance through the Export-Import Bank, in the construction of the great steel mill of Huachipato, previously described, when thousands cheered the speakers' expressions of appreciation, seemed conclusive to me.

3

However, the good will created by the practical application of the good-neighbor policy through years of hard work and expenditure of money can be wiped out, and will be wiped out if the policy is abandoned. At the close of the war, when there was a disposition to reduce economic aid to South America, our enemies made the most of it. During the war, our foes said to the Chileans: "The Yankees are good to you now because they need you; as soon as they no longer need you they will drop you like a hot potato." When after the war, there were superficial indications of a lowering of interest on our part, the same foes said to the Chilean, "Remember what I told you? Haven't they dropped you like a hot potato?"

There was a perfectly reasonable explanation for the reduction in appropriations for South America at the time. There was a grave threat in the Far East from the communists, and the immediate danger and need were there, and there is a limit to what we can safely spend. Even so, I am sure the cut was unnecessarily drastic, too much out of proportion.

4

Our enemies, taking advantage of our seeming loss of interest, increased their activities until they reached a new height. However, it would be a mistake to ascribe all this criticism of the United States to the communists and Perónists alone. The wave of extreme nationalism sweeping over the world was especially strong in South America and particularly among students. These youths of Chile were neither communists nor Perónists. Passionately patriotic, many looked upon the "Colossus of the North" as a threat to Chilean sovereignty and independence. I have previously referred to the fate of the Technical Education Agreement I had negotiated and later denounced because of the campaign against it, based on a distortion of its purpose and the strange failure of the Chilean Government to clarify it. This, however, did not impress me as evidence of Chilean hostility to the United States. With this single exception, the attacks on me were confined to those of the Nazis during the war and to those of the communists after it was over.

5

My theory of the mission of a diplomat is that he should cultivate friendly relations with frankness, reason and justice, and I am convinced that so-called shirt-sleeve diplomacy is the most effective means. Long before I became Ambassador I had no sympathy with the theory of some that it is wise swaggeringly to wave the "big stick." I know of nothing more suicidal with the proud, self-respecting Latin Americans.

On the tenth anniversary of the presentation of my credentials I was invited to the capitol by the chairman of the Foreign Relations Committee and, suspecting it had something to do with the anniversary, I expected to be received in the committee room and congratulated. To my surprise I was ushered into the chamber of the House of Deputies, which was filled with members of Congress, diplomats and friends. I found Foreign Minister German Riesco in the chair, and I was taken to the rostrum. Chairman Cañas Flores spoke complimentarily of my services; he was followed by Raúl Juliet, ranking minority member, in similar vein; and then the Foreign Minister, who followed, startled me with the announcement that on the orders of the President he was giving me the highest decoration of the nation. Under our regulations, coming down from the first days of our Republic when some were dreaming of a king and a court, our diplomats are forbidden to receive decorations, but I availed myself of the stipulation that an ambassador may accept if a declination would be open to misunderstanding. I accepted with pride, and then, in conformity with the rules, deposited the decoration in the vault of the State Department until my retirement. Some of my staff warned that I would be rebuked by Washington, but President Truman wrote me: "I think you did perfectly right in accepting the decoration, and I also think that you deserve it. It makes me feel that we are well represented in Chile."

Editorially, the Chilean press was more than kind.

6

But it was not all cakes and ale. I was chairman of the United States delegation at the Economic Conference of the United Nations held in Santiago in 1951. There has been a feeling among not a few that it is unfortunate that the United Nations furnishes a tribunal from which the communists can spread their amazing falsehoods, and I was to find this illustrated in Santiago. Eddie Miller, Assistant Secretary of State for the Latin-American republics, who had prepared a speech for the conference, was refused permission to deliver it because it was "not on the agenda." He then planned to deliver it at the luncheon I gave at the embassy for the heads of the delegations, but the Polish delegate left after the last course, and the undelivered speech was given to the press.

That luncheon had features that were both amusing and amazing because of the conduct of the Polish representative, a militant communist. During the Conference he had been making daily attacks on the United States. It was at the time many North Americans were donating blood for the military hospitals, and the Pole solemnly declared that the economic status of the workers in the United States was such that they "had to sell their blood to get bread"; and because a pervert in California had been arrested for selling his daughter into prostitution, the Pole indignantly said that the North American worker is so poor that "he is forced to sell his daughters into prostitution to get money to keep body and soul together."

I had a ridiculous experience with him at my luncheon. I had invited all the heads of delegations, including the Russian, the Polish and the Czechoslovakian. I was convinced, however, that none would contaminate themselves by entering and breaking bread in an American Embassy—but all appeared. I was a few minutes late at my own party, arriving during the cocktail period, and the Russian and the Czech came to me at once in a gentlemanly manner. Having shaken hands with them, I looked around for the Pole. He was pointed out to me. He was talking with another guest, and I went up and stood by his side. The man with whom he was conversing called his attention to the presence of his host. Continuing to talk, he held out his hand sideways, without facing me, and then went on talking, without a word to me. Clearly the Pole was no gentleman by the Russian standard, since the Russian was pleasant, even cordial, telling me what had become of Ambassador Zhukov, and surprising me by saying he had read my *Jefferson and Hamilton*. The Czech, a tall, graceful, well-groomed man, did not seem to belong to the communist group, and I heard later he did not return to Prague, where his brother had been "purged."

But if the Russian was gracious and gentlemanly in my house, he followed the Stalinist line in his talks in the conference. He had the temerity to protest hotly against "forced labor" in the United States, and when everyone perked up with astonishment, he explained. Did we not put men in prison for the commission of crimes; and some in mental hospitals? Did not the men in prison have to work, and did not Yankee doctors give mild chores to patients as part of their treatment? Was this not forced labor? And men working in factories and fields—did they not have to work to get food and clothing, and was this not "forced labor"? Having made his point, he announced mournfully that the condition of workers in the United States was pitiful. For three years, he said, wages had been rapidly going down—when, in fact, they had been rapidly going up and were the highest paid in history.

If he expected to impress and deceive the people of Chile he had queer notions about the intelligence of the Chileans. These made merry over the absurdities, and the Chilean press reported his comments in a satirical vein.

7

In the spring of 1950 I went to Washington in advance of the official visit of President González Videla, since it gave me an opportunity to be of some slight service to our Chilean friends. I went on the ship that carried Admiral Holger, who was going as a representative of the Chilean Navy, in the hope of getting some cruisers and a tanker, which were greatly needed. Throughout the voyage I found him hard at work at a table on the deck making his preparations. I had written President Truman the strongest commendation of the officer and man, and in approval of his mission. I saw him frequently in Washington, where he encountered the usual red-tape obstacles, but in the end he got the cruisers. The fight for the tanker was more difficult and annoying, but the agreement on its sale was written and signed. After my return to Chile, the State Department cabled me that the Marine Commission had refused to release the tanker and that the Secretary of Commerce had agreed with the commission. This light brushing aside of a signed agreement was shocking, and I wrote President Truman, strongly protesting, for he had promised me in Washington to interest himself in the sale of the tanker. He replied promptly that he had given instructions that the signed agreement had to be respected. The press of Chile had reported the purchase, and the repudiation of the agreement at that stage would have been a sure way to weaken, if not destroy, confidence in our dependability.

Then another obstacle: the corporation that had owned the tanker announced that it had received a better offer and would not sell, despite the agreement. Again President Truman intervened. Finally the corporation submitted a fantastic lawyer's fee, though in the contract it was stipulated that the fee should not exceed a stated figure. When I was informed about this by the Chileans I advised them to stand on the contract.

It is petty things like this that can do infinite harm to our relations with our neighbors in the south.

8

It was at this time, too, that there was a threat to restore the customs duties on Chilean copper, which would have meant a loss in Chilean revenue the country could not afford. The State Department was opposed, but an election was approaching, and the senators and congressmen from some copper-producing states thought it necessary, in their political interest, to insist on the restoration of the tax. In company with Jack McFall, the liaison between the State Department and Congress, I canvassed some members of the House and Senate, pointing out the effect on public opinion in a friendly nation, and found that very few favored the restoration of the tax, but most were embarrassed because a deservedly popular Senator from a copper state was facing a close contest for re-election and thought the restoration of the tax would strengthen his position at the polls. He was a kindly man who had rendered services to most of his colleagues, and his appeal to them had caused embarrassment. Among others we saw Senator George, perhaps the ablest senator dealing with international affairs, and found him sympathetic and understanding. At any rate, the import tax was not imposed.

9

With the arrival of González Videla in Washington it was clear that my return home would be no vacation. We went to the airport to receive him. President Truman greeted him when he alighted, and both presidents stood on a platform and spoke over the radio. Then on to Blair House, where the Trumans were residing while the White House was being renovated. The sidewalks were lined with cheering people, Chilean flags were fluttering everywhere, large pictures of the visitor were displayed at street intersections, and on Pennsylvania Avenue, in front of the Municipal Building, a platform had been erected for the formal presentation of the key of the city. Across the street hung a huge Chilean flag that almost covered the front of the Washington *Post.* The President spoke briefly and gracefully.

A crowd, gathered before Blair House, cheered lustily as González Videla stood in the car saluting, after the fashion of our own political leaders. That night President Truman gave a dinner, with a very large company, at the Carlton Hotel, and the two presidents returned to Blair House, where the González Videlas were to spend the night. That night the two presidents came to know and like each other. Truman, at the piano, played Chopin and Mozart, the Chilean gave a less finished performance, Margaret Truman sang, and the Chilean draped a poncho over Truman's shoulders. Later the visitor told me that on that night he had met "a real human being."

González Videla delivered his major speech at a luncheon

at the National Press Club, which was packed with correspondents, reporters and editors. These men, who see so many counterfeits in public life, so many posers, are apt to be cynical and not easily impressed. They were prepared to hear an ornate discourse, with rolling rhetoric without substance, all icing and no cake. But the President spoke simply, frankly, forcefully, without any pretension as to style, and his analysis of the communist threat was impressive. He received a great ovation. Lingering in the club after the event and overhearing the comments of these men, I found them astonished and delighted.

That night the Chilean President gave an elaborate dinner for President Truman at the Shoreham Hotel, followed by a reception and dancing at the Pan-American Building, which became too crowded for comfort.

Then on to New York—more hectic than Washington. We drove out to the Rockefeller estate for a luncheon given by Nelson Rockefeller; the sirens of our police escort screamed all the way. The next day, driving through the East Side to the Battery and thence to City Hall, through cheering crowds, with bands playing and flags flying, the President made his formal call on the mayor. From there we went to the Waldorf-Astoria to the mayor's luncheon, at which the President adorned the mayor with the picturesque costume of the Chilean *huaso.* A luncheon by Arthur Hays Sulzberger at *The New York Times;* another by the Chamber of Commerce; another by the copper and nitrate companies; and one day, with the sirens of the police escort sounding weirdly, we were driven to the country home of Peter Grace for luncheon. Our next visit was to the more remote home of Roosevelt at Hyde Park. Here we found Mrs. Roosevelt waiting at the gate to greet the presidential party. We went at once to the grave. The President stood uncovered in a silence that was disturbed only by the chirping of birds; he was clearly moved. The grave is in the garden—a simple stone. Then to the house and the library.

That day the Chileans saw something of the simplicity of true greatness. Mrs. Roosevelt gave them a luncheon in her cottage on the grounds. It was excellent but quite simple, and when she moved among the tables, sometimes acting as a waitress, I am sure the Chileans were astonished and delighted by the informality.

This state visit was a triumph for González Videla, and it rendered a real service to Chile. The press associations evidently had reported to Chilean papers the slight services I had rendered in the matter of the cruisers, the tanker and the copper tax, since when our boat drew in at Valparaiso and we reached the top of the gangplank to descend, we were startled by the music of our national anthem from a military band. We stood waiting for the conclusion, and I sent down the request that the band follow with the national anthem of Chile. My emotions are not easily aroused, but this incident, so kindly meant, touched us all.

XXI

Yankee Capital and Chilean Economy

Four Chilean presidents said to me that Chile wants and needs the investment of North American capital. Millions have already been invested in Chile, to the economic advantage of the country. During my tenure the investors never failed to conform strictly to the laws of the land. No American ambassador, I am sure, was ever more fortunate in the caliber, character and judgment of these Yankee businessmen. I found that the managers, the executives of these companies, understood and liked the Chilean people and were as much interested in the economic health and stability of the country as any Chilean. Never once did they camp on the doorstep of the embassy asking its intervention in the occasional controversies with the government. They knew that as businessmen well known in Chile it was preferable that they fight out their own battles with the government, since the interference or intervention of the embassy would stress a political point involving the sovereign rights and dignity of the country. Many of them had grown gray in the shadows of the Andes and looked on Chile as their second home. They unquestionably treated their employees with greater consideration and paid them better wages than other mining companies. And they did not interfere with domestic politics.

Before I went to Chile it was charged that some of these corporations contributed to the campaign coffers of a presidential candidate, and the reaction was bad. However, in justice to these corporations, they had been pressured by important politicians to furnish money. In the presidential election of 1942 I formally notified our people that if they intervened in domestic politics and found themselves in trouble they could not count on the protection of the embassy. I found, as I knew I would, that the companies were delighted, since it not only saved them money but also the embarrassment of a refusal. In none of the three presidential elections during my time in Chile could any of them be honestly charged with intervening with money. Inevitably the charge was often made by our enemies, and this was especially true in the election of 1952, but I had the satisfaction of being told by President Ibáñez that he knew we had not taken any part in the election. I have taken this occasion to pay a tribute to these North American executives because I found their conduct exemplary and because of my indebtedness to them for their co-operation through a long period.

2

England, Germany, France, Belgium and Holland are all represented by investments in Chile, but the heaviest are those of the United States. The Chilean nitrate deposits are owned by North Americans, though English capital is also invested in them. The first Chilean producers of nitrate were the Jesuits many years ago, who sold it on a small scale for the manufacture of gunpowder. After the expulsion of the Jesuits there was little interest in nitrate for a long time. When, years later, a daring adventurer, José Santos Ossa, in search of silver, noticed that when he lighted his campfire at night the white substance on the ground spluttered and gave forth a blue flame, he concluded that there was nitrate in abundance, and he interested English and Chilean capital. For some years the British were largely in possession of the infant nitrate industry. A clever, picturesque English engineer, John T. North, enlisting British capital in the installation of then modern machinery, began a systematic creation of a foreign market. Waxing rich, flaunting his wealth, enjoying to the full the delusion of grandeur, he came to be known as the "Nitrate King." It was years later that the Guggenheim interests poured millions into the modern development of the industry, and the Chilean mines became among the greatest producers in the world.

The story of the development of these mines is as thrilling as the most sparkling pages of fiction. Behind it was not only money but imagination. The famous mines of Maria Elena are located in the desert. It is a grim, gray, desolate area where rain never falls and a torrid sun burns fiercely on the sands. The most modern machinery was installed at a great cost; a railroad was built to get the nitrate to the sea; water was piped down from the Andean heights; and, through the unstinted expenditure of money and the highest technical skill, the mines have prospered beyond precedent.

Not least among the problems was to make life at Maria Elena livable, and soon an oasis was created in the desert. Where nature never intended a blade of grass to grow or a flower to blossom, trees now give shade and flower beds scent the air. The workers were comfortably housed. Excellent schools were provided, financed by the company but under the supervision of the state. Because the region was remote from shopping centers, stores operated by the company without profit—actually, at a loss—were opened. An excellent, thoroughly equipped hospital was built, and staffed by skillful surgeons and physicians.

The workers in these mines have been thoroughly trained. A Danish writer, Haakon Mielche, visiting the mine, was impressed by the comment of Paul Kruger, the manager. "Listening to Kruger," he said, "I got the impression that the Chilean miners are archangels." In turn, Kruger was liked and admired by the men, since a less domineering, more kindly and considerate man I have never known.

The nitrate mines have poured millions of dollars into the coffers of the state. The Yankee investor, who has made all this possible, leaves by far the greater part of the profits in Chile in the form of wages, taxes and through other devices, one of which, until recently, was frankly discriminatory.

3

Marvels of daring and ingenuity, with a lavish expenditure of money, may also be seen in the development of the copper industry of Anaconda and Braden. The use of Chilean copper was not unknown even before the Spaniards appeared. The mines operated by Chilean capital in the nineteenth century were successful when its copper was on the surface but thereafter the mines had a precarious existence until North American capital acquired them and poured hundreds of millions into their development. A wealthy mining magnate, Señor Concha y Toro, who owned the so-called Braden mines of today, found he lacked the resources for their development, and he commissioned an Italian engineer, then residing in Chile, to interest foreign capital. This man contacted William Braden of New York, and a company was formed to purchase and operate the properties. It was forced to expend vast sums of money to produce properly. A cart road, thirty-five miles in length, was built first. To bring the machinery to the mines 2500 bullocks were used, and the cost per ton was high. A railroad had to be built at a heavy cost because of the difficulties of the mountainous terrain. But human ingenuity was put to a test in the building of a town for the accommodation of the workers, and Sewell is the result. It is built on a slope of the Andes, on the side of a volcanic cone, the site grim and seemingly impossible for human habitation. The challenge was met by the construction of apartment houses built on terraces. With no steps or streets, Sewell is known as "the town without wheels," since cars cannot be used.

With the housing problem solved, the builders had to provide for the comfort and entertainment of the workers, since they were fifty miles from Santiago. Soon a finely equipped hospital, staffed by the best of surgeons, was in operation. Dentists were brought in. Public primary schools were opened at the expense of the company but under the authority of the state. An industrial school for the technical training of the more ambitious of the workers was opened. Churches built by the company were provided. To meet the shopping needs of the workers, company stores were opened where provisions were sold at wholesale prices without profit. Cinemas were furnished where pictures were shown at low cost. Four social clubs were organized for the men, with rooms, light and heat furnished by the company, and beauty parlors to minister to the vanity of the women were made available. A summer camp for the children was set up at Coya.

The transformation of the desolate mountainside into a city was miraculous, the ingenuity of man pitted against the stubborn forces of nature, with man the victor. Such achievements by the two copper companies have greatly advanced the economic development of Chile.

4

Even so, the misinformed, playing politics with prejudice, find too little to commend in the investment of hundreds of millions of North American capital. These dwell upon the fact that copper and nitrate are Chilean resources—and so they are—and so they were through the many years that they lay fallow before foreign capital came in. Then, too, the ill-informed and others playing politics try to create the impression that all the earnings of the companies leave the country. This charge is fantastically untrue, since more than 90 per cent stays in Chile, and the investor who furnishes the money and takes the risk takes less than 10 per cent away. The wages of the thousands of workers stay in Chile, the heavy taxes retain more, and this is to be expected. But a resort was had to one device that was arbitrary. When the rate of exchange ranged from one hundred to five hundred pesos to the dollar, the companies were compelled by law to buy pesos to pay the workers at nineteen to the dollar. This injustice has been corrected.

For years the revenue from these mines has been Chile's greatest source. When the copper or nitrate mines are occasionally shut down by strikes, the loss to the government is appalling. That is the reason the communists, bent on creating economic chaos, unemployment and social disorders, concentrate their efforts on illegal strikes.

The Telephone Company, owned and operated by North American capital, was almost entirely free from harassment during my tenure. One law was enacted so manifestly unfair to the company that it was set aside by the Supreme Court as unconstitutional.

The Compañía Chilena de Electricidad, being a public utility, was less fortunate since public utilities everywhere are considered fair game for the politicians. When I arrived in Chile it owned and operated the streetcars and was much criticized because the cars were old and unsightly, but the unreasonably low fares fixed by the government made their proper maintenance impossible and they were running at a loss. The government purchased the streetcar system, but, finding it could do no better than the company, it abandoned them entirely and substituted busses. The government is well represented in the management of the electric company since the president of the board of directors is a Chilean, and Chileans are represented by other members of the board. Its power plants, operating under handicaps, had occasional problems with the government, which did not always co-operate, but these troubles were minimized by the straightforwardness of the manager, Joe Cussens, who was personally liked and trusted. At his marriage to a charming Chilean I had the pleasure of acting as his *padrino*.

5

A potato famine in Ireland years ago rendered an immense service to Chile and the western coast of South America. A retired English army officer with an estate in Peru, and in need of potato farmers, took advantage of the famine to contract for a large group of Irish farmers. The Irish colony was decimated by malaria, and most sought a more salubrious climate, but one, hardier than the rest, stuck it out. This was William R. Grace, a man of constructive imagination, with vision and rare ability as an organizer. From Peru he began the building of his industrial empire. Interested primarily in the nitrate of Peru, when the fortunes of the Pacific war transferred the nitrate field to Chile he entered the Chilean field. Dealing with merchandise, and seeking foreign markets, he concentrated at first on transportation, and long before the completion of the Panama Canal he had established a regular boat service between the two continents, via the Strait of Magellan. Because the success of a shipping company depends on an exchange of goods, he invested in the development of industries along the western coast, and Chile profited. During my time in Chile the Grace people operated a manganese mine near Coquimbo, a flour mill in Arequipa, sugar-washing plants in Iquique, Santiago, Valparaiso and Viña del Mar, where they also had a woolen mill, a vegetable oil and lard plant, and factories for the making of soap, paint and steel barrels.

At the turn of the century British capital had successfully

operated a textile mill in Chiguayante for fifteen years. En-
countering difficulties, it closed in 1917, but the skeleton remained until 1929, when it was taken over by the Grace
people. Within a short time, after it had been rebuilt from
the bottom up, it was the most important textile mill in the
country. This had called for the investment of large sums of
money for the most modern machinery. Meanwhile the Grace
people owned and operated two weaving factories in Viña del
Mar. At that time the Grace factories produced 40 per cent
of the textile production of the nation. In 1936 there was
installed at Chiguayante the first and at the time the most
modern spinning plant in the world, and Grace added to his
textile activities those of cotton printing.

Four years later I visited the plant at Chiguayante and
found it a beehive of industry, with 900 looms in use. It
was turning out a beautiful product. All these mills, made
possible by North American capital, are so intimately identified with Chile that few think of them as other than entirely
Chilean. When William R. Grace, who had transferred his
headquarters to New York, was a successful candidate for
mayor of that city he was attacked by his opponent as "more
South American than Yankee."

The Grace people have done more than any other in encouraging trade between the United States and Chile. For close
to a century their ships have plowed the waters of two oceans
carrying cargo. With the launching of the "Santa Sisters"
—a number of boats with comfortable accommodations, a famous cuisine, amusements such as games, swimming pools, pictures on deck at night—travelers on pleasure or on business
find voyages from New York to Valparaiso restful and delightful journeys along the western coast.

With the increasing relations between the United States and
Chile, Grace launched the Panagra Air Line, which now
makes flights between New York and Santiago in less than
one day. Never gambling with the lives of its passengers for
the sake of speed, it has a deserved reputation for safety. The
flight from Santiago to Buenos Aires over the second highest

hump in the world is picturesque and dramatic. Before present-day, powerful planes, when the flight was through a narrow pass, if there were a storm or heavy fog in the mountains, the planes were grounded at Mendoza until the pass was cleared. Once I had invited a large company to a dinner for Mr. Pearson of the Export-Import Bank, but that day the plane from Buenos Aires, with the honor guest aboard, was grounded at Mendoza because of a serious storm. I postponed the dinner until the next day, but the plane was still grounded. And the next, it was the same. Remarkably, the invited guests were able to attend on the fourth day. This was most unusual even in those days. With the new, powerful planes this is no longer necessary since these air-pressurized planes can fly over the top and avoid the pass when necessary.

Thus Grace has made a tremendous contribution to intercourse between the South American nations. Before the use of planes it was a real adventure, not without hardships, to travel between countries shut in by towering mountains, but now tourists and businessmen may go anywhere on the southern continent in comfort and with speed.

The Graces, Bradens and Guggenheims have rendered incalculable services to Chile with the hundreds of millions of dollars they have poured into its economic development.

6

I had hoped during my tenure that everything possible could be done to encourage North American capital to invest in Chile. Being a North American, with the knowledge that our industrial development was due in large measure to foreign capital during our first eighty years, I was unable to understand the Chilean fear of foreign capital, the fear that it would endanger Chile's economic independence. The investments in the United States from England, France and Holland did us infinite good and no harm. Chile can well use North American capital, as four Chilean presidents have said.

All that capital requires is the assurance of fair play, without discrimination, with freedom from prejudice. When foreign capital enters any country it is under the obligation to observe strictly that country's laws. If it sometimes feels that some of the laws are unjust, so long as they are on the books our investors must adhere to them scrupulously, and they do. On the other hand, they have a right to a reasonable profit on their investment, and should be free from discrimination and prejudice.

When I drove ex-President Herbert Hoover, a great engineer, to the airport in Santiago, he pointed to the Andes in the distance and remarked to me that in all probability billions of wealth was buried in those mountains, but that hundreds of millions would be necessary to bring it forth. There are great possibilities for investment in Chile. It is a lovely country in which to live and labor. The people, so similar in temperament, appearance and manner to the North Americans, think generally along our line. Once satisfied of a friendly reception and governmental stability, our capital would find in Chile a congenial atmosphere for investment, and this, I know, would be in the interest of the nation.

XXII

Sound and Fury Again

We return now to the political or diplomatic phase. The presidential election of 1952 was approaching, and the maneuvering of the politicians and political parties was threatening to undermine Chilean-American relations. The communists and Perónists, taking full advantage of the extreme nationalism of many, were hoping to use it as a screen behind which to do all the damage they could when negotiated agreements were under consideration in Congress. Availing themselves of the Korean War, the demagogues were protesting against our "demand" that Chilean boys be sent across the sea to die in our quarrel, when no such "demand" had been made or even considered. At the beginning of the Korean War it was assumed that we might ask our South American neighbors, members of the United Nations, to send armed forces, if only a token number, to assist; and finally two nations sent some soldiers. There were many Chileans who thought it would be wise to make a token offering. The Chilean Government did discuss with me the possibility—the subject was broached by the government, not by me—of sending a frigate or a squadron of planes. When I transmitted this plan to Washington the word came back that we had decided not to accept help from South America at that time, and the idea was dropped at the Moneda.

The next crusade of the communists and Perónists was against the proposed Mutual Security Pact, popularly known as the Military Pact, for hemispheric defense against communist aggression within the continent. Before the plan had been officially presented or negotiations begun, the communist and Perónist crusade against it began.

The primary purpose of the pact was to assist our sister republics to defend themselves militarily if attacked and, through as much conformity in material as possible, to simplify such assistance as we might conceivably be called upon to give. This meant that the equipment of the Chilean armed forces—land, sea and air—would be materially strengthened. It did not mean that Chile would be expected to send armed forces outside the country unless, in its sovereign capacity, it saw fit. It assuredly had nothing whatever to do with the Korean War. Even so, many obstacles were to be thrown in the way of negotiations.

On December 22, 1951, I saw Eduardo Irarrázaval, the Foreign Minister, and left with him an *aide-mémoir,* with an explanation of our motives. I recalled to him the words of Aguirre Cerda that all talk of continental or hemispheric defense "is mere theater" unless backed by practical action. The minister was clearly interested and pleased, and he promised to confer with the President at once—a promise which, like all his other promises, he kept.

Soon thereafter our negotiators from our armed forces arrived, eager to begin discussions with those of Chile. We were happy in our choice of negotiators. Admiral Wilkins for the navy, Colonel Dan Ellis for the air force—who, as Air Attaché in my time, had earned the confidence and respect of the Chileans—and Colonel Armstrong for the army, a very able officer, familiar with the ideas of our General Staff at the Pentagon. These could not have been improved upon.

On January 24, 1952, in the Red Room of the Foreign Office, these men sat down with the highest-ranking officers of the three divisions of the Chilean fighting forces for the opening of the negotiations. The Chileans were forceful men who could be counted upon to veto any proposition, detrimental to their country.

Irarrázaval opened the meeting with an explanatory statement on its objectives. Having in mind the misrepresentations of the technical education agreement, I began by saying, with great emphasis, that we were not *urging* the agreement but were *merely offering* it for consideration; and, in view of the misrepresentations in the street, to make it emphatic I closed by reiterating that we were asking nothing but offering something we thought advantageous to Chile, and that the Chilean Government, an independent nation, would determine on the agreement's acceptance or rejection. If, after consideration, it concluded that it was not to the advantage of Chile, it could be rejected without fear of incurring the resentment of my country.

Even so, from the very beginning, the communists and Perónists raised the hue and cry that we were bringing "pressure on Chile" to enter into an agreement detrimental to her interests; that it meant that Chilean boys would be sent to Korea to die in our quarrel; and because, for manifest reasons, Argentina was not included, it was our purpose to stir up trouble between neighboring nations—the last thing we would want.

The first meeting then adjourned to permit the Chilean officers to study the preliminary plan in detail, and two days later we met again, and an agreement was reached that the of-

ficers could proceed with the negotiations, the representatives
of the three divisions acting separately.

These negotiations were conducted in an atmosphere of
friendly understanding and informality. A number of minor
concessions were made to meet Chilean wishes, and on March
19, 1952, the first draft was turned over to Irarrázaval,
who presented it to the President the following day.

Almost immediately the foes of the pact began their campaign against congressional ratification, but on April 9, in the
Red Room, Irarrázaval signed the agreement with me, and
it went to the Congress for ratification or rejection.

Determined to do nothing that even malice could interpret
as an attempt to bring "pressure," we of the embassy sat
back and observed the developments with some curiosity. Almost immediately a split appeared in the President's own party,
and the pact was being debated with some acrimony in the
party conferences, with one segment insisting that its representatives in Congress be instructed to vote to kill the agreement. Manuel Trucco, then Undersecretary of State and a
leading member of the party, went before the conference
with a full and lucid explanation of its provisions that should
have satisfied the most cautious and suspicious.

To make the situation more difficult, the presidential election was approaching, and it was all too clear that some politicians were angling for the communist vote. In early May
there was a proposal to postpone the consideration of the pact
in Congress, which meant until after the election, months
ahead. On May 6 President González Videla assured me that
the pact would be ratified. But Washington, having in mind
the fate of the technical education agreement, and noting the
bitterness of the attack, became doubtful of the outcome, despite my assurance that ratification was certain, and suggested
that the Chilean Government be asked to drop the pact from
the congressional agenda.

With distaste, I conveyed this suggestion to Irarrázaval. I
was not surprised by his astonishment and indignation. He

had made ratification a vote of confidence, and if the government parties would not ratify an agreement signed by him and made an administration measure, he would resign. I knew he would.

The next day he went before the committee in the House of Deputies and asked for a report within three days. He found five of the seven members favorable and two opposed on the utterly false ground that the United States was "bullying Chile." So remote was this from the truth that during the weeks that intervened before final action was taken, I never once urged ratification on the minister. By straining a point, one possible exception may be noted. With a gentle reminder from Washington that unless Chile ratified by May 1 it would not get the advantage from the pact that year, since the appropriation for the purchase of the material for the armed forces had made this the deadline, I merely gave the minister the fact and urged nothing, though I was personally eager for Chile to get the benefit that year. Since it was clear to me that the pact would be ratified, I urged an extension of the time limit, and this was granted.

2

In the midst of the controversy, González Videla denounced the copper agreement which had been entered into on the request of Chile. The announcement was given a sensational interpretation by a part of the press, which said that Chile had "declared its independence" and that "the days of Yankee bondage" were over. This was carried in North American papers and naturally created the impression that our enemies led by the communists and some Perónists, were in control and that the Mutual Security Pact was doomed. A few in the State Department concluded that González Videla was hostile to the United States and thought it wise to abandon the project for Chile and to have the pact struck from the congressional agenda. I did not mention this to Irarrázaval and I dismissed as untrue the fear that González Videla was our enemy. Again I assured Washington that the pact unquestionably would be ratified in Congress—as it was.

At this time González Videla summoned me to the Moneda to explain his precipitate denunciation of the copper agreement. A North American businessman having no close contact with the State Department had publicly announced that the price of copper would go down, and this, thought the President, would make it impossible for Chile to sell at its own price in the European market. This had aroused his anger.

At length the pact came up for action in the House of Deputies, and my prediction was justified when it was ratified by a vote of 78 to 21. It gave the Chilean armed forces what they needed and exacted nothing from them but the defense of their own country.

Despite this, the clamorous opposition continued to the end. There was a hostile demonstration in front of my house which was not impressive. More serious was the mob, composed of no more than four hundred communists and Perónists in front of the capital during the voting of the deputies. Not content with jeering the United States, this mob capped its rowdyism with an act of incredible indecency.

One of the deputies, stricken with a heart attack, had died on the floor of the chamber. When the body was being borne out by his colleagues of different political parties, the mob jostled the bearers of the corpse and spewed forth insults to the dead. "To hell with him," they shouted, with loud laughter. When Sir Charles Stirling, the British Ambassador, who had been having tea in the capitol, was leaving, he was insulted and pushed about. His glasses were knocked off and trampled upon.

The fight of the enemies of the pact now centered in the Senate. Senator Carlos Ibáñez, then a candidate for President, spoke against it, giving some erroneous interpretations of the proposed agreement. He was under the impression that the pact would send Chilean boys across the sea to die—which was not true; that the pact infringed on Chilean sovereignty

—which was not justified by the facts; that it was deliberately designed to disturb Chile's "friendly relations" with the Argentina of Perón—which was untrue; that we were applying "pressure"—which was as remote as possible from the fact. Much later, after the election, I sent him a copy of my speeches opening and closing the negotiations, making crystal clear that we were merely "offering" the plan and not "urging" it at all, and least of all that we were applying "pressure"—and he was satisfied. However, his opposition in the Senate was disturbing and surprising, since, as a military man he knew the needs of the armed forces we were proposing in part to supply.

While awaiting action in the Senate, the communist and Perónist propaganda intensified and reached fantastic proportions. The communist paper was running my picture over the caption "War Hawk." It said we were demanding that Chile give up Arica and Magellan, that Chile send troops to Korea, and that we were demanding bases on Chilean soil!

It was at this time, as the vote in the Senate approached, that vicious propaganda pamphlets denouncing the United States were being poured into the Argentine Embassy and consulates for circulation. These packages came bearing the stamp of the Foreign Office in Buenos Aires. But in the midst of all this Senator José Maza, of the Foreign Relations Committee of the Senate, told me that his committee and the one on military affairs had unanimously recommended ratification, and within a few days the pact was ratified by a vote of 24 to 6.

The next morning was the Fourth of July. In accordance with custom, a Chilean military band appeared early to play our national anthem in the garden of the embassy, and a Chilean officer hoisted our flag while one of our military men hoisted Chile's. The traditional reception that day was more crowded than ever.

I have gone into this matter of the pact to illustrate and explain the character of the "hostility" to the United States, which, while neither important nor typical, sometimes tended to create an entirely false impression of Chile's attitude toward my country; and because of some pride in the fact that there was less delay in ratification in Chile than in several other nations, which followed tardily. Never once did I have reason to doubt the friendly feeling of the Chilean people.

3

The reference to the traditional serenade at the embassy on the Fourth of July recalls an amusing incident. The military band appeared in the early morning, and there was usually a similar serenade at the homes of the attachés of our armed forces. One year Colonel Dan Ellis, my Air Attaché, was rudely awakened at six in the morning by the servants with the unhappy tidings that the house was on fire! Ellis, still in his pajamas, was feverishly directing the removal of the furniture by the friends who had rallied to his aid when he was startled by the music of a military band, which swept into view from around the corner playing the national anthem. In the midst of the tumult and the shouting, with the fire blazing and making headway, habit asserted itself, and it was not until later that Ellis could smile at the absurdity of the scene as he stood in the midst of the confusion in his pajamas, at salute, until the end of the anthem, all illuminated by the burning house behind him. Not often has an American army officer stood at salute in his pajamas.

4

While realizing the importance of adequate military preparation for defense, I was, and am, thoroughly convinced that the best service the United States can render its friends in South America is through economic assistance. Our too great reliance on military might for defense against the encroachments of communism fails to take into consideration the reason for the progress the communists have made in countries in need of economic aid. Had a small portion of the billions we have spent in preparation for a war which the hydrogen bomb has made improbable been used for economic aid in countries that need it, we would have waged a more intelligent war against communism than we have. Our neglect in this field explains why we have been losing the cold war since 1953.

I was therefore happy when the Mutual Security Pact was followed with another more in accord with my own feeling. President Truman achieved a great deal, but nothing he initiated will seem more important historically than his Point Four program of technical assistance. This is a practical extension of the good-neighbor policy of Roosevelt and Hull. In the negotiation of this agreement none of our ill-wishers had the temerity to oppose it. From the moment it was announced from Washington, the Chilean public men, press and people, realizing its possibilities, gave it their hearty approval. There was not a dissenting voice and only a mild grumble from the communist camp.

In the Red Room of the Foreign Office, crowded with spectators, reporters and photographers, I signed the general agreement with Horacio Walker, the Foreign Minister, the agricultural agreement with Minister Moller and the educational agreement with Minister Leighton. I was especially pleased with the agricultural agreement, which, if effectively carried out, may reasonably be expected to revolutionize farming in a land abundantly blessed with a rich soil and to end Chile's dependence on a neighboring nation for meat and wheat.

I find among my papers an amusing souvenir of the signing of the agreement. I had been annoyed by a photographer who had thrust his camera almost under my nose when I was signing, and I could not understand why until I saw the picture in the press the next morning. I was smoking a cigar, and because there was no ashtray on the table, it did not occur to me to remove the long cigar from my mouth when signing; and since the cigar was big and my face small in proportion, the effect was a bit grotesque and certainly undignified. The photographer was more interested in the cigar than in the smoker. I have, however, kept that picture as a reminder of the signing of a pact for which Chile will surely have reasons to be grateful.

Very soon a large group of technicians arrived in Santiago and settled down to work in close co-operation with trained Chilean officials. I was not surprised, shortly before leaving Chile, to find that one of the major projects of the Point Four program may be the development of the great, scantily populated province of Aisén. It had belatedly been dawning on the Chileans that this long-neglected province offered enormous possibilities. Stouthearted colonists, like those who had developed the rich farming region of the south, could make it contribute mightily to the economy of the country. González Videla, when President, had discussed with me his thought of inviting colonists from northern Italy to people this region, but this was before the Point Four program and we were not in a position to help.

The climate of Aisén is healthful, and though there is much rain at times, this is equally true of the neighborhood of Valdivia, which is a garden spot. Much of it is heavily wooded, but much more profit can be expected from a scientific cultivation of the rich virgin soil. Wheat and meat products are most needed by the Chileans, and these are said to be "naturals" in Aisén. According to experts who have studied the possibilities, this long-neglected province can support 2,000,000 sheep and 500,000 cattle, thus ending the dependence on Argentina for meat.

After signing the Point Four program I had a long visit with President Ibáñez when I called to introduce our agricultural specialist in the embassy. I was not surprised when the President talked almost exclusively about Aisén and its future.

In signing the Point Four pact I had in mind the prescience and statesmanship of Joel Poinsett, our first diplomat in Chile, who knew that Chile's future depended on a full-scale development of agriculture. I recalled that he was a member of the first society organized under the Chilean Republic for the encouragement of scientific farming. An aristocrat by birth, a man of social stature and a statesman, he was primarily a farmer; and so, in signing, I was thinking of Poinsett as the first North American who had favored the co-operation of his country in the full development of the agricultural resources of Chile, and I knew that if he could have witnessed the scene in the Red Room that day, he would have been happy to find that this co-operation had at length been made possible.

XXIII

Presidential Mirror of Chile

Chile has been almost uniformly fortunate in the personality and character of its presidents. In the early days of the Republic there was a disposition to elect military men, but this has not been true for many years, and it alone sets Chile off from most of her sister republics on the continent. It was my privilege to serve through the administrations of three and for a few months into that of a fourth. Perhaps character sketches of these men may contribute to an understanding of the Chileans.

Aguirre Cerda, to whom I presented my credentials, had been elected at a time of political defeat for the traditional ruling political parties. He was the nominee of a combination of political parties of the Left, known as the Popular Front.

He himself was the leader of the Radicals—more radical in name than in reality.

Short of stature, a bit stout but not fat, he was not an impressive figure in a crowd. His character was reflected in his eyes, which were at times whimsical, at times cynical, most of the time good-natured, but they could register resentment and indignation. He was happily free from the affliction of many political leaders called the "divine afflatus." At heart he was an educator, with his feet set firmly on the ground in this field. I had noticed his modesty and something of his humility when he was sitting for the bust by Jo Davidson, the great sculptor. He merged easily with the plain people. Invited once to an agricultural fair and knowing that he was to be there, I looked about to find and greet him, but I could see no one surrounded by military uniforms, no one wearing a high hat, and I inquired when the President would arrive. "Oh, he is here" was the reply, and my informant pointed to a little man in a simple business suit leaning on the railing around an enclosure in which prize pigs were on exhibition. He had been hidden behind men of higher stature, and there was nothing to set him off from the many others.

His people were tillers of the soil. On the grounds of the great *fundo* of La Serena, near Los Andes, I have visited the little country schoolhouse where he began his education. Eager for learning, he passed through the university, and later studied at the Sorbonne in Paris. He adopted law as his profession, lectured at the university, interested himself in politics in support of his ideals and managed a vineyard which produced an excellent red wine. He was affectionately called "Don Tinto" by his friends, after the wine of his vineyard.

He was an educator in the true sense, with a constructive impulse in statesmanship. "To educate is to govern," he had said. This was his most characteristic sentence. Intensively and intelligently interested in education, he knew it to be necessary in a functional democracy, and he was profoundly concerned about public education. He urged manual training to provide the country with skilled labor. He set up a little trade school of his own for the training of the boys of the underprivileged, some recruited from among orphans living in shacks and under bridges. This reflected not only his mind but the heart of the man, and was dwelt upon by Cardinal Caro in his funeral oration as an illustration of his contribution to the building of a good society. On numerous occasions when I have heard him discussing the needs of Chile with foreigners, he put the greatest emphasis on the education and health of the masses. He believed that the future strength of the nation depended on wholesome food, proper clothing and sanitary housing. Tourists driving into the city from the airport in Santiago pass block after block of two-story houses erected for the workers by the state as a part of Aguirre Cerda's elaborate plan for the elimination of the slums. These houses, in healthy surroundings, with small gardens for flowers in front and for vegetables in the rear, are the monuments of this President. Unhappily his plans were retarded by the devastating earthquake that wrecked so many towns, forcing a diversion of funds to their restoration. Then came World War II to hold back so many plans, but housing projects for the workers loom large in the program of all the Chilean governments.

But Aguirre Cerda's program for national development was not confined to humane and idealistic projects. It included the mechanization of farms, the use of the most modern machinery, the importation of fine cattle. Because he had vision, he saw the need for the industrialization of the country. For generations, copper and nitrate had seemed to the shortsighted enough to supply the nation's needs. The export taxes defrayed a large part of the financial necessities of the government. But Aguirre Cerda had learned something from the near collapse of these two major industries at the close of the first World War, and he knew Chile could not depend on these alone. With 2,800 miles of Pacific Coast, the sea teeming with tuna and other fish to supply the markets of South America, there was no well-organized fishing industry; with very heavy demands for cement in building in this land of the sometimes quivering earth, there were not enough cement factories to meet the demand; with steel necessary for the re-inforcement of the cement, steel had to be imported; and with the streets of Santiago congested with automobiles, there were no tire factories.

Since private capital did not come forward to meet the demands of industrialization, Aguirre Cerda conceived it the duty of the government to encourage it financially and technically, and the Fomento Corporation was created to meet the need. It has more than justified itself. One of the largest cement factories in the hemisphere has been built; a great steel mill has been set up with credits from the Export-Import Bank in Washington; a tire factory, financed jointly by Chilean and North American capital, is now flourishing. It would be tiresome to enumerate all the projects it has sponsored. The Fomento Corporation has ushered in a new day in the economic advancement of the people, and on its tenth anniversary it was Aguirre Cerda, then dead, who received the homage. Such, the statesman.

He was a convinced and militant democrat, a strict constitutionalist, a consistent defender of the freedoms of the individual, a champion always of the common man. A Catholic, he favored the separation of church and state as beneficial to both. He maintained affectionate relations with Cardinal Caro. I am sure that when Cardinal Dougherty of Philadelphia visited Chile he expected that the man elected by the Popular Front would receive him with cold courtesy, but he was astonished by the tone of his conversation and pleased with the assurance that there would be no serious misunderstandings between the church and state so long as Aguirre Cerda was President.

I found him in complete accord with our interpretation of the significance of Hitler's march into Poland. On the numerous occasions when I discussed different phases of the struggle with him, I found him invariably helpful and co-operative. Only once did he sharply resent an action of my government. When plans were made in Washington to settle a threatened conflict between two neighboring nations, Argentina and

Brazil were joined by a third country as mediators, and Chile, one of the three in the A.B.C. group of Woodrow Wilson, was left out. Aguirre Cerda showed his resentment to me. I was as much puzzled as he that we should have retained the two nations under dictators and dropped the one militant democracy. A staunch patriot, he was very angry. "It is not nice," he said, and his expression was one of disgust.

Though a politician and a party leader, his personal behavior savored more of the pedagogue than of the politician. He was simple in his tastes and natural in his manner. One night I had an initial showing of a Lincoln picture at the embassy, followed by a buffet dinner. We dispensed with protocol at the dinner, and this was as he would have had it. His dignity was that of the mind and spirit, not entirely of manner.

I found him a most understanding friend of the United States, though he was keenly conscious of some of our inconsistencies. No one could have followed the unfolding of the Roosevelt policies with more appreciation. He hailed the good-neighbor policy as ushering in a new day in the relations of the American nations. He had a warm admiration for Roosevelt and he asked me innumerable questions about him. He felt he was trying to do for Chile what Roosevelt had done for the United States, but the burden was too heavy, and his time too short. More sensitive than Roosevelt to attacks, he suffered toward the end from the misunderstanding of his more humble followers whose impatience with the slow progress of reforms did not take into account the earthquake and the war, and the dissensions among his political allies. Even when he was a dying man, a victim of work and worry, he refused to spare himself, and when he fell at his post, his detractors were silent, and he went to his rest mourned by the masses he had tried to serve.

2

No one could have more thoroughly satisfied the eye as to how a President "ought to look" than Juan Antonio Ríos, who succeeded to the Presidency. Tall, slender, handsome, with dark hair and eyes, and always dressed conservatively and in perfect taste, he looked the part of a leader. Thoroughly devoted to the ideology of the Radical party, his was a moderating influence for caution. Where Aguirre Cerda was passionately interested in raising the economic status of the masses, Ríos was primarily interested in the economic development of the country. I suspect that the Fomento Corporation of Aguirre Cerda impressed him more than his housing projects, though Ríos made progress in this, while hampered by the war.

In the first days of his regime, when world problems had become paramount, he lacked personal experience in international politics, but he was wise in his choice of advisers and he developed rapidly, though he advanced cautiously. A very clever national politician, a good manipulator of men, he needed no advice on domestic issues. Like his predecessor, he rose from the ranks. His was a family of farmers and in his youth he had followed the plow and milked the cows. He received his education in Concepción.

In the beginning I found him difficult to know. Always polite and pleasant, he seemed a bit remote, perhaps suspicious, and a barrier was interposed between the meeting of minds. Gradually this feeling of aloofness disappeared, and during the greater part of his administration we were on the most friendly and even confidential terms, and toward the end these had developed into mutual affection. He impressed me always as a thoughtful man with the courage of his convictions, jealous of his prerogatives, as he should have been, and utterly devoted to his country. He never compromised his dignity in official contacts and public actions. On ceremonial occasions, this dignity was like a steel armor, the real man impenetrable to the multitude in the street. As he rode to the capitol to the opening of Congress, and on other ceremonial occasions, he looked every inch the chief of state—an institution more than a man—and this puzzled me, since I sensed in him a very warm human feeling. I noticed that when someone broke through the crust he was delighted.

Once, when on an inspection trip during the war, General Brett invited him to a flight in the famous war-scarred plane, the *Swoose*. Standing beside him, the General had him navigate the plane for a moment. On his return to his headquarters in Panama, Brett made him a member of the fictitious "Order of the Swoose," and had a beautiful diploma made on parchment setting forth that Ríos had qualified as an expert pilot on a flight on a certain day. I was asked to present it to him personally if I were sure he would not resent it. I knew he would be delighted—as he was. He laughed heartily, spoke with appreciation of Brett, and he placed the diploma on a mantel in his office, where it remained until his death.

Throughout his regime, with his critical problems pertaining to the war, he was frequently harassed by political complications and sometimes forced to the reorganization of the government because of the intransigence of coalition ministries, and when necessary he formed a Ministry of Administration, but, fortunately, during his regime he had but two ministers of foreign affairs.

Unlike his predecessor and successor he did not live in the Moneda, since it is not too cheerful as a place of residence. His predecessor had died there of galloping tuberculosis, and Ríos was concerned about his own health. He built a charming country house an hour from the capital, overlooking a beautiful countryside. He lived, and sometimes entertained there, driving back and forth to his office in the palace.

I came closer to Ríos during his official visit to the United States than ever before. Since, en route, he stopped over in several nations for wearisome ceremonies, luncheons, dinners, receptions, the reviewing of troops and numerous speeches, he subjected himself to a supreme test of physical endurance, and he had but recently undergone a serious operation. I learned that in Lima he had thrown off the cold armor of protocol, danced the cueca in the Chilean Embassy and impressed the Peruvians with his warm personality. Later I asked him why he did not act in Chile in public with the informality that had pleased the Peruvians, and his answer was illuminating. He said if he did so he would be criticized for lowering the prestige of the Presidency. "I can, and do, in the provinces," he said, "where the people are all friendly, but in Santiago the critics predominate."

In Washington and New York he was still the man of Lima and he made the same impression. We met him at the airport and drove him to the White House, where President Truman was waiting on the steps to greet him. From then on, through long days, he endured the torture of luncheons, dinners and receptions with seeming pleasure. At a luncheon at the country house of Peter Grace he delighted the Americans by dancing the cueca with an American woman who had mastered the art in Chile. A high honor was paid him by the City of New York when he was invited to make the speech at the formal designation of the old Sixth Avenue as the "Avenue of the Americas" and to review the first American troops returning from the battlefields of Europe.

But the hardships of the journey had been too much. On alighting from the plane in Santiago I found his color good, his eyes bright and merry, his manner alert, but he had been sustained through the hectic tour by will power and excitement, for very soon he was stricken, and he sank rapidly. He was too ill to receive ex-President Hoover, but I drove the American ex-President to Ríos's country home to leave cards, an attention I later heard Ríos had appreciated.

In two speeches in Washington and New York, especially at the luncheon given him by the Senate Committee on Foreign Affairs, I took advantage of the opportunity, in his presence, to remind the senators that Chile was not a nation under a dictator and that the delay in breaking relations with the Axis was inevitable under the processes of democracy. He never referred to these speeches in my presence, but during his

illness I learned from Admiral Merino, then Acting President, and Fernández, the Foreign Minister, that he had
spoken with warm appreciation to them of my action, which
had surprised and pleased him.

The Ríos Administration covered the most tragic period
in world history, when all liberty-loving nations were in peril,
and totalitarian elements were threatening the overthrow of
democratic regimes. This was unquestionably true in Chile.
The war, with its economic dislocations, gave pause to domestic
reforms in Chile, as in all other countries. Ríos will be
judged in history as a war president. Despite tremendous pressure from totalitarian elements of both the Right and Left,
and a misunderstanding by a large portion of the North American press, which rapturously cheered the South American dictators for their arbitrary action in our favor—with Lend-
Lease dangling before them as a prize—while criticizing the
Chilean Democracy for following a procedure prescribed by
law, Chile emerged from a critical period under his guidance
without having violated the Constitution or deviated one hairbreadth from the processes of that democracy for the preservation of which we were waging war.

This was the supreme triumph of his administration, and
history will so record it.

3

After the death of Ríos, elections were called, and Gabriel González Videla became President. Born in La Serena
of middle-class parentage, he received a university education
and studied law. Ambition and imagination led him into politics, and at an early age he became a member of the House
of Deputies and, soon thereafter, the president of the chamber. Clever, resourceful, energetic, dynamic, he distinguished
himself by his activities and his fluency on the platform.

Though of short stature, he was a fighter, and his hot
temper in his early days was not always under control, as on

the day he hurled an inkwell at a colleague. He took high rank as a strategist in the election of 1938, when he directed the successful campaign of Aguirre Cerda, and he was rewarded with the embassy in France and then in Rio. In Vichy he formed a warm friendship with Admiral Leahy, the Ambassador of the United States. Throughout World War II he was a militant supporter of the allied democracies. But, impatient for higher honors, he resigned his embassy to enter the Senate.

Immaculate in dress, graceful in manner, he was an attractive figure and had extraordinary charm. His face smooth-shaven, his hair dark, his eyes brown and keen, illuminating his countenance, he exuded cordiality, no less true in a crowd than in a drawing room. His personal charm was not unlike that of President Roosevelt, and even his political foes found it hard to resist. I am sure he weathered numerous political storms by the charm of his personality. Though I heard he sometimes became enraged, I was never to see him when he was not a symbol of serenity, though I once found him on the verge of an eruption.

A fluent and forceful speaker, he avoided Latin floridity and spoke simply, forcefully and with felicity. I found him most impressive in extemporaneous speeches, when he let himself go, and in the heat of an argument he seldom said the wrong thing. His mental processes were rapid, so much so that the casual observer might conclude that his cleverness was superficial, but on the numerous occasions I took North American bankers and businessmen to see him, they always expressed their amazement on finding him so intimately familiar with the business, economic and technical problems of his country.

Seeing him on purely social occasions, one might conclude that he was something of a playboy, and few would suspect the thoroughness with which he studied his problems. He was a hard worker, and on many occasions I found the Moneda throbbing with activity at night, with political leaders passing in and out.

His courage could not be questioned since he knew no fear. In times of tension, due to controversies with extremists, when the batteries of abuse were turned upon him, he appeared out of doors in public meetings, making himself an easy target. I recall an especially perilous time when rumors of a conspiracy against the regime were rife and he was the pet aversion of the most dangerous extremists. When it was announced that he would speak outdoors to a multitude, I asked him if he were not taking an imprudent risk. He laughed. "My speech tomorrow will not be conciliatory," he said. "I shall tell them bluntly what I think of them." He did—and nothing happened.

I am sure it can be said without exaggeration that during the critical days through which South America was passing in the early postwar period because of conspiracies of totalitarians of both the Right and Left, he was the foremost chief of state on the continent—a fighting champion of democracy. Certainly no chief of state in the world made such an aggressive personal fight against both the Fascists and communists. He followed a straight line on the supreme issue of the day. With a keen international vision, he understood the deep significance of what was going on in the world.

I can personally testify to his sincere admiration and respect for the United States. Having got the erroneous impression that I thought him unfriendly, he invited me to his apartment between the election and his inauguration. "I know," he said, "that the future of Chile, its industrial development, its economic well-being, is dependent to a considerable extent on the friendship and collaboration of the United States. Chile needs capital and wants North American capital, and she can guarantee fair treatment." He was to give proof many times that this was the line of his thinking, though the pressure of domestic politics sometimes interfered. I found his government co-operative with mine on almost every issue.

Though long a leader of the Radical party and a zealous champion of its fundamental theories, when he was President he rose above party lines when necessary and sought a government of national consolidation in a crisis. At such times, putting patriotism above partisanship, he invited the co-operation within the government of Liberals, Conservatives and Socialists. When some of his friends, thinking in terms of presidential politics three years before an election, would have compromised the democratic cause, he faced the fight with a daring that commanded their admiration. This courage and decision were underlined when he broke all contacts with the Communist party that had betrayed him and the country and handed their passports to the diplomats of Russia, Czechoslovakia and Yugoslavia.

Unlike Ríos, he lived in the Moneda. Though the rooms of the palace are large and lofty, the atmosphere is not one of cheer, but rather of austerity. The windows look out upon the business section of the city. If there are any cozy corners in the palace they escaped my notice. González Videla therefore took full advantage of the beautiful summer palace in Viña del Mar, going there usually on Friday evenings and remaining until Monday mornings, both summer and winter. There he found relaxation and sea air. The summer palace was designed for that very purpose. There he could take his plunge in the long outdoor swimming pool fed by the sea, lounge or stroll in the ample grounds, and entertain his friends at luncheons and dinners on the terrace looking out upon the Pacific. He was a good equestrian. He took part throughout the year in the activities of the Paper Chase Club, and in his red riding coat he made a handsome appearance.

4

Having served but a few months during the administration of Carlos Ibáñez, I shall not undertake a miniature of him. During the few months I was waiting for the acceptance of my resignation I found him always gracious and friendly. In moments of sternness or in facing opposition, he could look like a figure carved in granite, but I soon found that he had a warm smile and a comforting sense of humor. I shall have more to say about him in chapters to follow.

The character and conduct of the presidents during my mission in Chile gave me confidence in the reality and stability of Chilean democracy. They would have reflected credit on any people. The three I knew most intimately were able men, of political experience and character; all dedicated their energies to the public service; all thought in terms of the future, for which all hoped to prepare the country economically; all made progress in the industrialization of the nation; and all knew that the ultimate stability of the state calls for the lifting of the social and economic status of the masses. All were staunch champions of the democratic creed; all had vision that reached beyond the national boundaries; and all were zealous in the protection of the rights and dignity of the republic.

They differed in their personalities, their tastes and judgment, but fundamentally they were all of the same pattern. They had the courage of their convictions and maintained the dignity of their office without swagger or flamboyancy. All were friendly to the United States, and none subservient. All, of course, made mistakes and miscalculations, as is inevitable in these shifting days of readjustment throughout the world. From all, I received innumerable kindnesses and proofs of personal friendship. A composite of the miniatures of the presidents which I have attempted presents a realistic picture of the Chilean people.

XXIV

A Peaceful Revolution at the Polls

The Radical party had been in power for fourteen years, with three presidents, when more than a year before the election the country moved, a bit boisterously, into the presidential campaign of 1952. This party had the advantage of a tight organization that reached into every nook and corner of the country, and it functioned three hundred and sixty-five days of the year. The leaders were clever politicians whose fingers were never remote from the public pulse. It had the disadvantage of being occasionally embarrassed by divergent elements within it. It had been an aggressive party of opposition during the lean years, and its presidents sometimes found that with some of its leaders opposition had become a habit. It won its first election in 1938 through a combination of Radicals, the Socialists and Communists, but in 1952 the Radicals were not confident or united; the once strong Socialist party was divided into three segments bitterly warring with one another; and the Communists were hostile because of the stout opposition of Ríos and González Videla to their subversive activities.

In Pedro Enrique Alfonso the Radicals found a candidate of character and governmental experience with an excellent reputation for probity, but despite his long party service he was not to receive its united support. One segment of the Socialists supported the Radical nominee; another, more extreme, aligned itself with a left-wing group that was on speaking terms with the Communists. Officially the Communists supported the candidacy of Senator Allende, the Socialist, who had been an uncompromising foe of communism. Events proving that he would not receive the united support of the communists were foreshadowed early when Pablo Neruda, the communist poet, returning to Chile from his self-imposed exile, announced in an interview in Montevideo that his party would support General Carlos Ibáñez. This disclosure caused some distress among the communists, who repudiated the prediction, but the fat was in the fire.

The Liberal party alone presented what superficially appeared to be a solid front behind the candidacy of Arturo Matte, who, as Minister of Finance, had made an excellent impression on the country, but the campaign had not progressed far when a Liberal Deputy announced his support of Ibáñez.

The Conservative party had split on a social program, and when the majority renounced the traditional policies of the party, retaining the name "Conservative," the minority withdrew and formed another party, named "Traditionalist."

Never had a campaign stretched over such a long period. It was in full blast many months before the presidential nominations were made, and, in jockeying for advantage, there was a constant shifting of positions on numerous issues.

More unfortunate for the country, the long campaign made

it impossible for Congress to agree on any program to meet the rapidly increasing cost of living through an inflation gone wild.

The chaotic state of the political parties lost them the confidence of the masses and of numerous independents, who began to feel that Chile required a "strong man," independent of the old political parties. Nothing effective had been done to check the inflation or reduce the cost of living, which was mounting beyond the reach of the masses. Drastic reforms were necessary, and no party or politician was willing to take the responsibility. Indeed, any suggestion from these would have been viewed with suspicion as to personal or political motives. Manifestly, the only course offering any promise would have been to invite in expert economists and financiers from outside the country whose proposals could not possibly be ascribed to domestic politics or personal interest. This, in fact, was seriously considered by González Videla, but political opposition led to its abandonment. Halfhearted efforts to control inflation had been made without effect. Speculation in foodstuff was manifest. Thus the very poor were suffering and in a spirit of revolt. The finances of the nation were in a bad way. These conditions played into the hands of the communists and extremists. The conditions were ripe for a revolution at the polls when General Carlos Ibáñez announced himself as an independent candidate for President.

Though in his seventies, he looked like a well-preserved person in his fifties. He was a man of impressive presence, tall, robustly built, with strong features, a distinctly Germanic head. His manner was that of the military officer he was, though years had intervened since he had commanded a regiment. He would have stood out conspicuously in any crowd. Naturally he had his enemies, dating back to his dictatorship in the twenties, though I never heard anyone question his personal integrity. In the 1920s he had taken over dictatorial power in a *coup d' état,* and though he had rendered some real service to the country his rule had been ruthless. But during his regime the bankers of the United States were urging loans on all and sundry, and millions poured into Chile. With money abundant, his administration had made some notable improvements in the country.

However, the inevitable reaction came, and Ibáñez crossed the border to Argentina, where he settled down to a long sojourn. When the ban against him was lifted he returned to Chile, where he lived quietly, tending his farm near Talca. He then seemed an historical figure with "his future in his past," but in 1942 the Conservatives and Liberals, some of whose leaders had been exiled by him, nominated him for President. This was in the midst of the war, and whatever may have been his views, not a few of his supporters, especially in the south, were Nazi sympathizers. When he was defeated it was assumed that a period had been put to his political life, and it was something of a shock to many when he announced his candidacy for the Senate from Santiago and was elected. Meanwhile, he had aligned himself with the Agrarian-Labor party, then but recently formed and composed in large part of big landowners in the south of the country.

However, his party split on his presidential candidacy in 1952. He was not a consummate politician, or he would have announced his candidacy in Chile and not from Buenos Aires and would not have given out an interview there in mild commendation of the regime in Argentina. These tactical mistakes, however, did not affect the mass of the voters, who were more concerned with the mounting cost of living.

Few politicians or political writers could conceive of his election without the support of one of the old major political parties. A few splinter parties sprang up, unimportant in numbers and formed primarily to exploit their leaders rather than for the support of Ibáñez. These rather obscure leaders were so violent and irresponsible that they did him more harm than good. They featured extravagant denunciations of the United States, cultivated the communists blatantly with a pledge to repeal the Law for the Defense of Democracy, to confiscate the American-owned mines without compensation, to renew diplomatic relations with Moscow, to denounce the Mutual

Security Pact and to sell strategic war material behind the Iron Curtain.

These men, acting on their own, ignored Ibáñez and treated him with such scant respect that at length at a public dinner he rebuked them for running wild with pledges as to policies and intentions without bothering to consult him. Though he served notice that he alone would determine policies, these irresponsible leaders of the splinter parties went full steam ahead with their tirades against the Yankees and property rights.

Throughout the campaign they were charging—and telling Ibáñez—that my embassy was actively injecting itself into the campaign against him. The usual charge was made that North American businessmen in Chile were intensively participating in the campaign with money—which was absolutely false. At the very beginning of the campaign, which covered twelve months and more, I had instructed my staff that they were not to discuss the campaign outside the office or publicly express a preference. The North American businessmen were again warned against making contributions to the campaign fund of any party.

2

About six months before the election I was convinced that without a radical change Ibáñez would be elected. The opposition was divided. My judgment was not based on any imagined strength of the splinter parties. The strength of Ibáñez was with the masses suffering under inflation who were not interested in tirades against the United States or its investors. They were thinking about the high cost of living and little else. Word reached me from the country districts that the workers on the *fundos,* who had once been the backbone of another party, were making no secret of their support of Ibáñez, and, more impressive to me, owners of factories, hostile to him, told me that most of their employees were for him. The feeling of the housewives of the very poor seemed especially significant.

One day the wife of a member of my staff went to market and was forced to await her turn in line. She decided to pass the time by asking five women of the very poor their preference in the election, and without a single exception they were all for Ibáñez. Asked their reason, their reply was significant. "How much was bread when Ibáñez was President in the 1920s, and how much is it now?" How much was meat, and now? These simple women could not understand that world conditions, due to the war, made impossible an early return to the prices of the 1920s. This line of reasoning had great effect.

It therefore seemed clear to me from the beginning that this election could not be judged by traditional standards, and that an emergence of the masses with a protest vote was pending. Almost six months before the election I reported to Washington that unless there were some radical and improbable change in the trend, Ibáñez would be elected despite the opposition of all the major parties. My associates thought this incredible, basing their dissent on the tradition that no one can be elected in Chile without the support of one of the major parties. At first Washington was as incredulous as my staff, but regularly for six months I reiterated my prediction, giving reasons. I know politics and something of mass psychology, and I could sense the underground movement of a revolution at the polls. This was not based on the irresponsible harangues of the extremists of the splinter parties, and, in fact, they were to account for no more than 100,000 votes of the 450,000 that went to Ibáñez. The 350,000 were not influenced by the attacks of the extremists on the United States; they were thinking about the cost of living.

After the election, I was congratulated by Washington for the accuracy of my prediction.

During the twelve years of my tenure in Chile before the election of 1952 I had met Ibáñez but twice, and very casually then. At the Hípico race course, during the visit of Vice-

President Wallace, I noticed General Ibáñez standing aside from the crowd and pointed him out to Wallace. "Should I meet him?" he asked. "By all means," I replied, and I introduced them and they shook hands. It was not until the last week of the campaign that I met him again at a reception at the nuncio's, when, moving about in the crowd, I found myself face to face with the candidate. He seemed that night as cold as marble and he did not smile when we shook hands. I knew he had been deceived by the extremists, who had told him, no doubt, that the embassy—and myself especially—had been active against him.

3

During the two months intervening between the election and the inauguration, the extremists among his supporters had their inning. In sensational interviews and speeches they were presuming to outline the policies to be adopted, without reference to the incoming President. Again the spigot of hate of the Yankees was pulled out and the poison poured forth. Again the people were assured that the new administration would confiscate the copper mines without compensation; that the Law for the Defense of Democracy would be repealed; that diplomatic relations with Russia would be instantly resumed; that Chile would begin the sale of strategic war material on a large scale behind the Iron Curtain; that the Mutual Security Pact would be immediately denounced. These self-annointed leaders spoke ex cathedra.

These sensational and false foreshadowings of what was to come made a very bad impression in Washington and, indeed, through the free world. I did not believe that these sensationalists spoke for the new President, and so informed Washington.

Unlike my colleagues, I did not call on Ibáñez to congratulate him until his election was made official by the action of Congress, since, with a plurality, he did not have a majority, and Congress had the constitutional right to choose either of the two highest on the poll. Pending congressional action, it seemed clear to me that the hurried congratulations of the Diplomatic Corps could be interpreted as an attempt to influence the action of Congress. To congratulate him on his election before he was officially elected impressed me as premature. I had no doubt that Congress, with its usual common sense in such cases, would give the victory to the man who headed the poll, but it seemed an interference in the domestic politics of Chile to congratulate the head of the poll until he was officially declared the victor. I was attacked by the extremists for not anticipating this event.

When Congress acted, I immediately asked for an appointment to see Ibáñez. I called to extend congratulations. He lived in a big rambling house outside the fashionable section. A guard of *carabineros* was stationed outside. Crossing a small court, I was shown into the house by one of the President's friends. Like so many Chilean houses, it had no central heating, and in the hall, before entering the room where the President-elect was sitting, I was advised to keep my overcoat on. In the rear of the room a number of his friends were engaged in lively chatter, and near the door sat Ibáñez with a single man. He rose when we entered and shook hands. I explained why I had not called before, and then took up the numerous fantastic charges against the embassy, the North American industrialists and myself, and I think pulverized them, one by one. Before I left, his manner had changed to one of cordiality and I had the satisfaction of hearing him say, "I have never thought that you or your embassy interfered in any way in the election."

As I expected, I found his position entirely different from that of those who had presumed to speak for him without his authorization. The interview lasted half an hour and was entirely friendly. He rose and summoned the photographer, and we posed for pictures. A little later I saw him again at his house to invite him to the reception I was planning for Eleanor Roosevelt. He took a small, much thumbed notebook from his pocket, and after glancing through it, he accepted with pleasure. During the eight months I remained in Chile after presenting my resignation in Washington, I saw him several times and I always found him cordial and understanding.

I have dwelled on the campaign and election of 1952 to emphasize the fact that even under critical conditions the Chilean people do not deviate from the democratic line.

Despite the cordial relations established, there were rumors that an attempt would be made by our enemies to convert the inaugural ceremonies into an anti-Yankee demonstration, which I knew would not reflect the feeling of the Chilean people, and I had a plan to prevent anything of the sort.

XXV

Mrs. Roosevelt's Chilean Triumph

Everything indicated that the inaugural ceremonies would be notable. Perón announced he was sending a delegation from Argentina, impressive both as to official status and numbers, headed by his vice-president and foreign minister, accompanied by about twenty others. Other South American countries could not compete with this, but some sent their vice-presidents as special ambassadors. The sending of large groups on special occasions had seemed to me an imposition on the host nation, laying upon it a heavy burden of expense and entertainment, and I told Washington that I wanted a small but select delegation which I wished headed by Mrs. Roosevelt, with General Bradley and one or two others. I suspect the State Department was flabbergasted since we had never before sent a

woman as special ambassador to an inauguration or coronation. However, I insisted, and President Truman agreed, but
for understandable reasons General Bradley could not leave
Washington at that time. Mrs. Roosevelt would be supported
by General John Hull, ranking next to Bradley. Since our
policy is not to send special ambassadors, I was designated as
such, but I always featured the head of the delegation as the
special ambassador, Admiral Leahy on one occasion, and Mrs.
Roosevelt on the other.

The announcement in the press created something of a sensation, and most of my colleagues were delighted. "My God,
what a master stroke," exclaimed the Ambassador from Vene-
zuela. The arranging of the program for Mrs. Roosevelt kept
the embassy dizzy for days, for there was a tremendous pressure upon it for the privilege of entertaining her. Our em-
barrassments never ceased, since after every minute of her
time had been assigned we found that President González
Videla wished to have her for dinner on the Sunday of her
visit. I had gone to the Moneda to invite the President to the
reception I was giving for Mrs. Roosevelt, but expected him
to refuse, since it was his rule not to attend functions at the
embassies. He gave an amusing explanation of his declination, but said that he and his wife were very fond of Mrs.
Roosevelt and wished to give a dinner in her honor on Sunday. Meanwhile, she had accepted a dinner invitation from
Mrs. Santa Cruz, wife of Chile's representative in the United
Nations, and this had not been arranged by the embassy. The
President suggested that perhaps he could persuade Mrs. Santa
Cruz to transfer her dinner party to the Moneda. Obviously
I could not make the suggestion to her, and I replied that he
alone could arrange the transfer with any degree of grace.
He went to his desk and telephoned Mrs. Santa Cruz, who
agreed. Since González Videla would leave office on the fol-
lowing day, this would be his last dinner in the Moneda, and
the next night Mrs. Roosevelt would attend the first dinner
given by his successor at the palace.

2

On October 31, at three-thirty, we went to the airport to meet Mrs. Roosevelt. A large crowd, with women predominating, headed by Amanda Labarca, who had been associated with Mrs. Roosevelt in the United Nations, had gathered, and as she descended from the plane a resounding cheer greeted her. After she had personally greeted many of the women, we drove her to the Embassy Residence, where she would be our guest during her stay in Chile. After a few minutes' rest, we drove her to Santiago College, where she was met at the gate by Elizabeth Mason, the principal, and four small children, two Chilean and two North American. The auditorium was packed with students and their parents and she was given a rousing ovation. A student delivered a speech of welcome, which was remarkable both in substance and style, and Mrs. Roosevelt responded gracefully.

She was then presented with a beautiful Chilean flag by two students, one being the daughter of the new President. After another ovation on leaving, she was taken to the salon of the college for a tea and reception by the American Womens Club, where every woman, it seemed, insisted on a personal chat with her. Talking with scores, after a tiresome journey sitting up in the plane, she showed no signs of weariness.

3

We hurried her back to the embassy for a press conference. Though we arrived before seven, the hour fixed for the conference, the room was already filled with reporters and radio people, with their paraphernalia in readiness. When, promptly on the stroke of seven, she appeared there was a gasp of astonishment, since punctuality is a little unusual in Chile.

She sat beside me on a davenport. Carlos Griffin, of my staff, sat directly across the table from her; he amazed and delighted her with the rapidity and perfection of his translations of questions and answers. She was perfectly composed when she announced, with a smile, that she was ready. The radio men held their instruments almost in her face, since the interview was going on the air. For nearly an hour she submitted to questions, some a bit delicate, and she replied with ease. Her answers could not have been wiser had they been dictated by the State Department after deliberation.

Once only did she cease to smile, and looked stern. We had decided it would be a mistake to exclude the reporter of the communist paper, which would have had much to say about the freedom of the press if we had. This communist reporter broke in once to ask if Mrs. Roosevelt approved of our alleged resort to bacteriological warfare, as was being charged in the communist propaganda. There was a dead silence in the room; most of the reporters showed their disapproval. Her answer was brief but barbed, the reporters broke into applause, and the communist asked no more questions. "My God, what a woman," I heard from the crowd.

She gave no indication of a desire to terminate the conference, but instead left it to the reporters to decide. When they put a period to the conference and she went upstairs to dress for dinner, we served refreshments, and the communist reporter consumed his full share.

It was at the press conference that she won the admiration and partiality of the press, which was to feature her throughout her stay.

Within an hour, the delegates from the United States who, with their wives, had accompanied Mrs. Roosevelt arrived for dinner. The party included General John Hull, General Walsh of the Inter-American Defense board, Admiral Bledsoe, the president of the Export-Import Bank, and the son of General Walsh. That night, after her hectic afternoon, Mrs. Roosevelt was in high good humor and the dinner was gay, but at eleven we shooed the guests home and sent her to bed.

4

On November 1 Mrs. Roosevelt's workday began at eight-thirty, when she shut herself in her rooms with Helen Steele, a secretary at the embassy, and for an hour dictated her "My Day" column directly on the typewriter. At ten o'clock, accompanied by Patricia, she was on her way to the Quinta Normal Health Center and the Trudeau Tuberculosis hospital. Nothing impressed the Chileans more than her sincere interest in all she saw. She inquired minutely about the management, chatted pleasantly with the doctors and nurses, and visited a number of the wards to speak to the patients.

At noon she was on her way to the Chile-American Cultural Institute for a luncheon in her honor. Impressed, as too few of our public men have been, by the notable achievements of the institute, she made a short, happy speech on the cultural relations of nations. Beside her sat Maria del Canto, then Minister of Education, whose life had been dedicated to educational work.

Back then to the embassy, where she received Professor Stevenson, who brought his boy, stricken with infantile paralysis. The child had been treated at Warm Springs by Roosevelt's personal physician and had so far recovered that he was able to get around on crutches without braces. His small sister presented Mrs. Roosevelt with flowers and delivered a pretty little speech.

At four o'clock, off to the Foreign Office to arrange the presentation of credentials. A great crowd, gathered in front of the Moneda, gave her a warm welcome. It was the first of numerous popular ovations. Mrs. Roosevelt sat on a sofa with Acting Minister Garcia Oldini, and they talked in French. By the time we left, the crowd had greatly increased in front of the Moneda and the ovation she received when leaving was tremendous.

At seven o'clock the reception at the embassy began. A very large and distinguished company including government officials, the Diplomatic Corps, officers of the armed forces, and

Chilean society crowded the rooms. General Ibáñez appeared with his wife and young daughters and remained late, mingling with the company, chatting with Mrs. Roosevelt, while Patricia entertained the young girls, who were delighted with what was probably their first grown-up party. Cardinal Caro appeared early and talked with Mrs. Roosevelt through an interpreter. It was ten o'clock before the last of the guests had left and we sat down to a family dinner. Showing no signs of weariness, she talked entertainingly of affairs at home until midnight, when she went to her room.

5

On November 2 Mrs. Roosevelt received callers until eleven, when she and Sybil were driven to the Municipal Theater, where the women of Chile paid homage to one of the greatest of their sex. Some time before, Mrs. González Videla, as honorary president of the women's organizations, had written me asking permission to arrange this tribute. Arriving near the theater, they found the streets so congested with thousands that it was with the greatest difficulty, and with the aid of the police, that the car was able to reach the entrance. The moment the car appeared pandemonium broke loose; the ovation continued, growing in volume, until she disappeared inside the theater.

This was packed to the top gallery. When, accompanied by Mrs. González Videla and Sybil, she went down the middle aisle to the stage, the ovation that had begun outside was matched by that of the women within. The President's wife, Graciela Mandujano, an outstanding worker among the underprivileged, and Amanda Labarca paid glowing tributes to the guest of honor, and she replied in a speech that struck precisely the right note.

A huge throng was waiting outside to give her another clamorous welcome when she emerged. We were a bit late in reaching the British Embassy for a luncheon with Sir Charles

346

and Lady Stirling. There was hardly time to reach the Moneda to present credentials to González Videla.

Again a huge crowd had assembled in the plaza and a great roar of cheers and shouts shook the air as Mrs. Roosevelt left the car. During a momentary wait in the palace she was urged to go to the window opening on the plaza to see the crowd. The moment she was seen, the crowd roared with enthusiasm, and she stood and waved. As she left the palace, the ovation was continued. On the sidewalk were two small children with their mother, and the photographers asked Mrs. Roosevelt to pose for a picture with the youngsters. Agreeable always to reporters and photographers, she complied, but one of the boys, intimidated by the unusual attention he was receiving, tried to pull away, but his mother dragged him back.

Leaving the palace, running behind schedule, we began the drive into the country to a reception for her at the beautiful home of the Cousiños. En route, we stopped at the Villa Maria Academy, run by American nuns. Though close to an hour late, we found the Mother Superior and a group of nuns waiting at the entrance to the grounds to receive her and conduct her to the auditorium, where the students had been waiting patiently. After an enthusiastic reception, a pretty Chilean girl delivered a beautiful speech of welcome in English, and after a graceful reply by Mrs. Roosevelt we were on our way again.

On then, at full speed, to the house of the Cousiños, where the reception had been in full blast for two hours. The dinner at the Moneda was drawing near, and though reluctant to leave this charming spot, she was forced to go, though not before she had greeted many and inspected the house, which had been designed by a North American architect. The visit had given her some idea of the charms of the Chilean countryside.

Back then to the embassy to dress hurriedly, and off to the Moneda for the dinner. The guests were personal friends of the retiring President's, and there was an agreeable absence of the stiffness of state occasions. The talk was not hampered by fears of political indiscretions, for this was the last dinner the President would give in the palace. The usual throng was waiting outside as we arrived, and when we left a little after midnight even more had gathered, though there had been no announcement that Mrs. Roosevelt would dine with the President that night.

6

Driving to the capitol on November 3 for the inauguration of Ibáñez, we passed through dense crowds that swarmed into the street, impeding traffic. They disregarded the police, who tried vainly to prevent them from surrounding the car. They were massed in front, behind and on the sides, and they knocked on the windows to attract Mrs. Roosevelt's attention. Not a few mothers held small babies up against the windows that they might see her. The cheering was deafening, and clearly came from the heart.

With great difficulty, Pepe, using the utmost caution to prevent injury to the people, reached the gates of the capitol grounds, and here the tribute was the greatest I have ever seen. The windows of the houses across the street were filled with cheering men and women. Great as was her ovation outside, it was matched by that which greeted her on entering the Salon of Honor of the capitol—as great as that which greeted the new President. The people on the ground floor rose. Those in the gallery shouted greetings. The only ovations at the capitol were those given the retiring and the new President and Mrs. Roosevelt.

On leaving the capitol for the visit of congratulations to the new President in the Moneda, there was such congestion and confusion that Pepe was unable to reach the entrance with the car, but the Brazilian Ambassador came to the rescue with the offer of his. We drove through a rather narrow street packed with people from building to building. They swarmed into the street, beyond the control of the police, surrounding and peering into the car, and again babies were held against the windows. We could move only by inches. But it was a demonstration of real friendship, plainly a sincere tribute, and Mrs. Roosevelt enjoyed it and understood. These people were pouring forth their affection for the Roosevelts. On finally reaching the Moneda, we found the same huge crowd and heard the same lusty cheering. With the energetic aid of the police we finally reached the entrance, filed into the Red Salon, where Ibáñez and his ministers smilingly received the guests. Mrs. Roosevelt talked quite a while with the new President, wishing success for his administration and happiness for himself and family.

Returning to the embassy, we had a simple, quiet lunch, since we all needed a brief rest before going in the afternoon to Cousiño Park for the military review. The streets en route were lined with cheering people. We sat for almost three hours during the impressive military parade.

And that night we attended the dinner given by the new President for the special ambassadors sent for the inauguration. We had planned to skip the reception that followed the dinner, but since we did not sit down at the table until almost eleven, when we rose the people were pouring in for the reception, and the approach to the stairs was so congested that we were barely able to force our way through. But when the stairway was reached we found it packed tight from wall to wall, with people ascending leaving not one inch for people going down. No protocol officer was in sight, nor anyone in authority, and we seemed destined to stay. Happily, Mr. McKinzie of the British Embassy saw our plight and came to the rescue. He had powerful shoulders and sharp elbows, and he fought his way down, with our party just behind. When we finally emerged from the crush, I found my tie hanging down, and my suit looked as though it had been put through a wringer.

7

Very early on the morning of November 4, Mrs. González Videla appeared at the embassy and took Mrs. Roosevelt to inspect her fine housing projects. She had worked on this with commendable persistency and success. They went first to the quarters where the very poorest lived miserably in shacks, and Mrs. Roosevelt went into these unsanitary habitations and talked with the women, who were both astonished and pleased. Thence on to the attractive houses built by Mrs. González Videla's initiative.

On the return trip, a stop was made at the Plaza Bulnes, where Mrs. Roosevelt had been invited by a large group of women interested in the United Nations. This stop was scheduled for ten minutes, since at one o'clock we were to lunch at the Polo Club, where Arturo Olavarría, the new Foreign Minister, was giving a luncheon for the foreign delegations to the inauguration. A woman was making a speech and it was impossible to leave until she finished and Mrs. Roosevelt replied. I was concerned lest our late arrival at the Polo Club be offensive to Olavarría, and I telephoned Patricia, who was with Mrs. Roosevelt. She sent two notes to the platform, but the speaker, engrossed in her talk, did not read them. There was nothing to be done—nothing but for Mrs. Roosevelt to abbreviate her speech. Finally they reached the embassy, where they found me waiting on the curb, and without their leaving the car, we hurried on to the club, where about 800 were lunching on the terrace.

Immediately on leaving the table, we drove to the polyclinic —a Chilean Red Cross, perfectly equipped—established and maintained by the North Americans. As always a crowd was waiting in the street to catch a glimpse of Mrs. Roosevelt. Having made a thorough inspection and talked with the women in charge, she was hurried on to Marie Schultz's Madre y Hijo, a maternity hospital which had rendered notable services to both Chilean and American women. Again the people were waiting in the street. Mrs. Roosevelt was so impressed by the work and system that she lingered longer than our schedule permitted.

A busy day—but it was just beginning. From Marie Schultz Hospital she was driven to the Sweet Memorial, a settlement house, also founded and maintained by North Americans, where working mothers could leave their children under expert care while they were at work.

It was five o'clock when we reached the embassy, but even then Mrs. Roosevelt sat down with Miss Steele for an hour of dictation, and at seven we were on our way to the home of Raúl Aldunate, where, out on the lawn in the moonlight, our guest first saw the cueca danced.

Then, as fast as the car would go, to the Crillon Hotel, where the Zonta Club, composed of women in business and the professions, had arranged a reception. The street in front was so densely packed with cheering people waiting to see Mrs. Roosevelt that it was no easy task to reach the entrance. Here she made another speech. The dinner for the President, to be given at the Carrera by the visiting delegations, was now very near.

Back then to the embassy to dress for dinner. We had become accustomed to the cheering for Mrs. Roosevelt, but I was astonished when on entering the room where cocktails were being served before the dinner the guests welcomed her with an ovation. President Ibáñez, in a happy mood, greeted her warmly. It was half past one before we reached the embassy, and that night, for the first time, she admitted to feeling "a little tired."

Mrs. Roosevelt wore simple dresses except at dinners, but she reserved for the dinner for the President a beautiful gown made from a sari given her in India. The afternoon before the dinner she came downstairs in a state of consternation. The dress she had planned to wear called for golden slippers, and her maid, in packing, had overlooked them. Here was a diplomatic problem without precedent. Could golden slippers that would fit be found in Santiago? It was a holiday, and the stores were closed. Sybil, however, had a happy inspiration. She had met a man who represented a fine shoe factory, and perhaps he could be found. He was located. The situation was explained to him. Yes, he would act at once. He would go immediately to the factory and bring an assortment of golden slippers. Within an hour he arrived with huge boxes, and out of these were poured many pairs of golden slippers, and all attractive. One pair was found that fitted, and Mrs. Roosevelt asked the price. The gallant Chilean was shocked. "Rather than have you pay for them I would take them back," he said. "They are a present." She laughed and thanked him.

And so it came to pass that at the first dinner for the new President Mrs. Roosevelt appeared in golden slippers of Chilean manufacture. The reporters loved this incident and reported it in feature articles.

She had won the admiration of the newspapermen that first day when, with such simplicity, frankness and cordiality, she had faced a large group of them, asking no quarter, replying instantly and fully to every question, and waiting for them to terminate the conference. Then, too, she had formed a high opinion of the Chilean reporters. It was she who was featured throughout the days of the inauguration. I am sure the string of ovations that greeted her everywhere came partly from a desire to salute the memory of her great husband, but partly, also, to pay tribute to perhaps the greatest living woman in the world. Her interest in Chile was not an affectation. This interest of the Roosevelt family went back to the far-off days when one of the Delanos pitched his tent to stay in this lovely land between the mountains and the sea.

I have described her triumph because it was unique. She was the first woman ever to be sent as a special ambassador to an inauguration or coronation, and none of the distinguished men sent on such occasions ever scored such a personal triumph.

We found her a comfortable guest. The maid who waited on her had much to say about her simplicity and kindness, which won the girl's affection.

After the event, the State Department, which had been,

not unnaturally, a bit startled by my insistence that Mrs. Roosevelt be sent to head our delegation, and possibly a bit doubtful, congratulated me on the result, calling it "a stroke of genius."

The Roosevelt name is magical in South America.

XXVI

Farewell to the Andes

Before the inauguration of President Eisenhower I had placed my resignation in his hands. This was the same pattern I had followed in 1937, 1941, 1945 and 1949, since it is obligatory for all chiefs of missions to submit their resignations at the beginning of a new administration. My resignation had been refused by President Roosevelt three times and by President Truman twice, but I had been politically active before going to Spain, and mine was a political appointment. I therefore had no doubt that my resignation would be immediately accepted in 1953, as was to be expected under our system. We went, as usual, in late December to our pleasant summer retreat in Villa Alemana, sure that by the middle of February we would be on our way home. This seemed so certain that

354

we shortened our vacation to hurry back to Santiago to supervise the packing of our accumulations of twenty years. The Chilean press editorially was expressing the hope that I would be continued in my post, but it did not understand the unwritten law of North American politics.

It was during this waiting period, after our return from Villa Alemana, that Milton Eisenhower, the new President's brother, and John Cabot, in charge of Latin-American affairs in the State Department, arrived with their wives on their continental tour of observation. The Eisenhowers were our guests at the embassy. We found him amiable and Mrs. Eisenhower charming and sweet. Though not well at the time, she went through the ordeal of functions with the cheerful courage of a trooper. There was no such popular reaction to the visit of the President's brother as had marked that of the Wallace visit or that of Mrs. Roosevelt, but he was cordially received.

Every effort was made to make his visit pleasant and profitable. The entire staff of the embassy was assigned exclusively to his service, and he was briefed exhaustively. Hundreds of leading Chileans met him at the reception I gave for him, and the North American colony arranged an entertainment, mostly musical, at which he spoke. We were a bit disappointed when, in an interview with the press at the end of his journey, he confined his praise to Bolivia and Argentina.

2

Meanwhile the Ibáñez Administration was functioning and I was still Ambassador, though momentarily expecting the acceptance of my resignation. The new regime began with Arturo Olavarría as Minister of Foreign Affairs. He was an able lawyer and a clever politician. We had had a mild disagreement on a war issue when he was Minister of the Interior, but at his initial reception for the Diplomatic Corps he received me cordially, and during his tenure our relations could not have been more agreeable.

During this period I was able to be of some slight service to him. In February 1953 the crew of a British ship had demolished a shelter house on Concepción Island in the Antarctic put up by the Chileans on ground the British claimed as their own. The incident aroused great indignation among the Chileans, all the greater because of the false rumor that in the House of Commons the protest of the Chilean Government had been dismissed contemptuously. In the heat of the controversy the threat was made to take the incident before the Organization of American States.

One night Olavarría, accompanied by two men from the Foreign Office, came to my house, and the position of Chile was explained in detail. The submission of the dispute to the Organization of American States could have thrown the door wide open to the Antarctic claims of numerous nations, creating bitterness and accomplishing nothing. At the end of a long conference I agreed to act as an unofficial liaison between the minister and Sir Charles Stirling, in an effort to find an amicable solution. I urged direct diplomatic discussions between the two governments that could be conducted in an atmosphere of serenity and reason, remote from domestic politics and the excitement of the street. Since I was known as a friend of both parties to the controversy, something was probably hoped from my unofficial intervention.

Unfortunately, at the beginning of the controversy Sir Charles Stirling left the capital on a fishing expedition into the south, and nothing definite could be done until his return, though discussions were begun with the ranking officer of his embassy. It was clear from the beginning that neither side wanted seriously to disturb the traditionally friendly relations of a century. Progress was being made when Olavarría was replaced by Oscar Fenner, who was in accord with the plan on which Olavarría and I had agreed, and in the end, through the diplomatic channels I had urged, the incident was closed without real damage having been done. Three years later, Olavarría in a letter to *El Mercurio* (April 12, 1956), reviewed the incident, referring to the conference in my house and the part I had played.

Oscar Fenner was a specialist in laws dealing with the army. He was new in the diplomatic field, but he continued in office during the remainder of my tenure. He had a pleasing personality and was able, reasonable, conciliatory—a man of fixed principles, with an abundance of that common sense that is so often more effective than diplomatic finesse. The Diplomatic Corps found him delightful to work with and I found him convinced that it was in Chile's interest to maintain the most friendly relations with my country. He was intensely patriotic, and the Chileans could rely on him for a firm maintenance of his country's rights and dignity. He carried no chips on his shoulders, but there was no subserviency to either Washington or Buenos Aires. I saw him frequently, and always in a comfortable atmosphere of informality.

3

The most dramatic, and even spectacular, incidents of the closing months of my tenure grew out of the unfortunate official visit of President Perón, the dictator in Argentina. No one was more unpopular in Chile. His visit was not in response to a Chilean wish. He had told the Chilean Ambassador, then retiring from his post, that he was going to an Argentine province on the boundary of Chile, and since he had long wished to revisit the country, it would be convenient at this time. He pointedly asked the Ambassador to so inform President Ibáñez. There was no escape from extending the fished-for invitation without a direct affront. The time for the visit, which Perón had fixed, was badly chosen, since it would be during the last week of a political campaign in which he wished to get his finger. On his arrival, I was at Villa Alemana; I congratulated myself on being out of the capital and under no obligation to attend functions in his honor.

The popular protest against Perón and his tyrannical regime began even before his arrival. The editor of *La Nación,* the government organ, had gone to Buenos Aires to get an interview with the dictator, and its publication was a major sensation. The purport of it was that there had to be an economic union between Chile and Argentina—for which, within reason, something may be said—but he did not stop with that. He left no doubt that he had in mind a political and ideological union as well. This sounded unpleasantly like a none-too-modest proposal that Chile be absorbed by Argentina. He criticized San Martín and O'Higgins for not having merged the two nations in the beginning, and he implied that the time had come to correct the blunder.

Not unnaturally, the Chileans thought this intolerable impertinence. *La Unión* of Valparaiso denounced the insolence of the suggestion in a powerful editorial carrying a denunciation of the dictator and his despotic regime. *El Mercurio* and *El Diario Ilustrado* in Santiago did so less harshly but quite as emphatically.

Congress was then sitting in extra session, called for a specific purpose, and the editor of *La Unión,* a member of the House of Deputies, fiercely denounced the interview and Perón from the floor of the chamber. The President closed the extra session, as he had a constitutional right to do. Thoroughly aroused, members of Congress proposed calling another extra session on their own for the specific purpose of dealing with Perón's fantastic ideas, but with indignation at white heat and the certainty that bitter things would be said while Perón was a guest of the nation, the plan was put aside.

Meanwhile, Perón had arrived in Los Andes. A crowd of curious idlers had gathered. Descending from his plane, the dictator, with the characteristic vulgarity of his type, flung Argentine money into the crowd, and this insult intensified the public resentment.

All this I observed from afar. When Perón's party whizzed through Villa Alemana on its way to the cavalry school in

Quillota, Pepe alone of my household saw the motorcade speed by. Unhappily, circumstances made it unavoidable for me to meet the pro-Nazi dictator. The President had to honor his guest with a reception and my invitation from that quarter was a command, so I went to Santiago; and, since my presence in town would be known, there was no escaping the reception in the Argentine Embassy. I was delayed in reaching the embassy, and when I arrived the room was packed with my colleagues, who were scarcely recognizable in the thick cloud of tobacco smoke; the chattering was deafening. I could not locate the two presidents to greet them, and the clamor was so great I could not make myself heard when I tried to make inquiries. At length, with the aid of my elbows, I reached Perón and Ibáñez, shook hands, and withdrew into the crowd. Even so, that evening a radio station, not unfriendly to the dictator, solemnly announced that "when the American Ambassador entered the Argentine Embassy a dead silence fell upon the room." The noise had been so great I had not heard the silence.

One incident during Perón's visit created less indignation than amusement. An organization of women supporting candidates in whose success the alien dictator was interested, had divided, and the foreigner felt called upon to persuade the factions to reunite for the election. Summoning the two leaders of the warring factions to the Argentine Embassy, he pointed to a suitcase on the floor and told them it contained 200,000 Argentine nacionales and was theirs if they reunited their factions. When they took the money, and the story spread, the two leaders of the factions were denounced by the other women "for disgracing Chilean womanhood"; and one of the ladies involved indignantly denounced the story of the 200,000 nacionales with the triumphant declaration that it was only 100,000! Chile trembled with laughter from the mountains to the sea.

I could see that Perón had a certain charm of manner, was graceful in bearing, ingratiating, rather handsome in a way, and debonair, but he bore no resemblance to a serious statesman and rather suggested the idlers and playboys that frequent café society in New York.

The Perón visit was a fiasco, but his subservient press in Buenos Aires glowingly described the "emotional, almost hysterical" acclaim with which he had been received in Chile!

4

On July 28, six months after I had submitted my resignation, President Eisenhower accepted it in a note referring to my services through twenty years—to those in Spain "in difficult times" and to my extraordinarily long service in Chile. On my return to Washington, Secretary Dulles asked to see me, and in a long, highly complimentary conversation my contact with the government ceased. The President's letter fixed September 1 as the date of my retirement. A Democrat could not have asked more generous treatment from a Republican administration.

During the months of waiting there had been little to do but to mark time. In late July the sale of Chilean copper had fallen off because of the price fixed by the government, and one mining company planned to reduce the production to the demand. This would have thrown 1500 miners, involving at least 3000 people, out of employment and could easily have resulted in serious disorders. On the request of Minister Fenner, I urged the company to reconsider, and it generously consented. Through August I had a number of discussions with Fenner and the Minister of Finance on copper problems in general, but I was leaving in a month and could not speak for the new administration.

5

Since it has been necessary to review the unpleasant controversy over the rupture with the Axis it was a relief to find the restoration of diplomatic relations bringing in ambassadors from Germany, Italy and Japan, with whom it was possible to maintain friendly relations. The first to arrive was Ambassador Fornari of Italy. We had been friends from Madrid days, when he lived across the street from me. He was a career diplomat of experience, and I had long liked and admired him. He was soon transferred, however, and his successor, Alberto Beria was equally agreeable and delightfully free from the offensive mannerisms that Mussolini had imposed on his diplomats. He had a charming wife and daughter, who recalled with nostalgia the delightful old house set in a large garden near Dublin, where they had lived when Beria was Minister to Ireland. They were especially homesick for this lovely place when they moved into the prosy Embassy Residence in Santiago, which was entered directly from the street. When the Ambassador abandoned the old residence and moved into the house of Agustín Edwards, with its lovely garden, the move somehow seemed symbolic of the change in Italy from Fascism to democracy.

Ambassador Von Camp, the new German chief of mission, was unmistakably German in appearance; he was tall, blond, punctilious. I had heard before his arrival that he had not been in sympathy with Hitler's plan for world domination and that his pet aversion had been the incredible Ribbentrop. A pleasant man, he was well received. The old German Embassy Residence, so long out of use, and in need of repairs, was not habitable at the time, and he took a modest house, where he was living when I left.

Beria began giving dinners and receptions as in prewar days, but the early death of the wife of the German closed the latter's doors to entertainment. The most colorful reception of early postwar days was that of the new Japanese Ambassador, Katsuhire Narita. He was a most agreeable man, in striking contrast with his wartime predecessor, who had forgotten to burn his personal diary on the breaking of relations. The women of his official household, young and pretty, contributed greatly to the notable success of his official bow to the Diplomatic Corps and Santiago society, as they moved about among the guests in charming Japanese gowns.

The war was over, and a new day had dawned—we all hoped.

6

During the nine months of President Ibáñez's Administration I saw him a number of times and always found him most cordial. The face, carved in granite, that I had seen before the election had softened, and he was warmly friendly with my country. The dire prediction of the pessimists that he would "speedily overturn the democratic regime" was immediately reduced to absurdity when he took a strong stand against communist subversives, against the repeal of the Law for the Defense of Democracy, against the denunciation of the Mutual Security Pact. He had adhered strictly to the traditional democratic processes during my last nine months in Chile. He had inherited a financial crisis, with inflation growing worse, and two years later he had the courage and wisdom to call in the economic, financial and managerial experts from the United States who had been so effective in Peru not long before, to advise on methods to bring order out of threatening chaos.

During these nine months I momentarily expected my recall. My correspondence with Washington had all but ceased. Political and economic reports went out from the embassy as usual, but I heard nothing directly from any ranking officer of the State Department. The morale of my staff had fallen because of the sweeping changes, announced and anticipated.

I could look back with satisfaction on fourteen years of effort to explain Chile and the United States to each other. If I had not always agreed with the policies of the Chilean Government, I had honestly tried to understand its point of view and transmit it to my government fairly. With none of the numerous governments of these years did I have any but the most amicable relations. I had a profound respect for the institutional life of the country. I had never swaggered with the "big stick" or so much as implied a threat, and I never forgot that I was dealing with a proud, sovereign nation as independent as my own. Then, too, I had a real affection for the Chilean people.

7

With the press announcement of my recall I had abundant proof that my friendship for Chile had been reciprocated, but in one small segment there was a violent exception—the communists were jubilant. During a secret conference of their leaders in Valparaiso—which was not as secret as they had thought—they had been told that one of their purposes was to drive me out of the country. Consequently their organ, *El Siglo,* gloated over my recall and, not content with that, they chalked on the walls of the city the words "Mr. Bowers, go home."

But aside from the communist paper, the Chilean press was running editorials, articles and letters that were gratifyingly flattering. These began with editorials in *El Mercurio* and the *Ilustrado,* followed in similar vein by papers over the country. Editorials on my retirement in *The New York Times* and the Washington *Star,* transmitted by the press associations, were reprinted in the Chilean papers. The most unique compliment came from the Chile Club, composed of the English, the Americans and Chileans who spoke English, when we were awaiting recall at Villa Alemana. It elected me president for the ensuing year!

The departure of a diplomat in Santiago entails a severe test of physical endurance because of the long procession of dinners, luncheons and cocktails. Such attentions from colleagues are to be expected, for they follow a pattern, but many of these were from Chilean friends, former ministers and former Chilean ambassadors. Luncheons were given by the Chilean Academy of History and Geography, by the British Cultural Institute, by the Chilean Institute, by the Chile-American Society, which had given me a luncheon on my arrival fourteen years before, by the North American Women's Club and the corporations representing North American investments.

My colleagues gave the usual luncheon at the Union Club, where my long-time associate, Dr. Hugo Pena, after a pleasant speech, presented to me, on behalf of the corps, a large silver plate bearing the crest of Chile and the signatures of all my thirty-eight colleagues. I was pleased to find among these the signatures of Von Camp of Germany, Beria of Italy and Narita of Japan.

President Ibáñez honored me with a luncheon in the Moneda, where, contrary to his custom at the time, he spoke briefly.

At the Cousiño Palace, Foreign Minister Fenner gave a luncheon that was notable in that, among the government officials past and present, were seventeen former foreign ministers with whom I had been associated; and also Leon Subercaseaux, home after a long wartime career in the embassy in London. He had ridden with me as Chief of Protocol when I presented my credentials years before. The eloquent speech of Minister Fenner was but an expression of his personal friendship.

Perhaps the most significant, because unofficial, luncheon was the one at the Union Club of the Chileans, sponsored by Cardinal Caro, Fernando Alessandri, the President of the Senate, and Gregorio Schepeler, the Chief Justice of the Supreme Court. The large dining room was filled with ministers of the government, the ranking officers of the three armed forces, leaders and members of all political parties but the communist, and men prominent in the professional, business and social life of the community. Ernesto Barros Jarpa, former Foreign Minister and my friend since my arrival, spoke with his usual felicity. This gathering of the Chileans without whose understanding my mission would have failed pleased me, and in my speech I tried to express my affection for Chile and my admiration for its democratic institutions. All these numerous speeches were published in full in the press.

The day before I left Santiago I made my farewell call on President Ibáñez, who again thanked me for my friendship with his country. The same day I called on Cardinal Caro, who had been my friend consistently throughout my long tenure.

That evening we drove to Valparaiso. We sailed for home on the *Santa Isabel*. My staff, accompanied by their wives, had driven down from Santiago to see us off.

As the ship began its homeward journey and the city began to dim in the distance, we agreed that we had never been so happy or so much among real friends as in this lovely land between the mountains and the sea, and we knew that we would miss the towering Andes in the background and the flaming sunsets on its peaks.

Index

A.B.C. group, 323
A.B.C. magazine, 232
Abelli, Crystal, 126
Abyssinia, 152, 270
Academy of Mathematics, 224
Adams, John Quincy, 143, 149
Africa, 28, 119
Agrarian-Labor party, 40, 159, 160, 335
Agricultural Society, 264, 265
Aguirre Cerda, Pedro (president of Chile), v, 8, 25, 27, 38, 60, 61, 62, 63, 68, 72, 73, 74, 76, 129, 144, 228, 252, 260, 267, 282, 309, 319-23, 324, 328; *quoted*, 64
Aisén, Chile, 317
Alameda, Santiago, 46, 278, 279
Aldisio, Salvador (statesman), 272
Aldrich, Winthrop, 259
Aldunate, Raúl, 351
Alessandri, Fernando, 145, 161, 364
Alessandri Palma, Arturo (president of Chile), 21, 33, 37, 41, 42, 50, 98, 111, 112, 140, 141, 143-57, 160, 162, 166, 180, 231, 248, 272; *quoted*, 151, 152, 154, 156
Alfonso XIII (king of Spain), 272
All-American cables, 76
All-American Housing Conference, 10, 11
Allende, Senator, 39, 333
Allies, 60, 109, 121
Almagro, Diego de (soldier), 188
Alpine troops, Argentine, 124
Ambassador's Wife (Cerruti), 273
American Association of University Women, 212
American Embassy, Santiago, 6-7, 33, 115, 126, 147, 171, 172, 245
American Historical Society, 222
American States, Organization of, 39, 228, 356
American Womens Club, 343
Amunátegui, Domingo, 222
Amunátegui, Gregorio Victor, 222
Amunátegui, Miguel Luis, 222
Anaconda copper industry, 301

Anderson, Marian, 52
Andes mountains, 10, 12, 47, 302, 307, 365
Annapolis Naval Academy, 190
Antarctic, 356
Antofagasta, Chile, 4-5, 76, 127
Antonio Coloma, Juan, 37
Appian Way, Rome, 238
Aranha, Dr. (Brazilian foreign minister), 63, 80
"Araucana, La" (Ercilla), 216
Araucanian Indians, 16-17, 18, 22, 194, 217
"Arauco Domado" (Ona), 217
Arequipa, Peru, 304
Argentina, 10, 14, 31, 41, 65, 69, 78, 79, 88, 93, 108, 110, 120, 123, 124, 125, 147, 155, 202, 229, 284, 310, 314, 317, 322, 335, 341, 355, 358
Argentine Embassy, Santiago, 314, 359
Arica, Chile, 4, 314
Armour, Norman, 124
Armstrong, Colonel, 310
Arrau, Claudio, 52
Asquith, Herbert H., 207
Atlantic ocean, 93, 107, 108, 110
Aurora (newspaper), 223, 224
Avenue Bernardo O'Higgins, Santiago, 49
Avenue of the Americas, New York, 326
Avenue Valparaiso, Viña del Mar, 233-34
Axis Powers, v, vi, 33, 63, 66, 68, 70, 71, 75, 76, 77, 78, 87, 88, 89, 93, 97-113, 114-30, 159, 270, 326, 361

Bahía, Brazil, 12
Balfour, Arthur James, 39
Balmaceda, José Manuel (president of Chile), 33, 146
Baltimore (ship), 127, 191, 192
Banco Edwards, 225
Banishment of the Carreras, The (Vicuña-MacKenna), 222
Barcelona, Spain, 90

Index

Index

Elizabeth II (queen of England), 55
Elliot, Mrs. Fraser, 214
Ellis, Colonel Dan, 310, 315
Encina, Francisco, 223
Encio, Maria de, 133
Encyclopaedia Britannica, 221
England, vi, 35, 39, 54, 58, 78, 88, 99, 124, 152, 159, 189, 207, 299, 306
English, 19, 20, 21, 22, 24, 27, 56, 60, 78-79, 189, 206, 270, 356
Enrique Alfonso, Pedro, 333
Enríquez, Enrique, 134
Ercilla, Alonso de, 216
Errázuriz, Archbishop, 146
Errázuris, Matías, 84
Escorial, Spain, 51, 52
Escudero, General, 104
Escuela de Servicio Social, 211
Esmeralda (ship), 192-94
Espinoza, Dr. Heriberto, 202, 204
Evarts, William M., 106
Export-Import Bank, 198, 287, 289, 306, 322, 344

Fahs, Ned (attaché), 202
Fairbanks, Douglas, Jr., 260
Falangist party, 39, 40
Far East, 289
Farellones, Chile, 55
Farrell, General Edelmiro J. (president of Argentina), 123, 124
Fenner, Oscar, 356, 357, 360, 364
Fergusson, Erna, 28, 56, 217
Fernández y Fernández, Joaquín (minister), 113, 114, 117, 118, 119, 121, 123, 124, 125, 128, 129, 162, 327
Fifth Column, Chile, 63-64, 65
Figueroa, Ana, 201, 210
Figueroa, Pedro (friar), 133-34
First Years of the Revolution in Chile (Amunátegui), 222
Fiske, Mrs. Minnie Maddern, 127
Flores, Cañas, 291
Flores, Miguel, 240
Fomento Corporation, 287, 322, 324
Fontaine, Joan, 260
Foreign Office, Chile, 45, 52, 63, 65, 75, 76, 102, 111, 310
Foreign Relations Committee, 290
Forever Amber (Winsor), 241
Fornari (Italian diplomat), 361
"Fourth Party," England, 39, 40
Fox, Charles James, 208
France, 39, 48, 54, 59, 68, 88, 91, 116, 151, 299, 306, 328
French, 24
Franco, Francisco, 66, 70, 71, 88, 234, 270
Free French, 116
Frei, Senator, 40
French Revolution, 271

Gallardo Nieto, Galvarino, 226
Gana, Blest (writer), 219
Ganderillas, Larraín, 279

Gandarillas, Manuel José, 224
Gandy, Dr. Theodore, 286
Gasparri, Pietro, Cardinal, 146, 248
Gasson P. (artist), 88
Geneva, Switzerland, 209, 266
George, Senator Walter F., 295
Geraldine, Mother, 277
German Club, Concepción, 70
German Embassy, Santiago, 65, 92, 103, 107, 108, 118, 125, 126, 137, 361
Germany, 20, 24, 59, 65, 67, 75, 78, 80, 97, 98, 99-100, 102, 107, 119, 299, 361
Germans, 20-21, 22, 40, 206
Gibbons, James, Cardinal, 252
Gibraltar, 270
Godoy, Arturo (boxer), 86
Godoy, César (deputy), 161
Goering, Hermann, 269
Goldwyn Girls, 242
Gone With the Wind (motion picture), 68
González Videla, Gabriel (president of Chile), v, 38, 51, 52, 157, 161, 166, 167, 169-70, 198, 227, 283, 285, 293, 295-97, 311, 312, 313, 317, 327-30, 333, 334, 342, 347; *quoted*, 35, 329
González Videla, Mrs., 346, 350
Gorst, Sir John, 39
Governors Island, 239
Grace, Peter, 296, 326
Grace, William R., 304, 305, 306
Grace Company, 196
Graf Spee (ship), 62
Graham, Sir George, 82
Graham, Horace, 128
Graham, Mrs. Horace, 126
Grammatica, Emma (actress), 52
Gran Federación Obrera, 40-41
Granada, Spain, 29
Grange school, 277, 278
Grau, Admiral Miguel, 193
Grayson, Kathryn, 244
Great Britain, *see* England
Greeks, ancient, 36
Griffin, Carlos, 343
Grove, Marmaduke (president of Chile), 39
Guatemala, 108
Guedalla, Philip, 271
Guggenheim interests, 300, 306
Guiñazú, Dr. Ruiz (minister), 79-80
Gunther, John, 154
Guzmán, Dr. (minister), 72

Halifax, Lord, 66
Hall, Carlos (counselor), 173, 174
Halsey, Admiral William F., 259, 262-263
"Halsey and Nimitz and Me," 263
Hamburg, Germany, 108
Harriman, Averell, 122
Harrison, Benjamin, 191
Havana, Cuba, 69, 77, 99, 118, 232, 285
Havey, Father William, 277

ABOUT THE AUTHOR

CLAUDE G. BOWERS *was United States Ambassador to Spain from 1933 to 1939, and this experience served as the basis of his previously published* My Mission to Spain (*1954*). *After he left his Spanish post, he was reassigned to Chile, and the present book is in part an account of his fourteen years as our Ambassador there.*

Prior to his diplomatic career he had been a distinguished newspaperman in Indiana and New York, where he was editorial writer on the Evening World. *In 1928, he was keynote speaker and chairman of the Democratic National Convention. In addition to diplomacy, newspaper work and politics, Mr. Bowers has written ten books of political history, including such notable works as* The Tragic Era, Jefferson and Hamilton, *and* Party Battles of the Jackson Period.